Pastoral
Teaching
of Paul

Pastoral Teaching of Paul

W. E. Chadwick

Foreword by
Warren W. Wiersbe

KREGEL PUBLICATIONS
Grand Rapids, Michigan 49501

The Pastoral Teaching of Paul by W. Edward
Chadwick. Copyright ©1984 by Kregel Publications,
a division of Kregel, Inc. All rights reserved.

First Kregel Publications edition . . . 1984
Reprinted 1985

Library of Congress Cataloging in Publication Data

Chadwick, W. Edward (William Edward), 1858-1934.
    The Pastoral Teaching of Paul.

(Kregel Pulpit Aids)

  Reprint. Originally published: The Pastoral Teach-
ing of St. Paul. Edinburgh: T. & T. Clark, 1907.
    Includes index.
    1. Pastoral theology—Biblical teaching. 2. Paul, the
Apostle, Saint. 3. Bible. N.T. Epistles of Paul—Criti-
cism, interpretation, etc. I. Title.
BS2655.P3C5   1984   253   84-7123
ISBN 0-8254-2325-2 (pbk.)

Published in the United States of America

CONTENTS

Foreword **by Warren W. Wiersbe**   xix

Preface   xxi

INTRODUCTION   1

The growing demand for greater efficiency in the Christian
   ministry, *in* the Church and *by* the world   .   .   1
Efforts to meet this demand, by special training, by books
   on Pastoral Theology and Ministerial Life   .   .   3
Our Lord ever the one Perfect Ideal for ministers   .   .   5
Among those immediately commissioned by Him we know
   most of St. Paul   6
Our materials for the study of His ministerial methods and
   teaching are ample   7
The special value of such a study at the present time   .   11
The stress St. Paul lays upon elements in ministerial work
   apt to be comparatively neglected to-day.   .   .   14
His example may lead us to supply certain pressing needs :—
   1. The need of more efficient teaching based on more
      adequate knowledge   16
   2. The need of a more intimate acquaintance with the
      thoughts and ideas of those among whom we
      minister   18
   3. The need of a deeper consciousness of sin, and of the
      evils of sin   20
   4. The need of more spiritual power   .   .   .   22
   5. The need of a revision of our "judgment values" in
      regard to the "important" and the "unimportant" .   23

Contents

Chapter 1

THE MINISTER OF CHRIST, A WORKMAN

PAGE

The Christian minister not only a workman, but an "artist" whose personality enters into all his work . . 25

Contrast with the mechanical service of Jewish and heathen priesthoods 26

Personality, as the vehicle of moral influence, an essential element in the spiritual religion of the Old Testament as of the New 28

The stamp of St. Paul's personality upon all his work . 30

I. *The Instrument with which the Minister works* . 32

The Gospel : its ideas and its powers . . . 32
    (*a*) 2 Cor. v. 11–vi. 10. The Gospel in the ministerial life 32
    (*b*) 2 Cor. iv. 2. The appeal to the conscience . 35

II. *The Material upon which the Minister works* . . 40

St. Paul's knowledge of human nature great . . 41
    (*a*) Generally : as seen in 1 Thess. v., Rom. xiv. . 42
    (*b*) As affected by local and other influences : as seen *e.g.* in *Galatians* and *Philippians* . . 49

Our need to study the characteristics of rich and middle-class and poor ; of town, country, and suburb ; of the South, Midlands, and North 54

III. *The Minister's object as a Workman* . . . 57

    (*a*) Christian maturity. The formation of Christ in men 58
    (*b*) Christian perfection. The full development of man in Christ 58
    (*c*) The building up of each and all into the perfect unity of the Body of the Christ — the Ideal Society 59

Contents

Chapter 2

THE PASTOR AND HIS PASTORATE

THE MINISTER'S CONCEPTION OF HIMSELF AND OF THOSE TO WHOM HE MINISTERS

PAGE

The salutations in the Epistles not formal, but chosen according to special circumstances, relationships, and needs . 64

I. *The Minister's conception of himself* . . . 65

The personal name, endowment, consecration (offering), influence, and responsibility 67
The employment for Christ of natural and acquired endowments 67
St. Paul's ready use of (*a*) his Hebrew training, (*b*) his knowledge of Greek life and thought, (*c*) Imperial ideas, customs, and privileges of his Roman citizenship . 67
    Examples : (*a*) in Acts xxi., xxii. ; (*b*) in *Philippians* . 67
The call to self-improvement in order to offer a more worthy offering 70
St. Paul's description of his position relative to the Divine (God, Christ) : *e.g.* as apostle ; as servant (δοῦλος) . 72
St. Paul's assertion of his Divine commission . . . 75
Our need for this conviction at ordination . . . 76
How to maintain the conviction through the years of ministry 77
The perpetual spiritual endowment . . . 78
    (*a*) of *Light*, for guidance 79
    (*b*) of *Strength*, for influence . . . 80

II. *The Minister's conception of those to whom he ministers* 81

How this influences his work for them . . . 81
St. Paul's different descriptions of those he addresses . 81
The probable reason : evidences of development of conception 83
    (*a*) of the individual 84

PAGE

(*b*) of the Universal Christian Society, and
(*c*) of the right relationship of the individual to the
Society 84

St. Paul's growth in Christian statesmanship, and the need
of this by the minister to-day 84

St. Paul's descriptions taken from the Old Testament : the
continuity between the Covenant People and the
Christian Church 86

The descriptions of both societies and individuals to be
regarded as ideals : parallels in the Prayer Book : the
value of the method 89

The Ecclesia the Ideal Society 90

The present need for the right discharge of social relationships 90

The "local" Church a training-ground for citizenship . 91

A social "heresy" of to-day—a perfect society out of imperfect members 93

St. Paul's stress on individual responsibility . . . 94

The Church a "purposive" society 95

The terms used by St. Paul 96

(*a*) οἱ ἅγιοι : the effect of a true interpretation on
the doctrine of Baptism . . . 96

(*b*) οἱ κλητοί : the "Divinely" "called" : two
present tendencies, (1) to the want of a sense
of *unity* in life, and (2) to a materialistic view
of life 98

(*c*) οἱ ἀδελφοί : a brotherhood implies (1) a Fatherhood, (2) a regeneration to a new common life :
the degradation of the term to-day : the failure
of modern secular "brotherhoods" : true
brotherhood possible only in union with
Christ 101

(*d*) οἱ ἀγαπητοὶ Θεοῦ : this thought an inspiration to
the pastor : the value of the individual : the
appeal to the lonely : to-day man treated as a
machine, or an instrument : the Christian
dear to God as "accepted in the Beloved" . 104

"Grace and peace" : the ministry to be a channel of these :
Can *our* ministry be so regarded ? . . . 106

Chapter 3

CONCEPTS OF MINISTRY

PAGE

The various titles used by St. Paul to describe his ministry . 108

These describe "functions of service," rather than formal
"offices" 109

The analogy between the human organism and the "Body of
Christ": the conditions of health in each: the due
exercise of all the organs 109

The "differentiation of function" in the developing organism:
How far is "specialising" in ministerial work justifiable? 111

    (1) *Apostle* (ἀπόστολος): the *legatus a latere*: the
personal responsibility: how our ministry may be
"apostolic": nearness to Christ: a direct commission
and equipment: we must represent Christ worthily. 113

    (2) *Servant* and *Minister* (δοῦλος and διάκονος): both
imply the *usefulness* of service: unity of the Divine
and human purpose of service: the stress laid upon
this unity in the Ordination Services . . 117

Difference in meaning in δοῦλος and διάκονος, permanence of
position and activity in work: the "Servant of the Lord"
in Isaiah 120

The demand to-day for proof of the usefulness of our service:
the stress upon service in our Lord's teaching of "the
Kingdom": to St. Paul service essential to the
Christian life in the Christian Society; close connection between his teaching and our Lord's . . 123

    (1) δοῦλος and its cognates: the "purchased" slave
of Christ: the minister His property: how we
may, and may not, be "slaves to men" . 127

      δουλεύειν in Gal. v. 13 (the bondage of love);
in Phil. ii. 22 (fellow-slaves for the Gospel);
Phil. ii. 6 (the humility of Christ) . . 130

    (2) διάκονος and its cognates: the comprehensive-
ness of St. Paul's conception of ministry:
our Lord's spirit and example of service:
the discharge of every function a διακονία . 132

Contents

PAGE

Eph. iv. 12. Universality of ministry in the
Church : the special ministry of specially
endowed men : their equipment for this   .   134

The demand ·by the State for efficiency for service in its
citizens, and present efforts to secure this : the unemployable has no place in the Ideal Society : the need
for growth in efficiency in the ministry   .   .   138

2 Cor. viii., ix. Alms-giving a διακονία : need (1) of clear
teaching on this subject, (2) of scrupulous care by the
minister in regard to "money-matters"   .   .   .   139

2 Cor. iii. 1 ff. The ministry of personal influence and
example   141

2 Cor. iii. 7–9. Certain contrasts of ministry .   .   .   142

(3) *Herald* (κήρυξ) : the Gospel must be announced
before it can be either explained or applied. (*See
Chapter VIII.*)   145

(4) *Prophet* : the high value set by St. Paul on this
function of ministry. (*See Chapter IX.*)   .   .   147

(5) *Preacher* : how the English word represents several
words in the original Greek : St. Paul's sense of the
importance of preaching. (*See Chapter VIII.*)   .   147

(6) *Teacher* (διδάσκαλος) : St. Paul as a teacher a wide
subject : we cannot isolate the function : the
teacher's task—(1) discipline, (2) instruction : its
connection with that of the pastor : the pastor must
learn to teach : present general inefficiency, yet
increasing need and responsibility   .   .   .   148

The sacredness of the work : carrying on the work of Christ
through the Holy Spirit — the Spirit of wisdom and
understanding, etc.   151

St. Paul on teaching. Rom. ii. 21 ff. (a mirror for all
teachers) ; Eph. iv. 20 ff. (teaching and conduct) ; Col. ii.
6 ff. (the results of teaching)   153

(7) *Ambassador* : instances of the idea in St. Paul :
our mission partly to subjects alienated from, if not
inimical to, their lawful sovereign : "the ministry of
reconciliation" : we represent Christ   .   .   158

(8) *Steward* (οἰκονόμος) : no idea more fruitful : all that
"responsibility" implies : the idea in the Ordination
Services   160

Our Lord on the qualifications of a steward : St. Luke xvi.

Contents

PAGE

I ff. and xii. 42 ff.: St. Paul on stewardship, 1 Cor. iv. 1 ff., the steward's task to dispense, also to furnish himself with the means—both a θυσία ζῶσα   .   .   .   162

"Stewards of the mysteries"—of the Sacraments, yet of more   166

Faithfulness the primary qualification of a steward   .   .   167

Instances of οἰκονομία in St. Paul: 1 Cor. ix. 17 (of preaching the Gospel), Eph. i. 10 (as representing Christ in the manifestation of God's will), Eph. iii. 2 (in administering the grace of God), Eph. iii. 9 (for making clear God's method), Col. i. 28 (in the house of God towards others), 1 Tim. i. 4 (in this same house to promote God's ordering)   168

(9) *Worker unto the Kingdom of God:* St. Paul's humility in association with others: the "social work" of the ministry and of the Church, towards the establishment of the Ideal Society   .   .   174

Importance of St. Paul's teaching upon "the Kingdom": its inspiration for the social worker: the social problem an ethical one—a problem of character   .   .   .   177

(10) *Soldier:* St. Paul regarded his work as a warfare: Eph. vi. 11 ff., the completely armed Christian a standard for self-examination: Is our work as ministers of Christ sufficiently militant against evil? the temptations amid which many of our people live: the danger of "undermining" .   .   .   178

(11) *Husbandman:* "pastoral" work hard and continuous toil: the different functions of the γεωργός, yet all dependent on the blessing of God; the parallels in the Gospels: we are not owners but occupiers, who must render fruits: the many analogies between "pastoral" work and the labour of the husbandman .   182

(12) *The Skilled Master Builder* (σοφός ἀρχιτέκτων): St. Paul's conception of edification: the overseership of the "clerk of the works": for what he is responsible: the quality of the materials: what can and can not be "sanctified to the Master's use": the choosing of the workers: what "organisation" implies   .   187

ΑΙΩ'ΚΩ: the Christian who is no Christian; the incompleteness of all true knowledge and of all true work: "the strenuous life": the need of constant self-discipline and of constant renewals of Divine strength .   .   .   192

Contents

Chapter 4

THE ADDRESS TO THE EPHESIAN ELDERS AT MILETUS

A PASTOR'S CHARGE TO PASTORS

PAGE

The importance of the address : evidence of its genuineness ;
its great wealth of pastoral teaching . . . 195

St. Paul's thorough knowledge of the Church : insight the
key to foresight : because he knew he could warn and
exhort 196

Our need for insight—the result of close study and careful
observation 197

No formal arrangement, but three chief topics—St. Paul's
own ministry, the immediate future, the duty of the
elders towards themselves and their Church . . 198

The power of an appeal to personal example and personal
self-sacrifice 199

The pastor's need of humility, his sorrow for sin, his trials . 200

How St. Paul had worked : "admonishing" (to repentance),
"teaching" (to faith), and "testifying" to the *whole*
Gospel whether palatable or not . . . 201

"Bound in spirit," entire self-devotion to Christ regardless of
consequences 204

The "heralding" of the Kingdom : the social Gospel : the
unselfishness of St. Paul 207

How we may be "pure from the blood of all" : the faithful
preacher of "the whole counsel of God" : no incomplete
message 208

The pastor's regard to himself, and for the whole of his flock ;
the functions of the "Shepherd of souls" . . 210

How the value of the flock is reckoned : "the blood of God's
Own" 213

Individual liberty to be respected, and individual responsibility taught 213

The dangers of the future from outside and from within ; the
sources of heresy 214

The siege of the strongholds of iniquity : the need of constant
watchfulness : the care of the individual . . 215

The power of God : the inheritance among the sanctified . 217

No self-seeking or self-enrichment : the motto of Christ . 219

Chapter 5

THE LOVE OF SOULS

PAGE

Two conditions for pastoral work—(a) a call from God, (b) the desire to serve man, from a love of souls : the enthusiasm of humanity 221

An intelligent love desires the best for those loved : this, to the Christian pastor, the Christ-like character and life 222

True love never exists apart from hate : in the Christian from the hatred of sin 222

In the ministry of our Lord and St. Paul a threefold combination : (a) the call from God, (b) the love for man, (c) the hatred of sin 223

From his conversion St. Paul's work "philanthropic" in the highest sense 225

Neither the desire (a) to make men "orthodox," (b) nor "to do our duty," are sufficient motives for pastoral work . 227

The motives of the ministry to-day the subject of severe outside criticism 228

Love of souls involves warfare against evil, and therefore against destructive conditions of life . . . 230

Proofs of St. Paul's love of souls : his appeals (a) from the analogy of motherhood, Gal. iv. 19 ; (b) as a father, 1 Cor. iv. 14, 15, 2 Cor. ix. 2 ; (c) as a brother, Gal. iv. 12, vi. 1 ; (d) in his Epistles generally 231

The love of souls implies the rebuke of sin : the difficulty of this task, and the temptation to shirk it . . 236

The temptation to make inconvenience to ourselves the measure of wrong 239

Both old and new weapons needed in the warfare against sin 241

Why present-day philanthropic efforts so often fail : no clear conception of the sinfulness of sin, of the "wrath of God," and its inevitable results 242

The condemnation of those who make gain from the promotion of the means of temptation . . . 244

In his love of souls and hatred of sin St. Paul an inspiration and example 244

Contents

Chapter 6

THE MOTIVE POWER OF MINISTRY (1 Cor. 13)

PAGE

This chapter not to be isolated from those dealing with the endowments of the Church and its members . 245

Love not a "gift," but a spirit in which all gifts to be exercised, and which moralises and "Christianises" all gifts and actions 247

The danger of popular preaching and emotional hymns . 248

The need for moralising and consecrating the powers of the intellect and of personal influence 249

Self-sacrifice, even to the uttermost, useless, if its effects upon ourselves be its ultimate motive 250

The personification of Love a portrait of the Incarnate Christ : Love synonymous with Christianity . . 251

Particular temptations in the pastoral life—envy, ostentation, conceit, "unseemliness" 254

The pastor must be "other-seeking" : not soon angry : must not reckon up or remember wrongs . . . 256

He must never rejoice secretly at another's failure ; he must always rejoice at any progress towards the Ideal . . 258

He must always bear, always trust, always hope, always be patient, and all without limit 261

The permanence of Love, like that of the nature of Christ, and of what is essential in Christianity, amid all changes 263

The need to realise how imperfect our knowledge, and our expression of our knowledge 264

An exhortation to constant growth towards full development . 266

The confession and the faith of the earnest seeker after Truth 267

Chapter 7

THE PRAYERS OF PAUL

I. *True prayer a revelation of faith, ideals, efforts* . . 271

The connection of prayer and work 271

St. Paul a "man of prayer" before and after his conversion ; the change in his "spirit" of prayer . . . 272

Contents

PAGE

St. Paul's teaching on prayer : (*a*) communion with God ; (*b*) includes thanksgiving, intercession, and consciousness of God's presence ; (*c*) co-operation of the Holy Spirit in prayer ; (*d*) the office of the understanding in prayer . 273

Examples showing the importance St. Paul attached to prayer 275

The need of constant and earnest prayer in the ministerial life 276

II. *Examination of St. Paul's prayers* . . . 277

Rom. i. 8–12. The need of thankfulness : the two spheres of service : the spiritual influence of the pastor, his dependence on his flock 277

Eph. i. 15–19. The need of "wisdom and revelation" in the knowledge of God : the discouragements of the pastor : the issue of knowledge in power . . . 281

Eph. iii. 1, 13 ff. The need of the Divine power for further knowledge issuing in greater love : the "social" teaching of the prayer : the ideals of the Messianic Society, and the "fulfilment" of the individual in its fulfilment . 288

Col. i. 9 ff. The ideal Christian character : fulness of knowledge of God's will applied to life under the Spirit's guidance ; the need of perseverance and of thankfulness 295

Phil. i. 9–11. St. Paul's view of Christianity : the ministerial life to be one of abounding love, of growing knowledge, and of increasing keenness of moral perception : the pre-eminence of character, and the moralising of all the faculties of life 301

Chapter 8

PAUL ON PREACHING

St. Paul before everything else a preacher . . . 306

His account of his commission as such in Acts xxvi. . . 306

His testimony to the things in which he had seen Christ . 307

The purpose of his preaching to produce repentance and faith, its final object salvation — safety within the Messianic Kingdom 308

The preacher must first impart knowledge ; the conditions

PAGE

essential for this; the wide-spread ignorance among professing Christians of the contents of the Gospel . 310

The subjects of St. Paul's preaching mainly three: (*a*) the facts of Christ's life, (*b*) the preparation for Christ in history, (*c*) his own personal experience of Christ . 312

The value of the concrete and the strength of the personal appeal 316

St. Paul's preaching also included "admonishing and teaching," the first often a necessary preliminary to the second 317

St. Paul's knowledge of human nature, his sense of the value of discipline 319

Skill necessary to admonish with good effect . . . 320

St. Paul a great teacher, to him the Christian ministry educational in its design 321

The importance of the teaching function in the pastoral office: our Lord a great Teacher: the permanent influence of a teaching ministry 322

St. Paul always teaching: examples from the Acts and Epistles 322

The place of "teachers" in 1 Cor. xii. 28 and in Eph. iv. 11 (the conjunction of "pastors and teachers"): examples from the Pastoral Epistles 323

Preaching implies toil of the nature of a struggle, this toil must be according to the Divine laws of human nature (mental science) 326

Complaints of the ineffectiveness of preaching to-day: one cause the want of spiritual power from want of spiritual communion 327

St. Paul teaches the preacher the need of a definite end—"Every man perfect in Christ Jesus" . . . 328

Preaching must also be a bringing of Good Tidings—a declaration of the possibilities of man and of Society . 329

The Gospel contains the means for the removal of the many unnecessary evils in both 331

The task committed to the preacher explained by πληροῦν . 331

Chapter 9

PAUL ON PROPHECY

The subject of New Testament prophecy demands more study than it has yet received 333

PAGE

The prophecy, as the religion, of the Old and New Testaments in all essentials the same 334

Religion implies a revelation of the Divine Will : a universal religion implies a universal means of communication of that Will and a universal capacity for receiving it . 335

As the conception of religion rises, the appeal of religion is more and more to the highest human faculties . . 335

Evidence of the existence of "prophecy" throughout the period of the New Testament 337

Prophecy an expression, implying a revelation, of the will of God 338

By St. Paul it is always closely connected with the Holy Spirit and His gifts 338

" Prophets " in St. Paul, always next after " apostles " . 340

" Prophecies" in I Tim. i. 18, "prophecy" in I Tim. iv. 14 340

St. Paul on the *use* of prophecy : our need of more " spiritual " preaching 341

Detailed examination of prophecy in I Cor. xiv. 3-6, 24, 25, 32. [Parallel between prophets in the O.T. and scientific discoverers and teachers of to-day] . . . 341

Prophets in Ephesians : (*a*) ii. 20. The essential unity of the Church of (1) the O.T., (2) the N.T., (3) to-day : the Head in heaven : the body on earth : organs of expression of the will of the Head necessary now as ever. (*b*) iii. 5 ff. Revealers of the unfolding mystery : the mystery still being unfolded, therefore the revealer still necessary. (*c*) iv. 11. The prophet's part in the equipment of the saints, this also necessary now, as always . . . 349

The need of more attention at the present time to the higher functions of ministry : we, partly from force of circumstances, too apt to be absorbed in the lower . . 353

Chapter 10

PAUL ON WISDOM

" Wisdom," according to St. Paul, essential to the Christian, especially so for those in positions of responsibility : his insistence on this both direct and indirect . . 356

PAGE

What is the true, the Divine "wisdom"? special care needed
    in the use of the word 358

"Wisdom" in the O.T. and N.T. always implies ability and
    skill, which may be physical, mechanical, intellectual,
    moral 361

The need of wisdom by the Church and its ministers .   . 363

The difference between the "wisdom of God" and the true
    wisdom of man 364

True wisdom in man a moral quality implying humility and
    obedience 365

Passages showing that wisdom means skill in living : (*a*) from
    St. Paul, (*b*) from the Acts, (*c*) from the Gospels .   . 366

Examination of 1 Cor. i. 22 ff., i. 30 ff. : St. Paul a Realist : the
    sources and tendencies of Nominalistic Ethics to-day . 369

The need for a more adequate "moralising" of religion. Col.
    ii. 1 ff. ; Eph. iii. 8. Christ the Divine Mystery, Truth,
    Ideal, and the Incarnation of the Divine Wisdom . 372

The "inexplorable wealth of the Christ" is "the treasures of
    wisdom" : the dispensation of these the task of the
    minister 373

The revelation of the Divine Wisdom in the physical sphere,
    through the discoveries of science : the application of
    results to the service of man 375

The need of similar efforts in the moral and spiritual sphere
    by Christ's ministers, promising similar results : the
    rendering of a still higher and greater service to man . 376

Discoveries in psychology and sociology : man's welfare
    dependent on knowledge of their laws : obedience to
    these laws (which are Divine) man's true wisdom . 376

The need of training for the clergy in these fields of know-
    ledge, and of more earnest study in them .   . 378

Right conduct the ultimate aim of the pastor : the need for
    him to give more adequate teaching upon the art of
    living, founded on a true science and philosophy of life . 379

[Additional Note on μόνῳ σοφῷ Θεῷ in Rom. xvi. 27] .   . 380

EPILOGUE   383

SCRIPTURE INDEX   387

FOREWORD

We live in a day of "ministerial confusion" primarily because of the variety of "role models" before us and the increasing number of "how-to-do-it books" that keep coming from the presses. Each preacher and author is certain that his approach is not only the right one—it is the only biblical one! After all, it worked for him, so it ought to work for everybody!

The result? A host of confused younger preachers, as well a silent group of more experienced men who are wondering if their philosophy of ministry is right after all. We are seeing principles replaced by methods and success being measured only by statistics.

Because of this confusion, I rejoice that this work, *Pastoral Teaching of Paul* is now available to a generation of ministers who need what these chapters present. After all, Paul was not only a great preacher, missionary, and theologian; he was also a great pastor! It is time that our present ministerial generation recovered the pastoral vision of the Apostle Paul.

Let me point out that this book is not based on Paul's Pastoral Epistles. For an excellent study in that area, see *Practical Truths From the Pastoral Epistles* by Eugene Stock (Kregel Publications, 1983). Dr. Chadwick's book is based on the pastoral *ministry* of Paul as recorded in the Book of Acts and revealed in his Epistles.

I know of no volume that treats the "images" of the minister as this one does — the workman, the servant, the herald, the steward, etc. Dr. Chadwick's exposition of Paul's "Farewell Address" in Acts 20 ought to be read by every ministerial candidate prior to ordination, and at least once a year by every pastor *after* his ordination! The studies on "The Love of Souls" and "The Prayers of Paul" are musts for the pastor who truly wants a spiritual ministry.

You need not agree with all of the author's interpretations to benefit from his insights. I happen to disagree with his views on baptism, but I heartily agree with his concern that God's people in the local church realize that they belong to God and to each other.

William Edward Chadwick was a child of the manse, his father being an Anglican clergyman. Chadwick studied at Victoria University, Manchester, and Jesus College, Cambridge. He served as Vicar of St. Giles' Church, Northampton, as well as at St. Peter's Church, St. Albans. He was Select Preacher at Cambridge (1907) and Hulsean Lecturer (1909-10). For seven years, he served as English chaplain at Clarens-Montreaux, Switzerland.

Perhaps he was best known for his writings. *The Social Teaching of St. Paul* appeared in 1906, and this present volume in 1907. He wrote at least ten substantial volumes, many of them dealing with the social problems of the day and the place of the church in helping to solve them.

I commend this volume to you, not simply for reading, but even more, for serious study. I trust that it will assist you in gaining a better understanding of what it truly means to do the work of the pastoral ministry.

Back to the Bible Broadcast   WARREN W. WIERSBE
Lincoln, Nebraska

PREFACE

Two criticisms which will at once be made upon this book, and with complete justification, I wish to anticipate :—

(1) That it does not give by any means a complete presentation of St. Paul's "Pastoral Teaching."

(2) That it contains comparatively few references to the Pastoral Epistles—our chief source for that teaching.

To these criticisms I would reply :—

(1) To give a *complete* presentation of St. Paul's Pastoral Teaching would mean a commentary written with this object upon almost every verse of his Epistles, as well as upon almost all that refers to him in the Acts of the Apostles. My object has not been to attempt to do this, but rather to show how rich in pastoral guidance and inspiration St. Paul's life and teaching are. If I should lead others to work further in the field upon which I have entered, I shall have achieved no small part of my purpose.

(2) My reason for making comparatively little use of the Pastoral Epistles has been twofold : [1]—

(*a*) In order to deal with them adequately, from this point of view alone, they would have required a volume to themselves.

(*b*) I wished to show St. Paul *at work* as a Christian minister. I wished to lead my συνεργοὶ εἰς τὴν βασιλείαν τοῦ Θεοῦ to study the *principles* upon which St. Paul acted and the *methods* he employed, rather than to listen to his definite injunctions to other ministers.[2] I could not cover both fields of study. The one I have chosen is, I hope, not the less useful : certainly, I believe, it is up to the present time the field which has been less frequently worked.

W. E. C.

I have read carefully much of the recent literature both in defence of and against the Pauline authorship of the Pastoral Epistles, and with this result—that further investigation of this question seems to strengthen the view that these are genuine letters of St. Paul. The following list of scholars (given by Dr. Plummer in the *Guardian* of June 5, 1907) who accept St. Paul's authorship is interesting : " Alford, Beet, J. H. Bernard, Chase, Ellicott, P. Fairbairn, Farrar, Findlay, Headlam, Hort, Howson, Humphreys, Knowling, Lightfoot, Lilley, Lock, Murray, Plumptre, Ramsay, Rendall, Reynolds, Salmon, Wace, Westcott ; Blass, Godet, Huther, Meyer, Roos, B. Weiss, Wieseler, Wiesinger, Zahn. Many others admit portions as genuine."

---

[1] I am not unmindful of Augustine's advice : " Quas tres apostolicas epistolas ante oculos habere debet, cui est in ecclesia doctoris persona imposita." *De Doctr. Christ.* iv. 16.

[2] The address to the Ephesian elders is somewhat different ; their position was hardly analogous to that of Timothy and Titus.

INTRODUCTION

ἵνα ἄρτιος ᾖ ὁ τοῦ Θεοῦ ἄνθρωπος, πρὸς πᾶν ἔργον ἀγαθὸν ἐξηρτισμένος.—2 TIM. iii. 17.

ἔσται σκεῦος εἰς τιμήν, ἡγιασμένον, εὔχρηστον τῷ δεσπότῃ, εἰς πᾶν ἔργον ἀγαθὸν ἡτοιμασμένον.—2 TIM. ii. 21.

τὴν διακονίαν σου πληροφόρησον.—2 TIM. iv. 5.

DURING recent years the standard of public opinion with regard to the qualifications necessary for a due discharge of the various functions of the Christian ministry, and also with regard to the responsibility which those should feel who enter this ministry, has steadily risen. This is apparent both within the Church and outside it. Within the Church, indeed within "all the Churches," we have witnessed a sharpening of conscience as to the standard of efficiency to be required from those permitted to discharge those sacred functions, upon whose adequate discharge the welfare of the whole Christian body in great measure depends. Outside "the Churches" the Christian ministry is the subject of a criticism which every year seems to become more searching and more exacting. This criticism may be regarded as a demand that at least the immense responsibilities inevitably connected with this office shall be more fully realised. All this is entirely for good ; and the world can do the Church no greater service than to insist that both those who have entered the ministerial calling and those who are preparing to enter it should "demand of themselves."

To help those who would try both to make and to meet this demand—that is, who desire to increase their ministerial efficiency—many efforts have been made, and new efforts are constantly being made by all sections of the Christian Church. There is an obvious reason for this. The population as a whole is becoming far better educated than in the past. It is therefore essential that if the Church, in the widest sense of the term, is to be a competent guide and teacher of the people, it must possess a ministry fully qualified to perform both these most important services. With the growing demand for efficiency in those who occupy any kind of a position of responsibility, inefficiency will, quite rightly, be no more endured in the Christian ministry than in any other responsible walk of life.

At the old universities, honour schools of theology have been established, and to some of the new universities a faculty of theology has already been attached. The various religious bodies now maintain a considerable number of theological colleges, both for graduates and non-graduates. The standard of knowledge required by the bishops from candidates for ordination has also to some extent been raised; and recently, by different Churches and schools of thought, many earnest appeals have been made for more liberal pecuniary assistance in order to give a longer period of training with a view to obtaining a more scholarly race of ministers.

Another evidence of this same movement is found in the large number of books upon Pastoral Theology or upon Ministerial Work which have been published in recent years. Some of these books are quite general, while others either deal with the work in particular spheres, or treat of particular functions which the Christian minister must discharge. Thus we have books upon the work in the town, the country, and the suburban parish: we have also books dealing more particularly with the studies, the preaching, the teaching, and the pastoral visitation of the clergy. Many of these books embody the lessons of long and wide experience, and most of them will be found exceedingly helpful not only by those about to enter the ministry, or by those recently ordained, but also by older men. It is not sufficient to aim at, or even to reach ideals : these have also to be maintained. For the ministerial life, if it is to be *mai.·tained* at a consistently high level, needs constant inspiration and constant self-discipline ; and self-discipline presupposes self-examination. Again, self-examination, if it is to be efficacious, implies some high standard of reference external to ourselves. If it is true that "by our perseverance we shall win our souls," it is equally true that only by our own perseverance may we hope to win the souls of others. We need something more than the mere possession of clear and lofty principles, which may be regarded as rules for life and action : we need also to test constantly our own practice—in study, in teaching, and in dealing with individuals—by these principles. The true test of the value of any book upon the ministerial life or upon pastoral work is the help which it gives to us in doing this. Such a book should then furnish us both with inspirations to effort and with lofty standards of conduct.

Consequently, in most books dealing with the ministerial office or with any particular function of this, we shall find that the rules or principles they contain are drawn more or less directly from the New Testament. The advice which the writers presume to give is based upon the teaching and example of our Lord and of His apostles. This is inevitable if we regard our Lord as our one perfect and complete Ideal, and if we have any real belief in the inspiration of the New Testament. For the Christian minister the standard of our Lord must remain for all time the perfect or ideal standard; and the teaching of the New Testament writers upon "the salvation of souls" must ever remain, not only our chief authority for this task, but an authority besides which all others sink into insignificance.

Our Lord's earthly ministry, regarded as a discharge of the pastoral office, has in comparatively recent years been examined and explained in more than one book of great value. The study of such books cannot fail to be useful to those engaged in ministerial work, for in our Lord's conduct and teaching we have clearly set before us once for all the primary motives and the fundamental principles which must always inspire and guide those who would really and permanently help their fellow-men. But our Lord's ministry in human form on earth was exercised within a somewhat limited circle, and the applications of His principles recorded in the Gospels are comparatively few in number.

After a study of our Lord's own example, it is surely in the study of the lives and teaching of those whom He specially chose and commissioned to carry on His work that we may hope to find further applications of His principles, and especially when these men found themselves face to face with a greater variety of both needs and circumstances.

Of no other among those specially commissioned by our Lord have we so full a knowledge as we have of St. Paul : [1] and no one among them more zealously discharged the various functions of the ministerial office : no one brought to it richer qualifications, not only of zeal—the characteristic quality of his nature—but of education, and of that breadth of sympathy which, humanly speaking, only large knowledge and a wide experience of life can give : lastly, no one saw more clearly the universal applicability of the principles of Christianity—that it contained a gospel for the world, that in it was enshrined a philosophy and rule of life for the whole human race, and that it must ultimately overstep all barriers of class and caste and nationality and race. In our two authorities for St. Paul's life and teaching—the Acts and his Epistles—we have an immense wealth of material for forming a clear conception of how he regarded the work to which he believed himself to have been divinely called, and to which, from the time of his conversion, he devoted all his energies. If anyone wishes to see how great this material is, let him read through the latter part of the Acts of the Apostles and then through

---

[1] " Paulus ist die hellste Persönlichkeit in der Geschichte des Urchristentums." Harnack, *Das Wesen*, p. 110.

St. Paul's Epistles with this object in view, and I venture to assert that he will be astonished to find how extraordinarily rich this material actually is, especially when we consider the limited extent of these various writings.

The Acts of the Apostles[1] was evidently written by a warm admirer of St. Paul, by one whose hero St. Paul literally was. This does not necessarily imply that the writer of the Acts idealised[2] the portrait which he painted, it only implies that he watched carefully and untiringly every action and word of the man he so greatly loved and admired. We can also see how, not only from completeness of sympathy, but actually through being himself engaged in the same work,[3] the writer was able to understand St. Paul, to enter into his motives, to see why he acted as he did. The account of St. Paul's work in " Acts " is full of characteristic actions and sayings, it contains many minute details, sketched in by a single word or a phrase,[4] and often revealing

---

[1] I assume that St. Luke was the author of "Acts." The evidence which has led two scholars of such eminence as Adolf Harnack and Sir W. M. Ramsay to this position may be seen clearly set forth in the *Luke the Physician* of the first, and in the *Pauline and other Studies* (pp. 191–200) of the second.

[2] "The picture which he has given of St. Paul is not, according to the ideas of ancient days, such as a eulogist would draw, but is an *historical portrait.*" *Luke the Physician*, p. 137.

[3] "He joined St. Paul at once in the capacity of a fellow worker." ἐλαλοῦμεν. Acts xvi. 13. *Luke the Physician*, p. 147. St. Paul includes him among his συνεργοί in Philem. 24.

[4] *e.g.* συνείχετο τῷ λόγῳ. Acts xviii. 5. vg. *instabat verbo.*

more by implication than by elaborate description,
yet telling us far more about him than we should
have learnt from a whole page of description by
a less well-informed or less sympathetic writer.[1]

St. Paul's work, as it is described for us both
in the Acts and in his Epistles, was evidently a
continuous warfare, not only against such opposition as all must expect to meet who enter upon
missionary work, but against misunderstanding,
misrepresentation, and persecution from those who
ought to have understood, even to have furthered
his great purpose. Thus, besides having, as a
Christian missionary and teacher, to preach and
explain the gospel and to strengthen the faith of
those who accepted it, St. Paul had constantly
to meet such charges as those of inconsistency[2]
and self-seeking. In addition to the direct and
aggressive work of propagating Christianity St.
Paul had again and again to defend his own
honour and purity of purpose.[3]

These personal attacks St. Paul refuted by a
clear declaration of his motives, by an explanation

---

[1] "No one has yet been able to draw a convincing portrait of
St. Paul from his Epistles alone . . . the portrait given in the Acts
of the Apostles has always remained a concurring factor, because
the abundance of actual fact which is therein afforded still makes
it possible to pass behind the external action to the inward
motive." *Luke the Physician*, p. 139.

[2] Ramsay, *Galatians*, p. 256 ff., St. Paul as a " Judaistic " preacher.

[3] *e.g.* 2 Cor. i. 17, where the words ἐλαφρία, and τό Ναί ναὶ καὶ τό
Οὔ οὔ, and ii. 17, καπηλεύοντες τὸν λόγον τοῦ Θεοῦ, evidently repeat
charges brought against him.

of his methods, and especially by revealing his life's history—including the history of his religious convictions.[1] When principles were attributed to him which were not his, he replied by making known his real principles; when his honesty was questioned, he answered by explaining his methods; when his sincerity was impugned, he pointed to what he had done and suffered for the cause of Christ. In short, St. Paul was by his opponents driven to frequent *apologiae*[2] *pro vita sua* which contain a remarkably full self-revelation. To this constant compulsory self-revelation we may say that we owe the greater part of our knowledge of St. Paul's ministerial methods and ideals.

St. Paul was the last man in the world to advertise himself gratuitously, or to regard anything he did as an opportunity for self-glorification : but, for the sake of the truth he preached, and for the sake of the souls of those to whom he ministered, he must refute charges which, though made against himself personally, would, if not refuted, injure the cause he had so much at heart.

If I may for a moment anticipate a subject with

[1] *e.g.* Gal. i. 13–ii. 21, upon which *vide* Ramsay's notes : Phil. iii. 2 ff.

[2] The most complete of these is undoubtedly the Second Epistle to the Corinthians. On the charges against St. Paul which occasioned it see Plummer's Introduction, p. xvii. f. It is because it is so largely concerned with refuting these charges that this Epistle contains perhaps our most valuable revelation of St. Paul's ministerial ideals.

which later I hope to deal more at length, I would say that in repelling these personal attacks and in writing about himself—a process necessitated by these attacks—St. Paul was placed in a dilemma in which many a Christian minister finds himself placed to-day. On the one hand he recognises that, compared with the necessity of spreading the gospel, his own importance is of no account. The work is everything, he is nothing. When the matter in hand concerns the propagation of the truth, the advancement of the cause of Christ, to consider the feelings of the individual worker as of any moment would be a direct contradiction of a principle which Christ laid down and upon which He always acted.[1] On the other hand, human nature being as it is, by God's wisdom or ordering, St. Paul could not shut his eyes to the fact that it is the personal, indeed, if I may coin a word, the "particular-personal" influence which is of all instruments the strongest for effecting the purpose he wished to accomplish. And the paradox cannot be entirely resolved by saying that this personal influence means nothing more than the "particular - personal" influence sanctified, strengthened, and enlarged in or through Christ or the Holy Spirit. Such a theory will not explain the personal-magnetic influence of men like Mahomet, or Napoleon, or Bismarck. The solution demands another

---

[1] *e.g.* Phil. ii. 5 ff., cp. St. Luke ix. 53 ff.

explanation. There does seem to be an influence of personality upon personality apart from religious or moral qualities, as well as one which is mainly due to the possession of these, or which may be enormously strengthened by these. And this purely personal influence does seem to be capable of being strengthened or increased. Herein lies one of the greatest, if not the greatest of all the responsibilities of life. For the sake of the cause of Christianity the Christian minister must actually strengthen this personal influence, this power by which he attaches others to himself. But while he does this he must recognise that he is enormously increasing his responsibility for using this influence in a right direction, and guiding it towards a right object *beyond* himself. While he seeks to attach others to himself he must see that he attaches both himself and them more firmly to Christ.

But to resume my argument. For reasons too many to enumerate we shall find that, if we take those directly commissioned by our Lord, there is no one among these from whom we can learn what must be the ideals of the ministerial life, and the essential qualifications for pastoral work, as we can from St. Paul.

A study of St. Paul's life and teaching, made for the purpose of learning these, has I believe another strong claim upon our attention at the present time :--

Every man who takes up earnestly and whole-heartedly the life and work of a minister of Christ sooner or later discovers, either by a growing knowledge of his own nature and endowments,[1] or from an increasingly intelligent perception into the particular circumstances in which he finds himself placed, that, while neither consciously nor willingly neglecting any essential or even important duty, he yet comes, in practice, to pay special attention to the discharge of certain particular functions as of special value.

Again, no careful student of the history of Christianity can fail to have noticed that at different times we find more or less importance attached to particular parts or aspects of the minister's work. At one time the chief stress is laid upon the work of dealing with the individual soul, upon bringing home to the individual conscience the sense of sin, and of the need of our standing individually in a position of right relationship to God. At another time we find special stress laid upon the idea of the Church as a Divine Society, as the ideal society in which the mutual relationships of men may find their perfect and complete realisation. At one time

---

[1] Unusquisque igitur suum ingenium noverit, et ad id se applicet quod sibi aptum elegerit. Itaque quid sequatur, prius consideret . . . Quo etenim unumquemque suum ducit ingenium, aut quod officium decet, id majore impleter gratia. Sed id cum in omni vita difficile, tum in nostro actu difficillimum est. Ambrose, *De Off. Ministr.*, Bk. i. cap. xliv.

the Church appears to be engrossed with questions of organisation ; at another time her chief interest seems to lie in the purity of her doctrine, or the orthodoxy of her teaching ; at yet another time she seems to be chiefly engaged in considering and defining her true relationship to the State or civil power. And what is true of the Church is, of course, specially true of her ministers—her official leaders, who are, naturally, also her spokesmen. At one time these seem to be primarily engaged in philanthropic effort, in trying to ameliorate the material conditions of the poor ; at another time they seem chiefly bent upon proving to the world the strength of their position according to the authority of historic continuity ; at another time their chief interest seems to centre in showing the importance of public worship being conducted according to ancient precedent, that is in the details of ceremonial being arranged after certain traditional methods.

From a careful study of St. Paul's life and writings, made in order to find inspiration and guidance for the ministerial life as a whole, I have no hesitation in asserting that some spheres or parts of ministerial activity do appear to have been regarded by him as of special importance ; and that, both directly and indirectly, he does seem to lay special stress on the necessity of the enthusiastic performance of certain functions of the ministerial life. Thus we may, I think, say that St. Paul does not forbid what I may term "specialising" in that life, and that we may, from his teaching and his example, find at least support for laying stress on the performance of particular duties, these being chosen by us, or commended to us partly through our own consciousness of particular gifts or endowments, partly by our consciousness of particular needs in the sphere in which we are working.

I would go further than this, and would venture to urge that the ministerial functions upon which St. Paul seems to lay particular stress,[1] the activities which he seems to regard as of special importance, are such as the Church, if she is to be the true guide and helper of the people, stands to-day in peculiar need; but which, in practice, the average minister at present seems only too apt to regard as of quite secondary importance.

It has been stated that if we take the three great teachers of the New Testament, we shall find that in the early ages of the Church the greatest importance was attached to St. Peter, that during the Reformation the appeal was mainly to St. Paul, while in these later days the Church needs especially to meditate upon the teaching of St. John.

There is doubtless a measure of truth in these

---

[1] *e.g.* those in I Tim. iv. 13.

somewhat sweeping assertions, but they are far from containing the whole truth. It would be more correct to say that in no age can the Church afford to neglect any of the great presentations of the faith, and that she must at all times bear in mind the many-sidedness of the Christian life which is expressed in the New Testament, and is there presented to her as a perpetual admonition. We may recall the saying of M. Renan, quoted by Matthew Arnold, "After having been for three hundred years . . . the Christian doctor *par excellence*, St. Paul is now coming to the end of his reign." But when we survey the needs of the present, and, as far as we can foresee them, those of the immediate future, we shall be inclined to hope and believe that Matthew Arnold's own opinion is much more likely to be true : " The reign of the real St. Paul is only beginning, his fundamental ideas will have an influence in the future greater than any which they have yet had — an influence proportioned to their correspondence with a number of the deepest and most permanent facts of human nature itself." [1]

First and foremost among the " facts " of human nature we may put the *needs* of human character. And I believe that one reason of the great value of St. Paul's teaching arises from his clear insight into these needs, and also from his conviction

---

[1] *St. Paul and Protestantism*, pp. 1, 2.

that in the "Gospel," using the term as a synonym for Christianity, lies the divinely ordained means for their supply. But, leaving the general needs of human nature, let us first try to fix our attention upon what experience teaches us to be the specially urgent needs both of man and of society at the present time. Then let us consider what qualities seem to be most generally wanting in much of the ministerial work which is being done to-day. For this work should surely have as one of its primary objects the supply of these needs—that is, of those defects in character to whose absence so many of our personal and social difficulties are due. An earnest effort to answer these questions will, I think, convince us, first, that to a great extent it is just those functions of the ministerial office upon which St. Paul does lay so much stress, which will supply these needs ; and, second, that unfortunately these are the very functions in whose adequate discharge the majority, especially of the younger clergy, seem to be failing to qualify themselves. In consequence we find that neither the needs of the Church nor the needs of the world are receiving that due supply upon which efficiency, and so welfare, depends.

1. First and foremost among present needs for the moral improvement of the people I should put that of "sound learning," of trustworthy

knowledge, and this in regard mainly to four objects :—1st, our own nature ; 2nd, God ; 3rd, our present immediate circumstances (the condition, and tendencies, and movements of the whole existing fabric of society and of social relationships) ; 4th, history.[1]   No one can study St. Paul's writings without noticing the immense stress which he laid, both directly and indirectly, both by precept and example, upon the *teaching* function of the Christian ministry.[2]   Again, a true man's prayers reveal his deepest desires and his highest aspirations ; and a true man will make every effort to accomplish and effect what he prays for.   In almost every one of St. Paul's prayers we find him making petition for growth in knowledge in his converts.[3]   And it is not always with regard to the amount or content of their knowledge that he prays, it is rather that *growth*[4] in the apprehension of truth may proceed in them.   I may mention in passing that more than once, when St. Paul speaks of γνῶσις as a valuable or useful possession or instrument,

---

[1] Out of 24 occurrences of γνωρίζειν in the N.T. 18 occur in St. Paul : of 29 instances of γνῶσις, 23 are in St. Paul : of 20 instances of ἐπίγνωσις, 15 are in St. Paul : γινώσκειν occurs 48 times in St. Paul's Epistles.

[2] Acts xv. 35, xviii. 11, xx. 20, xxi. 28, xxviii. 31 ; 1 Cor. iv. 17 ; Col. i. 28, iii. 16 ; 1 Tim. iv. 11, vi. 2, etc.

[3] *e.g.* Eph. i. 17, 18, iii. 18, 19 ; Phil. i. 9 ; Col. i. 9, 10.   See chapter on " St. Paul's Prayers," p. 271.

[4] *e.g.* Eph. iii. 19, γνῶναι . . . γνώσεως, "to know that which never can be known " (Westcott) ; Phil. i. 9, μᾶλλον καὶ μᾶλλον περισσεύῃ ἐν ἐπιγνώσει ; Col. i. 10, αὐξανόμενοι τῇ ἐπιγνώσει.

he leaves quite undefined the object of know-ledge [1]—a proof of his high regard for knowledge generally—as an endowment of the Christian life. To encourage growth in knowledge, and to assist it by dispensing the highest knowledge through adequate teaching, is evidently to St. Paul a primary responsibility of the Christian minister, indeed of every Christian. [2] But who with any wide acquaintance with the actual condition of things would dare to assert that these obligations, first, of constantly acquiring and assimilating, and secondly, of dispensing and of qualifying them-selves to dispense the highest and most essential of all knowledge are generally recognised, or are, in any sense of the word, adequately discharged by Christian ministers to-day? Of course we shall not fail to notice that in the stress which St. Paul lays upon the teaching function of the ministry he is only following closely in the foot-steps of our Lord. To the supreme importance which our Lord attached to the teaching office, especially by His own personal example, the gospel record is one continuous witness.

2. Another great need at the present time, if the work of the Christian minister is to be done efficiently, is that he shall be much more intimately

---

[1] Rom. xv. 14 ; 1 Cor. i. 5 ; 2 Cor. vi. 6, viii. 7.

[2] Eph. i. 17, πνεῦμα . . . ἀποκαλύψεως. "It is a teaching Spirit rather than a teachable spirit which the Apostle asks that they may have." J.A. Robinson, *Ephesians*, Kregel Publications. 1978. p. 38.

acquainted, not merely with the external and material conditions, but with the thoughts and aspirations of all the various classes or sections of the community. I am quite ready to admit that the majority of the clergy know much of the lives and thoughts of those who attend a place of worship, even of the homes and conduct of that much larger number who do not. And these, it must be remembered, belong to all the various so-called "classes" or grades of society. But what is the knowledge possessed by the average clergyman of the real intellectual difficulties of the great number of men who cannot accept Christianity as it is ordinarily presented to them in the pulpit? Or what is his knowledge of that very different class who seem to live for money, for pleasure, or society? Or, again, what does he know of that apparently rapidly growing number of men, at the other extremity of the social world, who often spend at least some portion of Sunday in reading socialistic or "labour" literature, or in discussing problems of politics or economics?

Now if we study either the Acts or the Epistles carefully, and try to pierce below the surface of the writing, we are constantly struck with St. Paul's intimate knowledge of the conditions, indeed of the "atmosphere" in which those are living whom he is addressing. And as our knowledge of the first century increases and we are able to appreciate better the many allusions[1] in St. Paul's Epistles we shall probably add largely to the numerous proofs of this which we already possess.   It was because St. Paul knew so deeply and so comprehensively the actual conditions of his age that he was able to use these very conditions so "wisely" in his great scheme of the Christianising of the Empire.[2] Here again we may notice a likeness between St. Paul and our Lord, for the Evangelists frequently, both explicitly and implicitly, draw attention to our Lord's knowledge, not only of individuals,[3] but of the thoughts,[4] the aspirations,[5] the peculiar temptations and sins[6] of the various sections of the community.

3. It has again and again been stated of recent years that while we have witnessed a wider diffusion of Christian sentiment, and, to some extent, a more general recognition of the claim of a Christian standard to be the standard of life, we have at the same time lost that sense of the deeper truths and the stronger convictions of Christianity which many of our forefathers

---

[1] As a proof of the value of increased knowledge of the conditions of the first century let anyone read the Epistle to the Galatians, first by the aid of one of the older commentaries and then by the aid of Ramsay's *Historical Commentary* on that Epistle.

[2] See Ramsay's essay on "The Statesmanship of Paul" in his *Pauline and other Studies.*

[3] *e.g.* St. John i. 48, ii. 24, vi. 64.

[4] St. Luke vi. 8.   [5] St. John vi. 15.

[6] St. Matt. xxiii. 13, 15, 23, 27, 29.

possessed. We carefully survey, widely lament, and from time to time attack the patent evils of society, that is as "imperfections" which may be largely remedied by further legislation ; but we forget that these are only symptoms of a deep-seated disease. St. Paul will show us the futility of such a method *by itself.* To study him is to be constantly reminded of the stress which he lays upon the reality, the power, the deadly effects of *sin.*[1] This want of the conviction both of the reality and of the power of sin is the source of most of the evils which abound to-day. Beneath the "phenomena" of evil which were sufficiently patent in such cities as Antioch, or Corinth, or Ephesus, St. Paul saw, pointed to, and rebuked *sin* as the chief cause of them all. This cause must be removed, and for its permanent removal St. Paul was convinced that the only efficacious instrument was the gospel. Who would venture to assert that Christian ministers generally, either in preaching or teaching, lay the same stress now as St. Paul laid upon this fundamental cause of both personal and social evils? Has it not been said, and with

---

[1] "It is one thing to say that the times are out of joint, to reckon with men's selfishness and vanity and greed as disagreeable but inevitable instances of life, to admit our own foibles and frailties, and to say that we know we are not what we ought to be. It is quite another thing to take the candle from Christ and look sin, within us and without us, straight in the face. . . . St. Paul says we wrestle not against flesh and blood, but against spiritual wickedness." Bp. Talbot, *Aspects of Christian Truth*, p. 222.

much truth, that the general consciousness of sin has become greatly weakened? Is the "ministry" wholly guiltless for this? Are we not all too ready to attack symptoms, and to blame circumstances and environment, instead of boldly exposing and attacking the disease at its root?

4. To-day we hear widespread complaints of the want of "spirit," of "energy," and of "power," both in Christian life and in the work of the Churches. One of the outstanding features of St. Paul's teaching is the importance he attaches to the presence,[1] the power,[2] the work[3] of the Holy Spirit, which to him is the Spirit of Christ,[4] if not actually identical[5] with the Christ of faith. Is there, I ask, any absolutely *a priori* reason why the presence of the Holy Spirit should be less real, or the power of the Holy Spirit less strong, now than in St. Paul's day? Once more, Is the ministry to-day sufficiently alive to the necessity of cultivating the conditions upon which both the presence and the power of the Holy Spirit seem to be dependent? The chiefest of all these is of course the careful maintenance of the closest possible union with Christ. When we hear the ministry blamed for want of "spiritual power," may it not be that the conditions whereby

---

[1] Rom. viii. 14, 16 ; 1 Cor. iii. 16, vi. 19, xii. 13 ; 2 Cor. vi. 6, etc.
[2] Rom. v. 5, viii. 26 ; 1 Cor. xii. 8 ; Gal. iii. 2, etc.
[3] 1 Cor. ii. 10, 13 ; 2 Cor. iii. 3 ; Gal. v. 17, 22, 25, etc.
[4] Rom. viii. 9 ; Gal. iv. 6.   [5] 2 Cor. iii. 17.

this power is assimilated, maintained, and dispensed, are wanting? Upon these conditions we may learn much from St. Paul.[1]

5. Lastly, I believe that a careful study of St. Paul's ministerial teaching and ideals may give us a more true sense of the real proportion, of the relative importance among things which actually do interest, or should interest us. The following is a useful exercise for ministers of Christ :—First, to read slowly through an Epistle of St. Paul, noticing carefully, both in doctrine and ethics, the points upon which he lays special stress : secondly, to think over what we have spent time and energy upon during, say, the last month. The difference between St. Paul's "judgment values" and our own may be, indeed very probably will be, very great. But this difference will not consist chiefly in the objects to be attained ; it will be the difference in the means employed to attain these objects that will be found most striking.

These five examples, in each of which it seems as if a return to St. Paul's teaching and methods of work is required to-day, form only a very small proportion of the lessons we may learn from a study of his ministerial ideals. Many other

---

[1] Upon this subject there is much that will be found most useful in the chapter upon "The Law of the Spirit of Life in Christ Jesus," in *The Fifth Gospel*, pp. 138 ff.

lessons will come before us in the course of the investigation contained in the following pages. I have chosen these five to show that an examination of the Apostle's teaching, as a help to, and an inspiration for, our own ministerial life is at least worth attempting. How imperfect and incomplete the following study is, I know well. I trust, however, it may at least induce others to pursue still further this same investigation—one from which they cannot fail to reap a rich harvest of benefit, not only to themselves but for those among whom they are called to minister.

Chapter 1

THE MINISTER OF CHRIST, A WORKMAN

σπούδασον σεαυτὸν δόκιμον παραστῆσαι τῷ Θεῷ, ἐργάτην ἀνεπαίσχυντον.—2 Tim. ii. 15.

τοῦτο τὸ ἔργον Θεοῦ ἐστιν καὶ ὑμῶν, ὅταν αὐτὸ ἀπαρτίσητε.—*Ignat. ad Polyc.* c. vii.

THE Christian minister is a workman,[1] not a machine ;[2] he works with certain instruments, upon a particular kind of material ; and he works

---

[1] 2 Tim. ii. 15, ἐργάτην ἀνεπαίσχυντον. The word ἐργάτης is used also of a minister of the gospel in 1 Tim. v. 18 (a quotation from St. Matt. x. 10, cf. St. Luke x. 7). It is used in a bad sense, of St. Paul's adversaries, in 2 Cor. xi. 13 and Phil. iii. 2. In the Gospels it is used of ministerial work in St. Matt. ix. 37, 38, x. 10 ; in St. Luke in x. 2, 7. It occurs in parables in St. Matt. xx. 1 ff., and in St. Luke xiii. 27, also of an agricultural labourer in St. James v. 4. [In profane literature it is frequently used of a husbandman (whose work calls for far more resource than that of watching a machine) ; it is also used of a stonemason, of one who practises an art, of a judge, and of a medical practitioner.] It also occurs in Acts xix. 25, with τεχνίτης, where Bengel notes, "*alii erant* τεχνῖται, *artifices* nobiliores, *alii* ἐργάται, *operarii.*" N.T. *Commentary*, Kregel Publ. 1982.

[2] In the Church, as in the world, there is to-day a danger of machinery being the master and man the slave. "Here again matter has the mastery over mind : the mechanism of industry is not under our control, but runs away with us." Mackenzie, *Introduction to Social Philosophy*, p. 103.

Upon St. Paul, and so the Christian minister as an ἀρχιτέκτων, see Chapter III. p. 187.

in order to form or fashion a certain definite object — an object with a particular definite character. But the Christian minister should be not only a workman, he must be an artist,[1] in the highest sense of the word, by which I mean that he must be a highly skilled workman, and that his personality, or character, must enter into all his work and be impressed upon all his material. There are workmen who are little more than human machines, in whom there is much more of the machine than of humanity. Actually their only office seems to be to set, and keep in motion, some mechanical contrivance. Into their work, beyond the qualities of [mechanical] obedience, regularity, and endurance, no characteristic to which the term "human" can be applied needs, or ever appears, to enter. Such to a great extent was the work of the heathen priesthoods of the ancient world: to some degree this was also true of the work of the Jewish priests. These were chiefly engaged in maintaining a system of rites and ceremonial observances, which must be

---

[1] Here we may recall the well-known words of Gregory (*Reg. Past.* i. cap. 1). "Nulla ars doceri præsumitur, nisi intenta prius meditatione discatur. Ab imperitis ergo pastorale magisterium qua temeritate suscipitur, quando ars est artium regimen animarum."

On p. 322 of the *Int. to Soc. Phil.*, Mackenzie speaks "of the educative influence of the finer sorts of art," and of how "they afford opportunities for the employment of the highest kind of skilled labour and check the despotism of machinery"; he also says "the moral life is the most subtle and exquisite of the Fine Arts, and requires a genius for its right accomplishment."

regularly performed at certain appointed times and with a scrupulous obedience to certain fixed directions. Into the performance of these tasks the higher virtues and qualities of personality hardly entered. The religious system was largely mechanical, and the men who worked it might, with little detriment to the system, also become mechanical, indeed that they should become so was rather advantageous than not.

But this part of the religion of the Old Testament was only a fragment of the whole ; and it is at least open to question whether it was an essential part. May it not be regarded as having been almost a Divine concession to the weakness and immaturity of human nature in an age when, at any rate for the mass of the people, the higher conceptions and exercises of religion were too difficult, too far raised above the ordinary level of religious ideas to find at that time any general acceptance ?

It is clear that very frequently but a small part in this system was taken by the loftier and purer spirits of the Old Testament. On the contrary, many of the greatest of these stated their antagonism to it, or rather to the dangers inevitably connected with it, in no uncertain tones.[1] They saw how comparatively useless were these rites and ceremonies to further the *moral* improvement of the people—the end they themselves had

---

[1] *e.g.* Isa. i. 12-14 ; Hos. vi. 6 ; Amos v. 21, 22 ; Mic. vi. 6.

in view. A religious system into which the *personal*, necessarily, so little entered could have but little effect upon the moral nature of its devotees. As a means of raising and developing the moral nature and moral possibilities the power of this system was necessarily small.

[I hold no brief for the Higher Criticism, and it is far from my object to enter into any discussion of the truth or otherwise of different results reached by various Old Testament scholars ; but the close connection of an elaborate, and certainly somewhat material and mechanical, ritual system with what we are told of the character of the rest of the work of Moses, does seem difficult. Between the broad and lofty ethical standard, *e.g.*, of the Ten Commandments and the minute directions given for the punctilious discharge of daily, monthly, and yearly ceremonies in the Tabernacle, there does seem a somewhat wide chasm to be bridged over in any single human personality, however comprehensive his sympathies, and however great may have been his powers of adaptation to particular present national and religious conditions.]

I assume that the essential [spiritual] religion of the Old and of the New Testament is one and the same, and that Christianity is the true and genuine development, along the normal and divinely appointed line, of the religion of Elijah, Amos, Isaiah, and Micah. This religion, through the whole course of its history, stands pre-eminent

among religions, not only in the loftiness of its
ethical conceptions, but in the manner in which
the personality of each of its champions and
teachers enters into their efforts on its behalf.
This power of personality reaches its climax in
the personality of our Lord, and so great is
this that Christianity has been termed " the
religion of a Person " ; and it has been asserted
that " Jesus Christ is the Christian Religion."
But in varying degree the same importance of the
personal, or of character, holds good, both of
all the truly great spiritual teachers and workers
who preceded Him and prepared for His coming,
and of those who have followed Him in the progress and development of Christianity. Our Lord
alone had a perfect character ; in Him alone the
infinite possibilities of a perfectly ethical nature,
one perfectly moralised, were absolutely realised ;
but the ethical power or influence of the saints of
the Old Testament, of the New Testament, and
of the true saints of the Christian Church has
been in proportion to the measure of the Divine
in their character and personality. By " the
Divine " I mean the Divine Righteousness [1] which

---

[1] The righteousness of which St. Paul speaks in Phil. iii. 9,
where also he indicates its source, ἐκ Θεοῦ, and the condition of its
possession, ἐπὶ τῇ πίστει. As an example of the unity of N.T.
teaching with the higher ethical teaching in the O.T. compare
St. Paul's teaching here with that in Isa. lxiv. 6 and Ps. lxxi. 16.
[St. Paul draws attention to the result of this righteousness in
Phil. i. 9.]

It is only because he is convinced that this righteousness which

absolutely filled and entirely ruled and sanctified
the human nature of our Lord.   The ethical
power of the personality will be the result of the
possession of this Divine Righteousness, and will
act upon, and so influence other human personalities,
and this without destroying their free-will, except in
the sense in which it may be said that the more
a man is filled with good the less is he liable to be
influenced by evil.

Of no Biblical character is it more true than of
St. Paul that the stamp or impress of his personality is upon all his work, and upon all his
teaching.   And St. Paul pleads for this personal
influence [1]—of which one condition is personal
freedom—in others.   This is surely one cause
of his intense contempt for mere legalism, one
reason for his exhortation to stand fast in the
Christian freedom ; for Christ gives to every man
not only a fuller life, but therewith a larger and
more powerful personality and influence.   Every
letter of St. Paul's opens with his own name, a
reminder that the teaching which it contains is
truth which has passed through, and become
impressed with, his own personality.   The power

---

he possessed is not due to any merit of his own that St. Paul offers
his own conduct as an example for his converts ; 1 Cor. iv. 16,
xi. 1 ; Phil. iii. 17.   The awful responsibility of personal example
could hardly be more clearly suggested.

The τὴν ἐκ Θεοῦ δικαιοσύνην is one of the many proofs of St. Paul's
" Realism," upon which see my *Social Teaching of St. Paul*,
p. 142.

[1] 1 Cor. vi. 5 ; 1 Tim. iv. 12 ff.; 2 Tim. ii. 21 ff.

of a truth (especially in reference to preaching) may often be expressed as the product of the truth multiplied by the personality of him who utters it.[1]

Two points may here be briefly noticed :—First, that even when St. Paul couples another name with his own to describe the source of a letter, he generally very soon passes into the singular form of address :[2] secondly, that the singular form of address and appeal and reference is more common in his earlier than his later letters. It is in the two Thessalonian Epistles that the " we "—Paul and Silvanus and Timothy—is most frequently found.[3]   May we not assume from this that increased experience strengthened St. Paul's conviction of the power of personal influence and of the personal appeal in the work of the ministry ?

Before proceeding to consider the personality or personal character of the Christian minister at length, I would deal briefly with each of the three other subjects which I named at the opening of this chapter.

---

[1] As a proof of the greater importance attached to personality in the N.T. : Is God ever in the N.T. (apart from the Apocalypse) represented as employing an inanimate instrument to effect His purposes ?   Such representations are of course common in the O.T.

[2] *e.g.* 1 Cor. i. 1, compare i. 4, 10, 11, 12 ; Phil. i. 1, compare i. 3, 4, 7, 8, 9 ; Col. i. 1, compare i. 24, 25, 29.

[3] 1 Thess. i. 1, 2, 5, 6, 8, ii. 3, 4, 5, 13, 17, 19, etc. ; 2 Thess. i. 3, 4, 11, ii. 1, 13, iii. 1, 6, etc.

I. The Instrument with which the Minister works

Briefly, this is the "gospel";[1] but to the term we must give a comprehensive interpretation. It is "the truth,"[2] the ideal life, and the whole range of ideas and of spiritual and moral forces[3] conveyed in and through the message which he delivers; and this message is delivered both in conduct[4] and in speech. It is "the word of God,"[5] the one spiritual weapon of offence or attack which the Christian warrior employs. This word or message may be used and conveyed in many ways, and in its employment every kind[6] of "wisdom" (*i.e.* of skill)[7] is to be exercised.

Here I would refer to two passages which in this connection, as in others, should be most carefully studied by every Christian minister :—

(*a*) 2 Cor. v. 11–vi. 10 ("one of the most autobiographical passages in the most autobiographical of epistles"). The passage, whose subject is "the life of an Apostle," like the whole Epistle, contains a wonderful self-revelation. St. Paul describes his work as an effort to

---

[1] Rom. i. 15, 16 ; Eph. iii. 6.

[2] 2 Cor. iv. 2 [Eph. iv. 21, cp. St. John xviii. 37] ; 2 Cor. vi. 7 ; Eph. i. 13, etc.

[3] Rom. i. 16, 17 ; 2 Cor. vi. 7, x. 4.

[4] 2 Cor. iv. 2 (ἑαυτούς), vi. 3, 4 ff., etc.

[5] Eph. vi. 17 (ῥῆμα).   [6] Col. i. 28 (ἐν πάσῃ σοφίᾳ).

[7] See Chapter X. on "St. Paul on Wisdom," p. 356.

persuade [1] men ; his ministry is a ministry of reconciliation ; he is an ambassador on behalf of Christ ;
in the exercise of his ministry the greatest care
must be exercised that there be created no cause of
stumbling ; the minister's object is to commend
himself to those to whom he ministers.   With the
second part of verse 4 (chap. vi.) begins the section
to which I would draw special attention, for it
describes the means employed to effect the
purpose in view.   St. Paul first [2] speaks of
personal sufferings borne in the course of his
work : these are all examples of an extreme form
of self-sacrifice.   They are part of the filling up
of the sufferings (characteristic) of the Christ,[3] for
the sake of the Church : and, like the sufferings of
the personal Christ, they are a very important
instrument of witness to the world, that is in
regard to his sincerity, and also as to his conception of the vital importance of his work.   In
verse 6, St. Paul passes on to describe other
weapons for influence, other instruments for the
conversion of those who do not believe.   The
Greek is at once so concise and so full of
suggestion that the meaning can only be obtained

---

[1] The various terms and phrases in this passage will be found
more fully discussed under such subjects as " Ministry," " Ambassador," etc., in Chapter III.

[2] Note how ὑπομονή comes first, a quality essential for every
kind of suffering.

[3] Col. i. 24.   Note τοῦ χριστοῦ in contrast with Χριστός in
verse 27.

by a paraphrase. For instance, "pureness"[1] means not only purity of life, but also sincerity of purpose, both of which are absolutely essential for pastoral influence : "knowledge"[2] implies growing perception both of the meaning and issue of the whole sum of truth ; for all knowledge is knowledge of God, and therefore helpful to one whose life's object is to make known the will of God : "kindness"[3] has been well defined as "the special grace of the gentleman, placing others at their ease and shrinking from causing unnecessary pain" ;[4] by a spirit that is holy,[5] *i.e.* our spirit, the spirit in which we give our witness must be inspired and governed by God's Holy Spirit ; there must be love which is "free from affectation and formality"[6]—two most insidious vices, and therefore enemies of the ministerial life ; by speech, reasoning, argument, which has its source in truth,[7] and of which absolute truth is characteristic ; "by Divine power,"[8] for there is no power like that of a life which is full of Christ—the

---

[1] ἁγνότης, elsewhere in N.T. only in xi. 3 (an interesting passage).

[2] γνῶσις. Bengel's note is very curious, "γνῶσις sæpe dicit *aequitatem.*"

[3] χρηστότης.

[4] For this and one or two other renderings in this passage I am indebted to Dr. Plummer *in loc.*

[5] ἐν πνεύματι ἁγίῳ.   [6] ἐν ἀγάπῃ ἀνυποκρίτῳ.

[7] ἐν λόγῳ ἀληθείας. Did not Dean Stanley once assert that not to be absolutely truthful was the greatest temptation of the clergy ?

[8] ἐν δυνάμει Θεοῦ.

power of God ;[1] by arms of righteousness[2] which alone are to be employed ; whatever weapons may be used by others against us, those we employ must be absolutely righteous. Too often to-day means and instruments are employed for what are termed " Church purposes " which cause at least a cynical smile upon the face of the world.[3]

(*b*) 2 Cor. iv. 2. There are few phrases even in St. Paul more pregnant with meaning than the words, " by manifestation of the truth commending ourselves to every man's conscience[4] in the sight of God." These words may be said to describe both the means and the method whereby the gospel must be propagated—the Divinely appointed instrument and the way in which it must be used for the salvation of man. The instrument is nothing else than the truth, and nothing less than the truth ; and the more deeply we study the writings of St. Paul and

---

[1] I Cor. i. 24. [2] διὰ τῶν ὅπλων τῆς δικαιοσύνης.

[3] It is not necessary to particularise, but we can hardly imagine St. Paul engaged in promoting dances or card parties to " meet the expenses " of the Church in Corinth.

[4] It must be noticed that the Christian minister as a workman works both with and upon the conscience of those he tries to influence and form. Thus the conscience is both an instrument and material. Upon St. Paul's idea of the conscience see an excellent note in Sanday and Headlam's *Romans*, p. 60, in which the history of the conception of the συνείδησις is traced. The affinity of St. Paul's use to that of his Stoic contemporaries is noticed. Compare W. L. Davidson, *The Stoic Creed*, p. 144.

St. John the more surely shall we be convinced
of the wealth of meaning contained in this one
single word.   It is at once the real and the
ideal.[1] Often in the New Testament the ideal
is regarded as the only real.[2] It is also the
whole revelation of God to man.[3] It is the
abiding as opposed to the transitory, the perfect
as contrasted with the imperfect, the substance
as opposed to "that which is but the shadow
of a shadow."   It is the opposite to that which
of itself opposes itself to the Divine.   Then St.
Paul does not limit the method of manifestation,
any more than does the prophet in that striking
phrase "Arise, shine," for both strength and
light, alike necessary for manifestation, are
granted unto thee.   Again, this manifestation
of the truth is intimately connected with our
own personality—"commending ourselves."   It
is only the personal which affects to the fullest
degree the personal.   We speak of being
"affected" or "moved" by the beauties of
Nature and Art, we say that these "speak," or
"appeal," to us.   But, if we reflect, we shall
find proof which will convince us that Nature

---

[1] As "truth" is in Jesus (Eph. iv. 21), who is the Christ, so
when by manifestation of the truth we commend ourselves, it is
"Christ in us" which we commend to the conscience of
men.

[2] Phil. iii. 20 ($\dot{\upsilon}\pi\acute{\alpha}\rho\chi\epsilon\iota$), cf. Heb. xi. 10 ($\tau\upsilon\grave{\upsilon}\varsigma\ \theta\epsilon\mu\epsilon\lambda\iota\acute{\upsilon}\upsilon\varsigma$).

[3] For "it presents the right view of the ultimate relations of
man, the world, and God" (Westcott).

when described as really loved or "felt" has to
a great extent been "personified."[1] To the old
Greek Nature was full of personalities. To the
Christian poet Nature has a soul, and is something more than the mere garment of the
divine. There is a "presence" in Nature.
What is true of Nature is also true of Art, it is
the artist in his art—in music or painting or
sculpture or poetry—that affects us.[2] It is the
personal and never the mechanical, however
cleverly contrived, which touches us. We must
commend ourselves :[3] it is the sanctified personality which affects, and impresses, and influences
for good. Neither our Lord nor His apostles
offered truth apart from life. Our Lord constantly offered Himself; St. Paul, in a great
measure, does the same. It is the immanence of
the truth, which is not far from the immanence

---

[1] In Wordsworth's Ode of Immortality it is (stanzas iii. and
iv.) the Shepherd Boy, the Children, the Babe on his Mother's
arm, that most touch the poet ; and note the "personification" of
Nature in

> "Earth fills her lap with pleasures of her own ;
> Yearnings she hath in her own natural kind,
> And, even with something of a Mother's mind."

[2] It is this thought of personality being revealed through art
which makes many of Browning's poems so inspiring to the
preacher, *e.g. Fra Lippo Lippi*—

> "Here's Giotto, with his Saint a-praising God !
> That sets you praising,—"

compare his *Andrea del Sarto* and *Abt Vogler*.

[3] The *Ars Poetica* contains many a valuable lesson for the

of the Divine—"that which is born of the Spirit
is spirit"—which is mighty in effect.

Lastly, the appeal is to the conscience.[1]   I
will not enter here into the subject of St. Paul's
psychology, a fruitful field of study, and one
which hitherto, so far as I am aware, has hardly
received the attention it deserves.   Here I
would only notice that the appeal must be
directed to the highest faculty of man.   History
and experience (if examined) will be found
alike full of records of failure on the part
of well-meaning but ill-advised " good " people,

---

preacher ; but few more true than that contained in the
lines—

> " dulcia sunto
> Et quocunque volent animum auditoris agunto.
> Ut ridentibus arrident, ita flentibus adsunt
> Humani vultus : si vis me flere, dolendum est
> Primum ipsi tibi ; . . ."   (99–103).

Goethe, too, was right when he spoke of Das Menschenrecht,
and then asked—

> " Wodurch bewegt er alle Herzen ?
> Wodurch besiegt er jedes Element ?
> Ist es der Einklang nicht, der aus dem Busen bringt,
> Und in sein Herz die Welt zurücke schlingt ? "

May I also commend a study of " The Prologue for the Theatre "
in *Faust* to the preacher?   From it he may get some useful
hints.

[1] A study of the " Conscience " in St. Paul would belong to a study
of his ethical teaching and of his psychology.   Much that is
helpful will be found in the articles on " Conscience " and on
" Psychology " in Hastings' *Bib. Dict.*   Also in Lightfoot,
Philippians, p. 303.   The parallel between the Stoic τὸ ἡγεμονικόν
and the Conscience is interesting.   W. L. Davidson in *The Stoic
Creed* states, " the ' ruling faculty ' is conscience."

simply from forgetfulness or ignorance of this essential condition of success.[1] Then we must remember that in this reference to the conscience there is involved St. Paul's "doctrine of man" (another fruitful subject for study), but which I cannot stay to consider here, except to notice its similarity to our Lord's idea of man, especially in one particular—viz. His belief in the *possibilities* of human nature. Would our Lord have died for man, would St. Paul have given up his life to the service of man, had they not believed in these? This belief in man's possibilities is essential to the Christian minister, and must be carefully nourished by him; for he will meet with only too numerous cases which tend "to shake his faith in human nature." Beside St. Paul's faith in man stands his faith in "the truth," when rightly commended, to win its way and to do its appointed work.

There is one further essential condition of our work noticed in these words of St. Paul, and that is the consciousness of the presence of God

---

[1] On the necessity of appealing to the higher faculties, see Mrs. Bosanquet's *The Strength of the People*, p. 2 ff. "Leaders like Cromwell, who insisted that you could not even make a good soldier of a man without appealing to his higher faculties, owe their success to their profound knowledge of human nature. Great religious teachers, who have put their faith in spiritual conviction and conversion, who have refused to accept anything less than the whole man, have achieved results which seem miraculous to those who are willing to compromise for a share in the souls they undertake to guide."

—"in the sight of God." The thought is a favourite one with St. Paul,[1] and gives a dignity and solemnity to his work. The condition must be remembered by us, for we have only to connect anything with God in order to see how intrinsically important it is. We are thereby at once reminded that the final judgment upon both our motives and our actions, upon the choice of our weapons and the methods in which they are used, lies with God, as the final Judge of these.

II. The Material upon which the Minister works

We must now consider this more closely, and while we do so we must bear in mind the conception of the minister as an "artist." Briefly, the material is human nature; in one sense always the same, in another sense never the same : even the same "subject" is never for two days exactly the same. If we leave our material or our task, we cannot assume that in our absence others have not been working upon it; indeed, they are always working upon it contemporaneously with our own labour. And as our material

---

[1] St. Paul uses it of his preaching, 2 Cor. ii. 17 ; of his pastoral care of his converts, 2 Cor. vii. 12 ; of his remembrance of them, 1 Thess. i. 3 ; of the quality of actions, 1 Tim. ii. 3. He charges Timothy, also, "in the sight of God," 1 Tim. vi. 13.

is different in nature and differs in itself from time to time, it constantly calls for different treatment and for the use of different instruments. Then we must remember we do not find our material quite "in the rough." It has generally been worked upon by others before us, and we must take up the work, often with ugly flaws and evidences of evil workmanship, at every stage of development. The thoughts which here suggest themselves are many. For the sake of clearness I will, as far as possible, confine myself mainly to two : first, that we must know as intimately as possible the nature of our material ; secondly, we must know, as well as we can, the stage of the development of the subject at the time we work. This latter condition implies that we know what other influences have worked, or are now working, either in aid of or against our own purpose.

St. Paul's knowledge of human nature was great in two ways. First, he knew it intimately as we find it everywhere and in all ages very much the same ; he knew "our common human nature." Secondly, he knew it as affected by various particular local influences, both past and present—influences of race, nationality, tradition, climate, politics, religion, and economic conditions.

Of the qualities of what we mean by our common human nature he had a profound knowledge. Here again the likeness to our Lord is very striking. Our Lord's knowledge of human nature not only struck but astonished [1] His contemporaries. It has been the admiration of every careful student of the Gospels in all ages. To gauge St. Paul's knowledge of this subject we have only to read through any one Epistle, that is an Epistle addressed to the same hearers, and then try to count up the various traits of character implied, and the various influences of different kinds to which he proves that he knows these hearers to be subject.

(a) *St. Paul's knowledge of our common human nature*

(a) 1 Thess. chap. v.[2] St. Paul wishes to warn, yet, from his knowledge of the human heart, he knows that an indirect method, one by which the need for thought may be suggested and self-examination provoked, is often far more efficacious than a direct rebuke or even exhortation. The condition which in the opening verses he describes is an all too common one—a condition of which we ourselves are frequently quite unconscious, one of real danger, yet in which we imagine all is well. Briefly, the state is one of comparative insensibility to moral and spiritual

---

[1] St. John i. 48, ii. 24, 25, etc.

[2] Many of the exhortations in this chapter seem to be so peculiarly suitable for those in a position of special responsibility that some of the older expositors have been led to believe that they were originally addressed to the elders of the Church in Thessalonica.

forces, and to the meaning of phenomena of which these forces are the cause. The moral and spiritual senses are neither watchful nor in action. For any Christian such a state is dangerous, for the Christian minister it is absolutely inexcusable. Yet it is a state in which many seem to live. The Apostle (in verse 11) closes his warning with a command to mutual encouragement and mutual edification. Here again we see the Apostle's knowledge of human nature. Continuous censoriousness and fault-finding detract from life, and may actually encourage us to dwell upon evil. There are multitudes of men and women who would be far more benefited by encouragement than by criticism, and by assistance in building up their character rather than by attention being drawn to their blemishes or deficiencies. The next paragraph (verses 12 ff.) is full of warnings and counsels, each witnessing to a deep knowledge of human nature. In verse 14, St. Paul recognises three distinct types of character, and the different treatment required by each. To supply this treatment continuously is not easy. Human nature soon tires of helping others, hence St. Paul writes παρακαλοῦμεν,[1] which here seems to combine the idea of encouragement or "heartening" with that of exhortation. Of the

---

[1] The significance of παρακαλεῖν in the N.T. is often brought out by translating, "be the medium of, or act the part of, the Paraclete towards."

three types the first is that of those who have a tendency to get out of line or rank—the self-confident and self-willed, who find obedience to law and order a constant difficulty. These need "admonition."[1] Side by side with these is an exactly opposite class—those with little spirit[2]—who require a very different treatment, that of sympathy, help, and stimulus. Besides these there are the "weak," whom we must take hold of,[3] and to whom we must give good support. But whatever be the particular failing in any character its rectification will require infinite patience.[4] In verse 15, against retaliation, we have an indication of the ethical standards with which St. Paul had to contend and whose insufficiency he had to prove.[5] The same task is laid upon the Christian minister to-day. In the second clause of this verse is another striking proof of St. Paul's knowledge of human nature. "You must not retaliate, you must aim at what is

---

[1] νουθετεῖν : in the N.T. eight times and always in St. Paul (including Acts xx. 31). The minister has to "apply his mind" towards such to get them to apply their mind towards themselves.

[2] The difficulty of these is very clearly expressed in Prov. xviii. 14, ὀλιγόψυχον δὲ ἄνδρα τίς ὑποίσει;

[3] As the Holy Spirit helpeth our weakness (Rom. viii. 26) we must support the weak.

[4] μακροθυμία, a favourite word with St. Paul, and an essential quality of character for the ministry. "Long-tempered" gives the meaning. (On the need of perfect control of temper see Chrysos. de Sacerdot. iii. 13.)

[5] Among the Jews as indicated in St. Matt. v. 43 ff. : among the Greeks as expressed in Soph. Antig. 643.

beneficial towards one another *and towards all.*"
Some natures will rise to the duty of acting
beneficially towards those within the community
—whether of the family or the congregation [1]—
but they cannot rise to that higher philanthropy
which does not ask " What claim have they
upon me ? "

(*b*) Rom. xiv. This chapter is again a striking
witness to St. Paul's knowledge of human
nature, and of his skill in dealing with it for
good. His subject here is "over-scrupulous-
ness"; his exhortation is to mutual tolerance
between those who think differently upon a
matter in itself of no vital importance. Yet
experience teaches us that it is from such matters
that often wide-spread ruin ensues. Both in the
pains he takes to deal with this dispute and in
the *manner* in which he deals with it, St. Paul
shows his intimate knowledge of human nature.
He knows the value of peace and unity for the
progress of the gospel ; and he knows that frequently the most bitter dissensions and the
greatest hindrances to Christian work have their
origin in matters which are in themselves of very
small importance.

The advice in verse 1 is that of an expert in

---

[1] Parochial or congregational selfishness is a tendency, a defect
in professing Christians against which every minister should
strive.

character study. The "weak" or over-scrupulous
are to be received into full Christian fellowship;
they have done nothing wrong: but when so
received do not let them be the subject of
perpetual criticism. St. Paul knew how easy it
is to be half generous, to be partially liberal-
minded, to give, and yet at the same time to
take away.[1] To bring the "weak" into an
atmosphere of criticism will not tend to their
edification—the only end for which they can have
been rightly received. In verse 5 we have another
example of St. Paul's insight. He knows the
unwillingness of most people to take the trouble
to "think out" a difficulty. A dislike to mental
exertion is far more common than a dislike to
physical exertion. Very few professing Christians
will take the trouble to "think out" their "faith."
To provoke and encourage thought must be one
of the chief aims of the preacher and teacher.
Refusal to "think hard" will account for most
of the prejudices and not a little of the opposition
with which the pastor meets. In verse 10 the
natural tendencies of the "weak" and the
"strong" are sharply opposed. The narrow-
minded are all too apt to "judge," and with
them to judge usually means to condemn. The

---

[1] Chrysostom has in another connection some excellent advice
on this spirit (*de Sacerd.* iii. 16), Ἂν δέ τις τὰ μὲν ἐκείνων μὴ λαμβάνῃ
κ.τ.λ., and he aptly quotes the words of Ecclus. xviii. 15–17, τέκνον
ἐν ἀγαθοῖς μὴ δῷς μῶμον, καὶ ἐν πάσῃ δόσει λύπην λόγων κ.τ.λ.

broad-minded are equally inclined to " despise "
the scruples or difficulties of the narrow. This,
as St. Paul indicates, is tantamount to despising
the possessor of these scruples. And St. Paul
would know that it is he that is void of understanding who despiseth his neighbour.[1] We
never hear of our Lord despising[2] any man.
He was often grieved and sometimes angry, but
never contemptuous. Nor do we read of St. Paul
ever despising anyone,[3] though his life was one
long battle against narrow - mindedness, and
against the bigotry and prejudice that will not
see. The Christian pastor's duty is to save,
and he will hardly be earnest to save that which
he despises. It is the thought of the intrinsic
preciousness of man which rules in the New
Testament. In verse 13 we have yet another
proof of St. Paul's clear insight into human
nature. There are those who are weak from
other causes than narrow-mindedness. Human
nature is subject to a strange variety of temptations ; one of the most difficult things for some
people to realise is how what they themselves
can use with absolute immunity can actually be
a danger to others. But, surely, having realised
this, to refrain from its use is of all forms of

---

[1] Prov. xi. 12. The Heb. is בז, the LXX has μυκτηρίζει.

[2] This is the spirit of the Pharisees (Luke xviii. 9) and of Herod (xxiii. 11).

[3] On the contrary, see Rom. ix. 1 ff.

self - denial the most useful. Only, instead of abstaining, we are often tempted to question whether we are called to give up what in itself is not in essence evil, or to say " Let us teach them by our moderation to use this wisely," forgetting, through our comparative ignorance of human nature, that what is no temptation to ourselves may be an absolutely invincible danger to them.

In all the many exhortations which we find towards the close of each of his Epistles, and often more implicitly than explicitly, St. Paul shows his deep insight into human nature, into its narrowness and its breadth, its weakness and its strength. This insight is absolutely essential for the Christian pastor, and the want of it is one of the most common of all causes of failure in ministerial work. Whence can this insight be gained? Here, again, St. Paul will teach us. The first requisite is a deep knowledge of self, such as we find in Rom. vii. (which I cannot help regarding as largely autobiographical), and in other parts of St. Paul's letters, especially in Second Corinthians. The other requisite is a deep and broad sympathy with others, a sympathy founded on the widest possible knowledge, which issues in an ability to feel *with* others, rather than merely *for* them, and to see life from their point of view. The two powers, first of large versatility,

and secondly of careful spiritual and moral
" diagnosis," [1] must be most diligently cultivated.
St. Paul possessed both to a very high degree.

This deep and extensive knowledge of human
nature is one of the chief causes of the immense
value of St. Paul's writings to those whose life's
work is dealing with the souls of others.   To
obtain it is a chief reason for constant and careful
study of other writings which exhibit the same
characteristic.   We shall find this insight into
human nature pre-eminently in the Psalms, and,
if to a somewhat lesser degree, in the Prophets.
One side, if not the highest or deepest, is represented in Proverbs, also in Sirach and in
Wisdom.   Outside the Bible we shall find
Marcus Aurelius, Dante, Shakespeare, Bunyan,
Goethe, Browning, Thackeray, and George Eliot,
all worthy of study.   For it is not without reason
that these writers have been favourites with many
of the greatest preachers.

(β) *St. Paul's knowledge of local and other peculiarities*

This is another proof of St. Paul's intimate
knowledge of the material upon which he worked,
I mean his knowledge of the peculiarities of
the different populations to whom he ministered
or wrote—peculiarities arising from differences in

---

[1] This is an art which the physician of souls must cultivate as
essential for his efficiency.

such formative influences as race, religion, political experiences and position, trade, and education. Of course St. Paul's own education and experiences fitted him to appreciate and assimilate rapidly these various peculiarities. The ability to do this is most valuable, and that we may strengthen this ability, by giving wide intellectual and political interests, is one of the chief reasons why, previous to and beneath a theological training, a broad general education should be regarded as an essential preparation for the Christian ministry. It was because of the sympathy resulting from his wide knowledge of Judaism, Hellenism, and of Roman Imperialism, from his being entirely at home in, and thoroughly conversant with, the ideas and ideals of these three worlds of thought, that St. Paul could, in the best sense of the words, become all things to all men. The most frequently quoted instances of St. Paul's power of differential treatment are his speeches in the synagogue of Pisidian Antioch, to the Lycaonian peasants, and to the Athenians. But these alone give us an entirely inadequate conception of the wonderful versatility and adaptability of the Apostle. To three such very different audiences most speakers of any ability and with much practice would have spoken quite differently. It is rather in the minutiæ or details of his appeals and in the illustrations of his arguments that we find the strongest evidence of St. Paul's ability to make use of local interests and idiosyncrasies. To appreciate this power fully, as well as to appreciate the pains which St. Paul took to employ it to advantage, we require, besides an intimate knowledge of his speeches and epistles, an equally intimate knowledge of the particular conditions of those to whom each of these was addressed. We must know how these people lived and were governed, under what religious and political influences they were living, upon what they mainly occupied their energies, and about what they were chiefly thinking. We must, in short, be able to throw ourselves into the atmosphere and environment in which they were. Until within recent years our knowledge of the conditions of St. Paul's time has not been sufficient to enable us to do this at all adequately. We have known the broad features of its political and religious positions, but it is only lately that we have obtained such a knowledge of the details of life in various localities that we can appreciate, not only allusions made to these, but arguments strengthened by reference to them, on the part of St. Paul.

As an illustration of how our increasing knowledge of the first century enables us to appreciate St. Paul's teaching more fully, I would draw attention to the many notes in Professor Ramsay's *Historical Commentary on Galatians*, where light is again and again thrown upon the reason for

St. Paul's use of certain expressions. That reason we can now see was St. Paul's intimate knowledge of the life and customs of the cities in which "the Churches of Galatia" were situated.

A few examples must suffice :—

(a) Ramsay compares St. Paul's language and arguments in Gal. iii. 7, "Ye perceive therefore that they which be of faith, the same are sons of Abraham," with those in Rom. iv. 11 f., "that he might be the father (εἰς τὸ εἶναι αὐτὸν πατέρα) of all them that believe, though they be in uncircumcision . . . and the father of circumcision to them . . ." He then points out that to the Galatians St. Paul uses a metaphor drawn from Greek law, i.e., that "it was specially and fundamentally on religious (οἱ ἐκ πίστεως) grounds that the Greek heir and son was adopted to continue the family cultus." [1] "For the Romans he employs a different metaphor, founded on the customary usage of the word *pater*. . . . A man may be described as the *pater* of all to whom his qualifications constitute him a guide and leader and protector." [2]

(b) Gal. iii. 15 ff. "An illustration from the facts of society, as it existed in the Galatian cities, is here stated." [3] "Let me take an illustration, brethren, from daily experience. Though it be but a man's Will, yet when it hath 'passed through

---

[1] *Historical Commentary on Galatians*, p. 341.
[2] P. 343.   [3] P. 349.

the Record Office of the city' no one can make it ineffective, or add fresh clauses thereto." "The Galatian Will, like God's Word, is irrevocable and unalterable : it comes into operation as soon as the conditions are performed by the heir."[1]   It was quite different in Roman law, where a form of Will secret and revocable had come into use.

(c) Gal. iii. (23–25).   "The Law has played the part of a 'servant responsible for our safety, and charged to keep us out of bad company.'[2] . . . When St. Paul compared the Law to a *paidagogos*, . . . he chose an illustration which would be clear to his Galatian readers. . . . This also throws some light upon the social organisation in the Galatian cities, for it places us in the midst of Greek city life, as it was in the better period of Greek history."

(d) Gal. v. 19 ff.   The list of "the works of the flesh."   Ramsay writes :[3] "In the list of fifteen faults there are three groups, corresponding to three different kinds of influence likely to affect recent South Galatian converts from paganism. Such converts were likely to be led astray by habits and ways of thought to which they had been brought up, owing to (1) the national religion, (2) their position in a municipality, (3) the customs of society in Hellenistic cities."   He then proceeds to show that the sins which St. Paul enumerates are exactly those most likely to be

---

[1] *Historical Commentary on Galatians*, p. 351.
[2] P. 381 f.   [3] P. 446 f.

fostered by the old Anatolian religion ; how, within the city life, there was special temptation to jealousy and strife ; and how the last two sins mentioned are just those "most closely connected with the society and manners of the Græco-Asiatic cities."

Other instances of St. Paul's evidently intimate knowledge of the life of the Galatians, and of his careful use of this knowledge, will be found on pp. 370, 393, 395, 443 of Professor Ramsay's *Commentary*.

What he has done in this way for the Galatian Epistle, other commentators (*e.g.* Bishop Lightfoot in his *Philippians*) have done, though less thoroughly, for other Epistles of St. Paul. But, as I said above, as our knowledge of the details of life both in Rome and in various provincial cities during the second half of the first century increases, our proofs of St. Paul's intimate acquaintance with the local religious and political peculiarities of these cities, that is of the idiosyncrasies of the particular human material upon which he was working, will be much increased.

If the Christian minister to-day would employ his energies to the best advantage he must take the trouble to acquire a similarly intimate knowledge of those among whom he works. This is of course especially necessary for the foreign missionary, and probably much of the want of success in foreign missionary work in the past has been due to forgetfulness of this essential condition.   Nor is such knowledge less necessary for pastoral work at home.   If we hope for success, we shall not appeal in exactly the same way to the educated and the uneducated, to the old and the young, to townspeople and country-folk, to the landsman and the sailor.   More than this, each similar class of society, except perhaps the most highly educated, exhibits striking differences in different parts of our own country, otherwise what do we mean by the "characteristics" of the Northerner, the Midlander, and the Southerner?   The explanation of these differences is to be sought partly in racial distinctions, but much more in the effects of environment.   I use the term in its fullest sense, and it must certainly include such influences as those of climate and occupation : and we must not think of the effects of environment only in the present, but of its influence upon past generations, and so again, indirectly, upon the present. For the environments of past generations are at least a factor in what we term hereditary influences.   For example, the general physique of the men of to-day in any particular locality is at least partially due to the climate, occupation, and manner of life of past generations.   Also environment supplies and, to some extent, limits ideas which influence conduct, and tend to form character.   Let me say in passing that I believe every Christian minister should have some clear if elementary knowledge of the principles of psychology, and of the psychology of society. By this knowledge his powers of dealing with individuals and also of teaching will be immensely increased.   If carefully put into practice, even an elementary knowledge[1] of this science will save him from much waste of energy, from almost countless mistakes.   When St. Paul illustrated and enforced his appeals to the Galatians by analogies drawn from customs with which they were familiar he was but using the method of "association of ideas," which every scientific teacher (one who has studied psychology) knows to be the best, if not the only possible method of implanting new ideas.

The true pastor will take great pains to find out what his people are thinking about, he will discover what is familiar to them.   Then by carefully attaching his teaching to the familiar he will gradually obtain admission for ideas which are comparatively, or even entirely, unfamiliar. This careful study of the thoughts and ideas of others serves another purpose.   It enables us to sympathise with those we would influence.   And sympathy is ever the true key to influence.   I have dwelt at some length on this subject, because only those who have studied the reason know why so much preaching and teaching, upon which infinite pains have been bestowed, is so ineffective.   It is because the meaning of much of

---

[1] For gaining this, John Adams' *Primer on Teaching*, or James' *Talks to Teachers on Psychology*, will both be found useful.

it remains unknown to the hearers, and it remains so because they have not already the ideas necessary to assimilate what is placed before them. The psychologist knows, as St. Paul knew, that it is the new *in connection with* the familiar, the mixture of new and old, which rouses and maintains *interest* — one essential condition for all successful teaching. If we study St. Paul's speeches at Antioch, at Athens, or before Herod Agrippa, we shall see that in each case he commences with that which is familiar and then proceeds from that which is familiar towards that which is comparatively strange to his hearers. We shall see the same skill employed in his letters, in which again and again he obtains admission for new truth by carefully connecting it with ideas which were evidently familiar. St. Paul is a master of method.

III. The Object of the Minister as a Workman

Lastly, the wise and true workman will have a clear conception of his object. As he stands before his material he will know exactly what he wishes to produce out of it. The model[1] to which he works will be before him, visible to the eye of his imagination, which is not always different from that of the eye of faith. All this is eminently

---

[1] 2 Cor. iii. 18, τὴν αὐτὴν εἰκόνα μεταμορφούμεθα . . .

true of St. Paul.   He knew exactly what he wished
to accomplish.[1]   He was perfectly clear about his
object, as the following passages will show :—

(*a*) Gal. iv. 19.   " My little children, with whom
I once more travail until ye shall have attained
to the fully formed life of the Christian." St.
Paul's object is here quite clearly defined by the
words, μέχρις οὗ μορφωθῇ Χριστὸς ἐν ὑμῖν. St. Paul
here likens himself to the mother, his Galatian
converts are like an immature embryo. " In the
Christian, Christ is to inhabit the heart (Eph. iii.
17), in him there is to be the νοῦς of Christ
(1 Cor. ii. 16), the πνεῦμα of Christ (Rom. viii. 9),
the σπλάγχνα of Christ (Phil. i. 8), and the body
and its members are to be the body and members
of Christ (1 Cor. vi. 13, 15)."[2]

(*b*) Col. i. 28.   " That we may present every
man perfect in Christ." Here, again, St. Paul
quite clearly defines his object, πάντα ἄνθρωπον τέλειον
ἐν Χριστῷ. And the words which follow should
not be forgotten, εἰς ὃ καὶ κοπιῶ ἀγωνιζόμενος κ.τ.λ.,
" to effect which I toil laboriously, struggling," etc.
We may also notice that while in the passage in
Gal. iv. 19 the end was " Christ in us," here it is

---

[1] 1 Cor. ix. 26, οὕτως τρέχω ὡς οὐκ ἀδήλως . . . " Scio quid petam
et quomodo, qui liquido currit, metam recta spectat et recta
petit." Bengel.

[2] Meyer *in loc.* (*E. T.* p. 256 ff.).   The whole of Meyer's long note
on this verse is excellent.   As a useful warning against what may,
unconsciously, take place in our work, Bengel's words, " *Christus,*
non Paulus in Galatis formandus," may usefully be remembered.

"us in Christ." The Christian minister must remember both these aspects of his purpose. Again, St. Paul's words here recall the words of Christ in St. Matt. v. 48, "Ye therefore shall be *perfect*, as your heavenly Father is perfect." The standard with both our Lord and St. Paul is infinitely high, and the truth contained in the paradox, "If you would succeed you must aim at the impossible," must not be forgotten.

From these two passages we may describe St. Paul's object as Christian *maturity* and Christian *perfection*. Both these passages, I think, refer to individual Christians, each of whom is to be brought onwards towards perfection. My third example shall again deal with the individual, but now as a member of a society, and as inconceivable apart from the society.

(*c*) Eph. iv. 13. Here we have the object of all Christian "ministering" (in its widest sense) and of all Christian living thus described: "Till we all (together) attain unto the unity of the faith and of the (full) knowledge of the Son of God, unto a full grown man, unto the measure of the stature of the fulness of the Christ," and in verse 15—a continuation of the same somewhat prolonged sentence—the object is again defined, "That we may grow up in all things unto Him which is the head—even Christ."

I may say at once that the passage in which these sentences occur is vital for any adequate knowledge of the Pauline idea of the object of the Christian ministry. As I shall deal with the passage at length in another connection, I will here confine myself to its bearing upon the object of the ministry. This is defined as an attainment in common (οἱ πάντες) unto three ends, each of which is preceded by the same preposition (εἰς), which are co-ordinate, and each of which further defines or amplifies the others. We may take the expression εἰς ἄνδρα τέλειον as central, and we must notice the almost paradoxical οἱ πάντες . . . εἰς ἄνδρα τέλειον, where οἱ πάντες is not "every one," or "all of us," but "all of us together." The individuals are to grow as the body grows. We may compare the growth of each member of the physical organism during the growing of the whole. In this growth *of*, and *into*, a corporate unity there is no loss of individuality, but actually a deepening and strengthening of it. To this we may compare the growing individuality of both the features and the character of a child. The analogy of the growth of the human body is probably in the Apostle's mind ; but the further we try to press this analogy, the more do we realise its incompleteness. Then the growth of each member contributes not only to the growth, but to the unity of the body. [The minister to-day may learn this lesson from St. Paul,—that a want of unity in an organisation or among a body of individuals is a sign of want of growth, of immaturity in one or more of the separate parts or members; they have not all grown together.] Then the idea of unity implies diversity, for not only each individual but the *individuality* of each individual has something to contribute to the perfect, the ideal unity; and this ideal unity is conditioned by, *i.e.* is dependent upon, faith *in*, and [full] knowledge of, the Son of God. *Εἰς ἄνδρα τέλειον* is a pregnant phrase, and must be interpreted both individually and *socially*.   In the process of the growth of the society each member must grow more perfect; and in this personal growth he will contribute to the growing perfection of the social organism.   I regard the third clause as explanatory of the second, *i.e.* the "perfection" of the perfect man is "measured" by the fulness of the stature of the Christ.

From all this it will be seen that here again St. Paul describes the work of the ministry, or of ministering, as taking part in a process whose end is perfection, or complete maturity; but in this case the object is the formation of a society, in whose growth unto perfection the growth unto perfection of the individual is being realised.   As I have already stated, the importance of the passage for helping us to keep in mind the object of our ministerial work cannot be exaggerated.   The difficulty in its interpretation consists in keeping in view at the same time the many ideas which the Apostle presents to our minds.   Briefly, we may say that the perfection of the individual is dependent on the perfection of the society, and *vice versa* the "saints" are to be fully equipped in order that the society may be built up.

Never was there a time when it was more important for the Christian minister to insist upon both these complementary truths. For to-day we are constantly met by two heresies, each of which is fatal to true progress. On the one hand we still see far too much individualistic Christianity, which is at least partly due to a want of a proper conception in the past of the nature and function of the Christian society in the great work of the regeneration of humanity. This individualism tends to religious narrowness, for it leaves not only undeveloped, but actually untouched, certain faculties of human nature so that these remain unsanctified by Christ, and unconsecrated to His service. This individualism is, strange to say, sometimes curiously manifested in a certain maimed form of sociability—in small, so-called "social efforts," in which, however, only particular and very limited aspects or functions of true social life find exercise. These are apt to take the place of, and so prevent, the realisation of the larger corporate life of the Church, in which every human faculty should find exercise, and so opportunity, for its development.

On the other hand, a heresy has invaded the Church which is to-day very prevalent in the world—that by the improvement of social arrangements alone, that is by a more perfect organisation of society (apart from or only attaching secondary importance to improvement in individual character, or the sense of individual responsibility) we can make progress towards an ideal state of society. The well-balanced and carefully proportioned teaching of St. Paul, which attaches equal importance to the individual and the social aspects of life and of the truth, is the answer to both these imperfect conceptions. For it teaches that the perfection of the individual and of society are independently impossible, indeed that each actually presupposes the other.

As we look back upon these three passages from St. Paul's teaching, we see that in each the thought of Christ is paramount. In the first, Christ must be formed in each individual ; in the second, each individual must be perfected in Christ ; in the third, the perfect man is only perfect when that perfection is measured by the measure of the stature or maturity of the fulness of the Christ. The moral is obvious—to the Christian workman Christ must be ever present. He is the one sufficient standard and example, towards which he must work—He alone is the Truth, which is the ideal.

Chapter 2

THE PASTOR AND HIS PASTORATE

Αὐτὸς δὲ ἐγὼ Παῦλος παρακαλῶ ὑμᾶς.—2 COR. X. I.

A very helpful way of learning St. Paul's conception of his work as a minister of Christ is to study, either together or in quick succession, the various addresses or salutations with which his Epistles open. By carefully combining these we may learn much about how he regarded his position, his Divine call, and his qualifications for the work he was trying to do. We may also learn how he thought of those whom he was seeking to influence and teach.

These opening salutations are, in the various Epistles, very differently expressed. This shows that they are not mere formal addresses or rhetorical introductions, but that each has been carefully chosen, either to express some particular aspect of the relationship which must exist between himself and his readers, or to remind them at once of some particular truth to which he felt it was necessary to draw their attention. I cannot notice every detail of all these addresses.

Two of the most full are those found at the head
of the First Epistle to the Corinthians and the
Epistle to the Romans.   To these two I purpose
mainly to confine my attention.

I. The Minister's Conception of Himself

The personal name at the opening of every
Epistle reminds us of a fact to which I have
already referred, namely, that it is of the essence
of Christianity, which in this respect is at one
with the Old Testament, that the communication
of the Divine message and of the Divine power
shall proceed largely through a human personality.
The great saying of St. John, "the Word became
flesh," has more than a single personal application.   Here the personal name—in St Paul's
case the post-conversion name—suggests the
whole personality in its completeness ; and, of
course, the personal implies the moral.   Hence
we may say that the Christian message and the
Christian influence proceed from a Moral Personality, through a moral personality, with the object
of moralising more perfectly other personalities.
In this connection we see the wisdom of the
authors of our English Church Catechism in
placing the personal name in the forefront.
Here is a definite personality brought into special
covenant with God, to be enriched by Him, to
be led to recognise its responsibilities, both in-

dividual and social (for baptism is admission into a society), in regard to faith, obedience, duty, and communion with God.

The " sacramental " nature of the human personality when consecrated to God's service is an interesting thought. The Church's definition of a sacrament is almost an exact definition of what the personality of a Christian and especially of a Christian minister ought to be. It should, as manifested in conduct,[1] be an outward and visible sign of the inward and spiritual grace by which it is endowed ;[2] it should be such that it can be regarded as a Divine gift,[2] bringing strengthening and refreshment to others ;[3] as such it may be said to have been ordained by Christ Himself to convey the light of His presence,[4] and His power,[5] indeed His life,[6] to others. The sanctified and consecrated human nature is a means and channel of the Divine

---

[1] St. Paul was not only an instrument in preaching the gospel but also, in his own person, the strongest testimony to its power (Lightfoot on Gal. i. 16). St. Paul also asserts that the fact that Christ lives in us (Gal. ii. 20) should be manifest ; and that the Galatians received him ὡς Χριστὸν Ἰησοῦν (iv. 14) ; cf. 2 Cor. iv. 11, " that the life also of Jesus may be manifested in our mortal flesh."

[2] Eph. iv. 11. " The gift was a double gift. Christ first endowed the men, and then He gave them, so endowed, to the Church." Westcott *in loc.*

[3] Rom. i. 11, ἵνα τι μεταδῶ χάρισμα ὑμῖν πνευματικὸν εἰς τὸ στηριχθῆναι ὑμᾶς.

[4] 2 Cor. iv. 6.

[5] 2 Cor. i. 5 ff. παρακαλεῖν here means to impart the strength of the Holy Spirit (ὁ παράκλητος) Who is the Spirit of Christ.

[6] Philem. 19, ὅτι καὶ σεαυτόν μοι προσοφείλεις.

grace,[1] it is also a pledge of the possibility of the same.[2]

St. Paul teaches us the necessity of the complete consecration of the entire personality, and therefore the consecration of those special natural endowments[3] with which in varying degrees each one has been enriched. Among these endowments we may think of race, nationality, wealth, social position, education, and experience. Each of these is a factor in our endowment which, rightly used, and sanctified by careful thought and moral consecration, may be employed to promote our life's purpose. In St. Paul's case this endowment, both natural and acquired, was unusually rich. We must notice how carefully and constantly he used it. And in this his example should be a perpetual inspiration to ourselves. It is well worth while to read carefully through the Acts and his Epistles with this single object in view—of proving to ourselves how continually he employed what we may term his " educational[4] advantages." A list of quotations[5] will show what immense use he made of the Old Testament, of which his knowledge was certainly great. He is always employing alike

---

[1] Phil. i. 24 ; Eph. iv. 12.   [2] Phil. iv. 9.

[3] τὰ σώματα ὑμῶν in Rom. xii. 1 will include these.

[4] We have only to read St. Paul's Epistles in chronological order to see that his education was always proceeding.

[5] Such as that found in an appendix to Westcott and Hort's *Greek Testament*.

the history, the literature, the aspirations, and the causes of failure of the nation from which he sprang. Of what he had evidently learnt as a "Tarsian" he makes little less use. For instance, again and again he introduces ideas which, if not directly derived from, were strangely parallel [1] to, those of the Stoic philosophy. These from their familiarity would catch the ear, and so at once claim the sympathetic attention of his Hellenic hearers. His knowledge of all that "the Empire" meant to one who was evidently proud of his Roman citizenship was also continually employed to suggest an analogy and so point a lesson for those by whom this same knowledge would also be possessed. [2]

But many a Christian minister who has considerable endowments is slow or unskilled in using these. On the other hand, St. Paul's readiness to do this must evoke our admiration. By readiness I do not mean anxiety to claim privileges, but the aptitude which comes from the thoroughly disciplined and versatile mind, and which is always alert to seize an opportunity. Almost at the same moment we may see St. Paul making use of very different factors in his endowment. I will take two instances of this :—

---

[1] Some of these parallels are pointed out in Lightfoot's *Philippians*, p. 287 ff. See also W. L. Davidson, *The Stoic Creed*, p. 165, etc. Also Johannes Weiss, *Die Christliche Freiheit*.

[2] On this subject see Bp. Westcott's *Some Thoughts from the Ordinal*, pp. 12 ff., beginning, "Christ . . . calls us through the circumstances of our life," etc.

(1) From the scene described at the end of Acts xxi. and in xxii., when his life was in imminent peril from the violence of the Jewish mob in the Temple court. Here within the space of a very short time we see St. Paul claiming his rights as a Roman citizen,[1] conversing in Greek with a provincial official,[2] and addressing in "Hebrew"[3] a hostile Jewish audience in such a manner as to obtain complete silence.

(2) Within the space of the comparatively short Epistle to the Philippians we again find St. Paul using to the full various factors of his endowment, whenever any of these will further his purpose, strengthen his argument, or help to obtain more consideration for an appeal. Writing from Rome to a Roman *Colonia*, he refers with pride to the progress of the gospel in the πραιτώριον;[4] he bids his converts behave worthily as "citizens" (ἀξίως . . . πολιτεύεσθε)[5] of the gospel of Christ; and he bids them remember that their commonwealth (πολίτευμα) is in heaven.[6] In chapter iii. he reminds (possibly) another section of his readers at Philippi that he was "circumcised the eighth day, of the stock of Israel, of the tribe of Benjamin, a Hebrew of Hebrews: as touching the law a Pharisee." But in this

---

[1] Acts xxii. 25, εἰ ἄνθρωπον Ῥωμαῖον καὶ ἀκατάκριτον ἔξεστιν ὑμῖν μαστίζειν;

[2] ὁ δὲ ἔφη Ἑλληνιστὶ γινώσκεις;

[3] προσεφώνησεν τῇ Ἑβραΐδα διαλέκτῳ.   [4] Phil. i. 13.

[5] Phil. i. 27.   [6] Phil. iii. 20.

same Epistle he is all the time conscious that he is writing to those who not only spoke, but were accustomed to think, in Greek, and who would appreciate the meaning of ὑπάρχει (used of the πολίτευμα). Lastly, we may say that the rich and varied list of the moral virtues which are to be realised in life is thoroughly cosmopolitan : things εὔφημα and the exaltation of ἀρετή would appeal to the Greek, things σεμνά would remind some of the old-fashioned Roman atmosphere which was still a tradition ;[1] things δίκαια would appeal to the erstwhile Jew.[2]

The noble exhortation in Rom. xii. 1 ff. is undoubtedly addressed to every Christian : for that reason it should not appeal less, but more strongly to the Christian minister.[3] The "body" is to be presented to God, and in the explanation we give to the term "body" (σῶμα)[4] we must remember the words τὴν λογικὴν λατρείαν ὑμῶν. Thus we may define the offering of the body

---

[1] The loss of things σεμνά is indirectly bewailed in Hor. *Odes*, Bk. iii. (odes i.–iii., also at the end of vi. :

"Aetas parentum pejor avis tulit
Nos nequiores, mox daturos
Progenium vitiosiorem.")

[2] Phil. iv. 8.

[3] "The clergyman is the layman *plus* all that is given and demanded in the loftiest and holiest calling possible to man." Littlejohn, *Conciones ad Clerum*, p. 17. (The whole address on "Clergy and People" will be found most useful.)

[4] "What God asks is . . . living men . . . the response of entire self-surrender,—the response of sacrifice to sacrifice." Gore, *Romans*, vol. ii. p. 97.

as including the thinking and feeling faculties, indeed as the sum of our natural endowments, which is the instrument and offering of the spirit. The translation "ourselves" in the Communion Office is perhaps the best explanation of what the Apostle summons, or encourages the Roman Christians to offer in return for the Divine Offering which he has in the previous chapters been explaining. It is well for us to ask what is this "self" which we express our readiness to offer consecrated to God? Have we enriched and enlarged it as far as we possibly can? Do we recognise the duty of constant self-enrichment and self-enlargement for the sake of others? This self-enrichment is a very different thing from "reading up" some particular book or subject in order to preach or speak upon it.[1] It really means constantly gathering from every quarter, carefully assimilating what we gather, and then as carefully using what we have assimilated. Only thus may we offer, as St. Paul offered, a rich personality, a wide and sympathetic influence, for the service of Christ. The knowledge gained from travel, from study, from thoughtful intercourse with various classes of society must be carefully "cerebrated" (this is a part of mental discipline); and then in our preaching and teaching and in our dealing with

---

[1] A great modern preacher has rightly insisted on the difference between "preparedness" and "preparation."

individuals we shall speak with far greater
acceptation. St. Paul has fully revealed to us his
own method and object in this respect. "Without being the slave of any, to win more I made
myself the slave of all. To the Jews I became
as a Jew to win Jews," etc. (1 Cor. ix. 20 ff.)

To his personal name St. Paul in every Epistle
except two adds one or more descriptions of his
position or his office. His favourite terms in
this connection are either apostle or servant, or
sometimes both, with the definitions "of Jesus
Christ," or "of Jesus Christ through the will of
God," added. In Romans we have "a servant of
Jesus Christ, a called apostle"; in First Corinthians, "a called apostle of Jesus Christ through
the will of God"; in Second Corinthians, "an
apostle of Christ Jesus through the will of God";
in Galatians, "an apostle (not from men nor
through a man but through Jesus Christ . . .)";
in Ephesians and Colossians, "an apostle of Christ
Jesus through the will of God"; in Philippians
(with Timothy), "servants of Christ Jesus"; in
First Timothy, "an apostle of Christ Jesus according to the commandment of God . . .;" in
Second Timothy, "an apostle of Christ Jesus
through the will of God"; in Titus, "a servant
of God and an apostle of Jesus Christ"; in
Philemon, "a prisoner of Jesus Christ."

Putting these various descriptions together, we

may state that in every case, before addressing
his readers, St. Paul is careful to make clear his
position from the point of view of his relationship
to the Divine, however differently this relationship may be conceived.[1] It is not " Paul," or
even " Paul an apostle," who presumes to teach,
or advise, or exhort, but " Paul an apostle, or
servant *of Jesus Christ*." The Christian minister
to-day cannot lay too much stress upon this
thought from the side of *responsibility*. From
this point of view he must keep clear to himself
and make clear to others his relationship to the
Divine. Doubtless the idea does add to the
sense of the " sacredness," " greatness," " importance " of our position [2] and our office, but
only in the sense of the tremendous nature of
our responsibility for the right discharge of our
stewardship. If St. Paul's teaching upon the
pastoral office was useful for no other purpose,
we should owe him the greatest gratitude for
insisting upon its essential connection with the
Divine. " Paul " writes, preaches, works. The
man's whole personality, with not a single factor
of it lost or unemployed, is engaged ; but it is not
Paul in himself that does this, it is not even Paul

---

[1] As "apostle" of Jesus Christ, as "slave" of Jesus Christ, as
"prisoner" of Jesus Christ.

[2] "St. Paul lays stress on this fact, not with a view to personal
aggrandisement, but only to commend his gospel with the weight
which he knows that it deserves." Sanday and Headlam, *Romans*,
p. 5.

as a servant, or apostle of Jesus Christ, but as these *by the will of God*. The addition of these last words takes us a great step farther. Our work is now placed in its true position in the great world order, in the unfolding and development of the great Divine Plan. The use of technical terms and expressions is full of danger,[1] but no one can doubt St. Paul's conviction of the existence of a Divine "Plan of Salvation" both for the individual and for society (the world). He was equally convinced that in the working out of this plan he had been called by God to take a definite place and part. From one point of view this plan may be regarded as a great progressing, and ever progressive *order*. In the working out of this order the Church in our own country, and so every separate parish and congregation, indeed every individual ministry, has its place, its definite work to do. To this work it has been called by "the will of God." To keep in mind this will and to do it is its greatest responsibility. For the fulfilment of the Divine Purpose Christianity is the Divinely ordained agency; of this agency every Christian minister is a servant. Speaking of the "wisdom" of God—which in this connection is very much

---

[1] The Christian teacher or preacher must always remember that

> "Denn eben wo Begriffe fehlen
> Da stellt ein Wort zur rechten Zeit sich ein."
>
> Goethe, *Faust.*

what is called the " Plan of Salvation "—Bishop Westcott writes : " This wisdom is seen in the adaptation of the manifold capacities of man and the complicated vicissitudes of human life to minister to the one end to which 'all creation moves.'" [1]

I shall not here stay to consider the significance of the titles "apostle" and "servant," as they will be considered among other "titles" by which St. Paul describes his position and his work.[2] I would only notice how each of these titles used by St. Paul suggests before everything else the *responsibilities* of the ministerial position. In discharge of the function of an apostle, or an ambassador, or a steward, or a "master-builder" there is a wide opportunity for the exercise of personal choice and therefore of personal responsibility, for the exercise of judgment and for the choice and adaptation of methods to particular circumstances. In each the idea of the mechanical is excluded.[3] In each, again, there is a strong necessity for the consecration of the whole man— intellect, judgment, conscience, will—to the service of Christ in the purpose of God.

In both Rom. i. 1 and 1 Cor. i. 1 we have κλητὸς ἀπόστολος. The significance of κλητός is probably exactly given by the words " not from

---

[1] *Ephesians*, p. 49.   [2] See Chapter III.
[3] The only time when St. Paul uses ἄγγελος of a Christian minister is in Gal. iv. 14, where there may be a reference to the scene at Lystra (Acts xiv. 12), when Paul was called Hermes.

($\dot{a}\pi\acute{o}$) men nor through (a) man," in Gal. i. 1. The conviction of the Divine origin of his commission is constantly present to St. Paul and constantly asserted by him. The occasion of his call is usually referred to the conversion of the Apostle, but in one passage at least[1] St. Paul seems to refer to a Divine preparation of himself for his work long antecedent to this. It has been noticed that this idea of κλῆσις is one which has its roots in the Old Testament, and is especially connected with the prophetic office. Gen. xii. 1–3 ;[2] Ex. iii. 10 ; Isa. vi. 8, 9 ; Jer. i. 4, 5, etc. This perpetuation of the sense of the "call" is one of the many indirect proofs of the continuity of the prophetic office, and of St. Paul's fulfilment among other functions of that of the prophet.

In her ordination services the Church has wisely laid stress upon the necessity for this conviction of the Divine call, and I suppose that at the time of ordination the sense of the conviction is usually intensely present. But an important question for continued practical pastoral efficiency is, "How may this sense or conviction of a Divine call be *maintained* and kept fresh through the long years

---

[1] Gal. i. 15 ff.

[2] The *action* of Abraham as a manifestation of God's will in conduct was "prophetic." Also "he looked for the city which hath the foundations" (Heb. xi. 10) ; and "the prophets were the living depositaries of the idea of the theocracy or kingdom of God." Davidson, *O.T. Prophecy*, p. 8.

of ministerial work, and often of at least apparent
ministerial failure ? " For this conviction must
be maintained if we are to endure to the end,
if we are to win both our own souls and the
souls of those around us. St. Paul knew from
experience what it was to see men [1] forsake the
work of the ministry ; he also knew what it was
to see one [2] forsake it, and yet take it up again.
That St. Paul maintained the enthusiasm of the
freshness of his call is proved both from the
Acts and from the contents of every letter that
he wrote.[3] As we read his life and his words
we are conscious, not only of a sense of responsibility which continues to be always fresh
and keen, but also of an abiding possession of
Divine help and strength to meet new and
constantly changing circumstances. One secret
of the maintenance of ministerial freshness and
energy lies in our determining to see the immense
importance of even the details of ministerial work.
By St. Paul the doing of each work, the meeting
of each opportunity, the using to the full each set
of constantly changing circumstances seemed to
have been regarded as nothing less than obedience
to a Divine call. Nothing that could be done
for Christ, however small the task or the oppor-

---

[1] *e.g.* Demas, 2 Tim. iv. 10.   Demas is called a συνεργός in
Philem. 24.

[2] Mark ; Acts xv. 38 ; cp. 2 Tim. iv. 11.

[3] Notice the zeal and energy depicted in Acts xxviii. 30, 31, and
in 2 Tim. iv. 17.

tunity might seem to be, was unimportant. To do what he could for Onesimus, and so for Philemon, or to write a letter to the comparatively small Church at Colossæ, was to St. Paul as essential as to write to the Church in Rome, or in Ephesus and the other Churches of " Asia." From him we learn that to maintain the sense of "the call" we must listen for it, and hear it in the successive experiences of our work just as carefully and as clearly as we did when we first entered upon our ministry. When St. Paul obeyed the summons to leave Antioch,[1] or the command to leave unevangelised certain parts of Asia Minor and to cross over into Europe,[2] or, in the face of imminent danger, to go up to Jerusalem,[3] he felt he was as surely obeying a Divine call as when he obeyed the voice of Jesus at his conversion outside the walls of Damascus. Another proof of this abiding conviction of the call may be seen in St. Paul's uses of the words δεῖ and ἔδει to express the sense of a Divine arrangement in which he must take his part.[4]

Together with this thought of the renewed call must go the thought of the perpetual spiritual endowment. This endowment St. Paul teaches us is twofold—that of light for guidance, and that of strength for effort and perseverance. A call

---

[1] Acts xiii. 2.   [2] Acts xvi. 6, 7.   [3] Acts xx. 22, xxi. 13.
[4] Acts xix. 21, xxiii. 11 ; Eph. vi. 20 ; Col. iv. 4.

is a summons to make a choice, and to the Christian the making of a right choice assumes the guidance of a Mind higher than that of his own. Also to obey the call and to continue in obedience to what the call demands presupposes to the Christian the power to obtain and to continue to obtain a strength greater than his own. When St. Paul prays for his converts that they "may grow more and more in knowledge till they attain to the perfect understanding of God's will," and that they "may be strengthened in all strength according to that power which centres in and spreads from His glorious manifestation of Himself,"[1] we may assume that he is asking for others an endowment of the value of which he has personal experience. When St. Paul asserts his possession of a Divine guidance, he seems also to assert its limitations. There are subjects and occasions upon which this Divine guidance may be claimed with unerring certainty. There are other circumstances in which it seems to be impossible to say quite surely that we are Divinely commanded to do this or to abstain from that.[2] St. Paul seems to say we cannot quote Christ's command or authority for every detail of conduct, the Gospel is not a "second Levitical code";[3] there are numberless occasions when we

---

[1] Bp. Lightfoot's paraphrase of Col. i. 9 ff.

[2] Contrast 1 Cor. vii. verses 10 and 12.

[3] " This absolute certitude is essential in the revelation of

must give advice—the very best we can give—but for which we cannot plead a direct Divine precept.   Under certain conditions some "commandments of men" may be most useful : but we cannot claim that they are "doctrines."[1]   Whenever possible we must not only fall back upon, but assert principles : yet there is a danger, if not a cowardice, in the readiness to make certain things "a matter of principle" when at least no Divine principle is really involved.

Beside the endowment of guidance to choose our path, there is the endowment of strength to persevere, a power which must include the strength to meet and overcome the opposition of all forms of evil.   To his possession of this endowment St. Paul bears constant witness. He possesses it as a continuous supply, he also obtains it in special measure to meet special crises—occasions when he was exposed to some extraordinary strain.[2]

---

central principles.   But it would be destructive of all that is valuable in human effort, if it extended to the minute details of practical life."   See T. C. Edwards, *First Corinthians*, p. 168.

[1] St. Matt. xv. 9 and St. Mark vii. 7 (upon which see Swete's note *in loc*).   The quotation is from Isa. xxix. 13. *Mark*, Kregel Publ. 1977.

[2] Contrast Phil. iv. 13, "through Him who constantly strengtheneth me," and 2 Tim. iv. 17, "on this occasion strengthened me." In 2 Cor i. 4 St. Paul speaks of "God who constantly supplieth to us that which is the characteristic virtue of the Paraclete," whereas in Acts xxiii. 11 and xxvi. 22 he speaks of special help afforded in particular crises.   In 2 Cor. xii. 9 we seem to have an abiding promise of help, possibly given at a definite time, in view of a weakness which might recur and when special help would be needed.

This strength the Christian minister must be careful to maintain ; for St. Paul does not lead us to think that he regarded its possession as in any way limited to himself or to a select few. But if it is to be acquired and maintained certain conditions must be satisfied. Like the possession and enjoyment of all God's gifts, this is conditional. It may be defined as the strengthening presence and power of Christ, which to St. Paul was little if at all different from what we should term the strengthening presence and power of the Spirit.

II. The Minister's Conception of those to whom He ministers

A minister's relation to his people, and his treatment of those to whom he ministers, or towards whom he holds a position of responsibility, will be largely governed by his conception of these people ; and this conception must be capable of expression in terms. From the salutations in St. Paul's Epistles we can gain most helpful inspiration for our own ministerial work from carefully considering how he expressed his idea of those to whom he was ministering. In his descriptions of them, or of their position (as in his descriptions of himself and of his own position), there is, again, quite sufficient variety to prove that St. Paul was using no mere mechanical or rhetorical formulæ.

These various appellations have been made a subject of study by various commentators, and by Dr. Hort in his *Christian Ecclesia* they have been very carefully compared. It seems at least possible, as we learn more of St. Paul's own growth into the fulness of Christian thought, and also of the special circumstances under which each letter was inspired, that we shall be able to state more certainly than we can at present why each particular description was chosen. Though we cannot consider these in detail, we must not fail to mark how St. Paul changes from "the Ecclesia of the Thessalonians which is in God the Father and the Lord Jesus Christ" in his *earliest* letters, to "the saints which are at [Ephesus] and the faithful in Christ Jesus," or to "the saints and faithful brethren in Christ at Colossæ," in his *latest* letters written to communities. Nor must we fail to notice how the transition from the one use to the other is marked by the employment of *both* terms in the two letters to the Corinthians. In the first we have "the Ecclesia of God which is in Corinth— them that are sanctified in Christ Jesus, called saints, with all that call upon the name of our Lord Jesus Christ in every place, . . ." and in the second Epistle we have "the Ecclesia of God which is in Corinth with all the saints which are in the whole of Achaia." We cannot say that as St. Paul's experience enlarged he became more "individualistic" in his teaching. Certainly his appreciation of the value and significance of the corporate unity of the Church did not become less. No letter urges more strongly the significance and the power of this unity than does the Ephesian letter; none is more insistent upon the necessity of strenuously maintaining this great truth.

Possibly the key to St. Paul's use in these salutations may be found thus :—With growing experience he became more and more impressed with the value of the idea of the one Universal Ecclesia. Earlier in his ministry he had spoken without fear of the "Ecclesia of the Thessalonians," and also of the position of individuals in reference to local Ecclesiæ. A little later we may notice the signs of a twofold growth. First, the separate Churches are growing larger and stronger, and this growth may have led to an unwise independence. Secondly, the Church as a whole is spreading more widely over the empire. With this second kind of growth there arose a danger of want of close connection between the separate Ecclesiæ, and also a want of union of each to a common, if invisible, Head or Centre. At the same time as these changes were proceeding a change was taking place in St. Paul himself. He had acquired a personal knowledge from actual residence at Rome of much that went on in that "heart of the empire." Also in the years immediately preceding his imprisonment, as well as during his imprisonment (from those who came to Rome), he had gained a wider knowledge of provincial life in many centres. St. Paul in consequence became more and more impressed with the value of a strong central government, and also of the closest possible connection between this centre and each member or group of members of the empire. St. Paul now applied those same convictions to the Church. He became equally convinced of the immense importance of the unity of all believers. His *chief* concern was not now the unity of the members of the Ecclesia in Philippi or Colossæ, though this was of great consequence;[1] it was rather the vital union of all these Ecclesiæ and of every member of each of them to Christ the great Invisible Head of all.

The more I study the forms of these various salutations the more am I compelled to admire what has been so aptly termed the " statesmanship "[2] of St. Paul. I am equally struck with how we can learn from that statesmanship truths which are of immense value for our present needs and circumstances.

Bearing in mind the changes of form in these

---

[1] Phil. ii. 1 ff., iv. 2 : in both these the idea is unity in Christ, or to Christ.

[2] See essay in Ramsay's *Pauline and other Studies*, also Lock's *St. Paul the Master Builder*.

salutations, let me take the following common experience from Church work in our own time. A new church is to be built and a new congregation formed in a district rapidly growing in population. The nucleus of this future congregation will be certain members of one or more neighbouring congregations. For a time the minister's chief object will be to concentrate as far as possible the thoughts and energies of his people upon building up a new " cause." The thought of the *internal* unity of the new local congregation must be pre-eminent ; the members must be bound to it and to each other. For a time their desire to emulate, even to rival already existing congregations, may possibly to a certain extent be encouraged. But when the new church is built and free from debt, and the congregation is formed, and when the lessons of the need of concentration upon their own concerns and of emulation of others have done their work, *then* the minister must lay stress on the part his people must take in the wider view and wider work of the gospel in the town, the diocese, the nation, the world. A study of St. Paul's method and language shows us how he saw the special needs of the moment, and how careful he was to bring to their supply just that particular aspect or factor of Christian truth or Christian life which was then essentially necessary. At the present time both among Churchmen and Nonconformists there is a growing conviction of the spiritual dangers connected with a narrow, even a selfish, parochialism or congregationalism. By thoughtful men in all "the Churches" it is being felt that the conceptions insisted upon by St. Paul in his later Epistles need most careful consideration. We must deepen and strengthen the sense of the responsibility of the individual towards the purpose and work of the Church Universal. This will imply that we must insist upon a conception of the Church as a unity far wider and more comprehensive than any local, or national, or sectarian expression of the Christian society.

We cannot insist too strongly upon the necessity of forming a true conception of the nature and the position of those to whom we minister, and also of the Divine purpose in regard to them. Our attitude towards a man or a society is finally governed by our conception of that man or that society—by what we consider they are, they were meant to be, and may become. By our "attitude" towards them I do not mean simply what we think of them, but our whole conduct in reference to them.

In St. Paul's descriptions of those to whom he ministers we must consider first the likeness of these descriptions or titles to those of God's covenant people in the Old Testament. Such terms as ἐκκλησία,[1] κλητοί,[2] ἅγιοι,[3] ἡγιασμένοι,[4] are familiar Old Testament terms, and to St. Paul and the first Christians their connotation would be governed by Old Testament associations. To St. Paul, as we have already seen, the Christian Church was the direct, genuine, or legitimate descendant of the Church of the Old Testament, whether in the days of Moses, or Isaiah, or the Return, or the second century B.C. To St. Paul the Christian Church had taken the place and must continue the purpose of the covenant people, with all the privileges and responsibilities of that people. This truth, which we must be careful to maintain, helps us to make clear the unity of God's purpose through the ages, and yet the very different methods employed for the furtherance of that purpose in different periods and under different conditions.[5] It enables us to explain the different steps and the various factors and elements in the long preparation for an absolute and a universal religion. This explanation, of course, assumes that we study the Old Testament by the light of the fullest knowledge available, and in connection with all that

---

[1] Upon the O.T. meaning of ἐκκλησία and συναγωγή and their Hebrew originals קָהָל and עֵדָה, see Hort, *Christian Ecclesia*, pp. 3 ff.

[2] Upon κλητοί, see Sanday and Headlam, *Romans*, p. 4, and Lightfoot, *Colossians*, p. 220.

[3] On ἅγιοι, see Lightfoot, *Philippians*, p. 81.

[4] On ἡγιασμένοι (as equivalent to קְרֹשָׁיו), see Deut. xxxiii. 3.

[5] Heb. i. 1.

can be learnt from the history of the surrounding
peoples.   Then the continuity of the history
becomes apparent.   Too often the Bible is
studied as if we had no knowledge of the history
of the Jews between Malachi and John the
Baptist, and as if there was a want of providential
guidance of the people during this epoch : whereas
in a very true sense it is the history of this period,
and of the period immediately preceding it, which
forms one of our greatest aids to the interpretation of the New Testament.[1]

We must remember that throughout the Bible
we are constantly presented with *ideals*.   This is
one secret of its power.   Both in the Old and
New Testaments men and societies are addressed
by names and titles which describe, not their
actual present condition, but what they are meant
to be.   It may even be said that, at least
occasionally, God is described as treating them as
if they actually were so.   Bearing this in mind,
we may say that one great part of every Christian
pastor's task is to induce people to live up to all
which the names by which they call themselves
implies.   A man calls himself "a Christian," or
"a Churchman."   Even if his life is not in accordance with what these words should imply, we do
not refuse to call him by these titles ; but we
have constantly to remind him of the obligations

---

[1] The loss sustained by the neglect of the study of the Apocry-
phal Books of the O.T. is incalculable.

which they suggest. Then, many of the Bible writers are intense "realists." Behind the actual they see the ideal (which *is* the real) actually existing, and they write of this idea as a *present* reality. Such a method is found especially in the second part of Isaiah, in certain of the Psalms, in St. Paul, and in the Epistle to the Hebrews. This method of describing individuals and societies by their ideal, rather than by their actual condition, explains many passages in the Prayer Book, especially such as are found in the Baptismal, Marriage, and Burial Services. If this use is not remembered, many passages in these services must appear not only unreal, but actually untrue.

St. Paul employed this method again and again, and the wisdom of the practice has been proved by experience. Often the best of all ways to induce people to become what they ought to be is to treat them as if they actually were so. We thus show them what we expect from them ; and we know that neither from ourselves nor from others do we get more than we demand.

The term ἐκκλησία has been so fully treated by Dr. Hort that I may refer to his book both for its history and its significance. If we take Dr. Hort as our teacher, we gain certain very useful lessons for guidance in pastoral work with regard to both the "local" and the "universal" *Ecclesia.* According to Dr. Hort, the *Ecclesia* is "the body of responsible citizens" called (*e.g.* out of their houses) to deliberate and act for the welfare of the State.   To this thought Professor Ramsay has added another which is also most helpful, viz. that in certain parts of the New Testament the Christian Ecclesia in a city is regarded as the true "city"; the civil, or heathen city is only a city "in a state of arrested development."[1]   Hence the Church is meant to be a representation or expression of society at its best—a society in which all the social functions and all the social relationships are perfectly discharged.   From this thought at once arises the lesson that the local "Church" should be a school in which may be learnt and practised the right discharge of these functions and relationships.   It is to be a "city" in which the meaning of such words as "citizen" and "citizenship" find complete expression or demonstration.   It should be a model of social life to the world surrounding it.   This truth is insisted upon, both directly and indirectly, under many forms and analogies by St. Paul, and not least in those Epistles in which the term ἐκκλησία is wanting in the salutation, *e.g.* in *Romans*, *Philippians*, and *Ephesians*.

There is no truth upon which we need to lay greater stress at the present time than this.   The cry of the social reformer is for the right discharge of social functions and relationships.   It is in its failure to discharge these that modern life exhibits

---

[1] Ramsay, *The Seven Churches.*

some of its chief weaknesses. A man exemplary for his industry forgets the responsibilities of fatherhood towards his growing children; he thinks that when he has found the money for the household expenses he has done the whole of his duty;[1] he is, also, too absorbed in business to take any practical interest in the duties of citizenship. Again, grown-up children— even those who earn good wages — are more commonly refusing to do their duty to their aged parents, by contributing to their support.[2] Boys and girls are becoming more anxious to cast off as early as possible the restraints of home life.

The "Church" as a school and training-ground for the right discharge of the various relationships of life may be a fruitful subject for pastoral teaching. Mutual improvement societies and debating classes held in connection with Churches have been in the past the nurseries for public life of many men who have taken an intelligent, useful, and honourable part in both municipal and national affairs. Possibly the encouragement given by Nonconformist Churches to their members to take office, the existence in these of more numerous offices, and the more demo-

---

[1] The schoolmaster is becoming more and more a "professional parent."

[2] This is a growing difficulty in the administration of the Poor Law.

cratic government of these Churches may to some extent account for the larger proportion of Nonconformists who, in comparison with Churchmen, at any rate in municipal or local affairs, seem to obtain office.   I mention these facts in connection with the thought (at least implied by St. Paul) that the local Christian Ecclesia must be regarded as a "model" society, and that the universal Ecclesia should realise our highest conceptions of society as a whole, a society in which we find the complete discharge of all social functions.

A study of St. Paul's teaching suggested by the majority of these salutations will provide the Christian minister to-day with an aid towards combating a social heresy which is at present growing in popularity.

Only in his three earliest Epistles does St. Paul fail to add to his salutation of the Ecclesia (in *Galatians* "Ecclesiæ") a remembrance of the individuals (*e.g.* οἱ ἅγιοι) of whom the Ecclesia was composed, or who were dwelling in the vicinity.[1]   And we notice that even in the three Epistles where there is no mention of the members in the salutation, St. Paul lays great stress upon individual responsibility.   In 1 Thess. iii. 12 he insists upon the need of the love of each to each ; in iv. 4 ff., upon the necessity for *personal* purity as a social duty ; in iv. 11, for the need of each to mind his own business ; in iv. 18 ff., upon the

---

[1] 1 Cor. i. 2 ; 2 Cor. i. 1.

need of each to encourage each. In 2 Thess.
iii. 6 he dwells upon the need of personal carefulness in conduct; in iii. 10, upon the duty
of personal industry; in iii. 14, 15, upon the
necessity of giving personal admonition. In
Gal. v. 15, St. Paul warns against personal bitter-
ness; in vi. 1, he exhorts to personal forgiveness
(in the true sense of the word); in vi. 2–5, he
speaks of the duty of personal service of each to
each, and yet of the personal responsibility (or
personal burden) which can neither be shifted
nor delegated. It would be difficult in the whole
range of St. Paul's teaching to find the necessity
for personal responsibility more clearly taught
than in Gal. vi. 1–10.

The social heresy to which I refer may be
briefly described thus :—That by some skilful
manipulation or arrangement of social *machinery*,
or of social organisation, the perfect "state"
may be evolved apart from individual responsibility for its perfection or its welfare.
The same idea may be expressed thus :—That
by some kind of social arrangement (to be
brought about by means of legislation), a perfect
society may be constructed out of imperfect men.[1]
This heresy contains just sufficient semblance of

---

[1] This is, of course, the fallacy which underlies so many so-called
socialistic schemes. The want of sufficient *moral* elevation in
individual members has gone far to ruin many co-operative
enterprises.

truth to make it all the more dangerous ι falsehood. The semblance of truth consists in this—the experience that good laws and good social organisation do tend to improve character. But good laws and a good social organisation imply a high elevation of character in those who frame them. And if they are to be really beneficial an equally high standard of character will be required in those who are to administer them. But in a democracy both the makers and the administrators of the law are ultimately chosen by those who have to obey the law. Thus we arrive at the conclusion that efficiency, both in making and administering the law, depends finally on the individual citizen, and therefore upon his character. This is why both our Lord and St. Paul lay such stress upon the building up of the individual and upon the responsibility which he personally must feel. In Eph. iv. 12, the "fully equipping"[1] of the saints precedes, indeed is an essential preliminary condition for, "the building up of the body of the Christ"—the Christian society.

Before leaving the thought of the Ecclesia we must notice that where it occurs in the salutation of an Epistle, only in Galatians (and there in the

---

[1] πρὸς τὸν καταρτισμὸν. Bp. Westcott has pointed out a wonderful agreement between St. Paul's description of the "building up" of the Christian society and the results of modern scientific discovery. The body is "built up" of millions of cells. Very many diseases of the body are diseases attacking cells, or groups of cells, forming part of the tissue of the body.

plural[1]) does it stand alone without further definition.   In First and Second Thessalonians we have "the Ecclesia of Thessalonians in God the Father and the (our)[2] Lord Jesus Christ."   In First and Second Corinthians it is defined by words which follow.   As the term was one in use, apart from a Christian connotation, by both Jews and Greeks, it was necessary for St. Paul to define *which* Ecclesia of Thessalonians, or which Ecclesia at (or in) Corinth, he was addressing.

The definition in First and Second Thessalonians is suggestive.   "The Christian Ecclesia is in God the Father—therefore a religious assembly marked off from all that is pagan, and it is 'in the Lord Jesus Christ,' therefore distinguished also from what is Jewish. The creed of the Thessalonian Church is here in brief."[3]   Thus the Ecclesia is a "purposive" or "constituent society"[4] whose purpose is to express belief in God as Father and in Jesus Christ as Lord.   I mention this to suggest that it is well for every minister from time to time to remind the Christian Ecclesia of every parish or district that it is a purposive society, and that the very justification for its existence depends upon its effort to fulfil its purpose.[5]

---

[1] ταῖς ἐκκλησίαις τῆς Γαλατίας.

[2] In 2 Thess. i. ἡμῶν is added to ἐν Θεῷ πατρί.

[3] See Findlay *in loc.*

[4] Giddings' *Inductive Sociology*, pp. 199 ff.

[5] More and more to-day the Church is called upon to justify its

We must now briefly consider the various terms which St. Paul uses in these salutations to describe the *members* of the Christian society, or societies, which he is addressing.

In the salutation of every letter to a Church—except in the First and Second Epistles to the Thessalonians and the Epistle to the Galatians, where, as we have seen, individuals are not mentioned—professing Christians are addressed as "saints" (τοῖς ἁγίοις). The modern associations of this word have been described as "little less than calamitous," so far as helping us to understand its significance by St. Paul. To those who can read the Bible in its original languages the word need cause no great difficulty, especially if they will use the best commentaries.[1] But the Christian pastor when wishing to place ideals before his people must remember that as a rule he speaks to those who have no knowledge of either Greek or Hebrew. The word "saints," as Dr. Maclaren points out,[2] has been "woefully misapplied both

---

existence from the utilitarian point of view—to show what purpose it serves.

[1] See especially Sanday and Headlam, *Romans*, pp. 12–15 ; Hort, *First Peter*, pp. 70–72 ; and Lightfoot, *Philippians*, pp. 81, 82. The following words from Sanday and Headlam's note should be remembered by the Christian teacher : "Because Christians are 'holy' in the sense of 'consecrated' they are to become daily more fit for the service to which they are committed (Rom. vi. 17, 18, 22), they are to be 'transformed by the renewing' of their mind (Rom. xii. 2)."

[2] *Colossians* (in the *Expositor's Bible*), p. 11 ff. I wish to express my frequent indebtedness to this excellent exposition. Its

by the Church and the world. The former has given it as a special honour to a few, and 'decorated' with it mainly the possessors of a false ideal of sanctity. . . . The latter uses it with a sarcastic intonation as if it implied much cry and little wool, loud professions and small performance. . . . Saints are not people living in cloisters . . . but men and women immersed in the vulgar work of everyday life . . . who are yet living lives of conscious devotion to God."

The practical lesson which the Christian minister to-day has to enforce is what the profession of Christianity must involve. As Bishop Lightfoot says : "Though the term ἅγιος does not assert moral qualifications as a fact in the persons so designated, it implies them as a duty."[1] Or, in the words of Dr. Maclaren, "We have here not only the fundamental idea of holiness and the connection of purity of character with self-consecration to God, but also the solemn obligation on all so-called Christians thus to separate themselves and devote themselves to Him."[2]

That people should have a correct conception of the meaning and implied consequences of the term "saints" is of importance, because in it is also implied what I believe to be the apostolic view of baptism. And certainly if "Church-

usefulness as a guide and inspiration to the working minister cannot fail to be great.

[1] *Philippians*, p. 81.   [2] *Colossians*, p. 13.

membership" is to be regarded as involving any real responsibilities, our people must be clearly instructed upon the meaning of baptism and in the obligations both of those who have been baptized and of those who bring children to baptism.[1] In 1 Cor. i. 2 we find ἡγιασμένοις parallel to and explained by κλητοῖς ἁγίοις. The former word evidently means those who have been admitted into union with Christ (by baptism) and continue in union with Him. The word is explicitly connected with baptism, as a condition of union with Christ, in Eph. v. 26:[2] it is also closely connected with baptism in 1 Cor. vi. 11. Hence baptism pledges the baptized to a life of separation from the defilements of the world, and to a life of consecration to God. In the case of infant baptism those who bring the child are pledged to instruct the child to fulfil these conditions in life until the child is able to fulfil them in its own person. The perfect tense does not refer merely to a continuous state, but also to a state which has had a definite beginning.

In Rom. i. 7 and 1 Cor. i. 2 we have κλητοῖς prefixed to ἁγίοις. In fixing the exact significance of this word "called" we shall do well to

---

[1] We need to insist that both Baptism and the Lord's Supper are *social* rites, involving social responsibilities, and are expressions of social ideas.

[2] See Westcott's note, *in loc*. "The initiatory sacrament of Baptism is the hallowing of the bride." What is true of the society must in such a case as this be true of each individual.

remember that in Rom. i. 1 we have "Paul a 'called' apostle."[1] The meaning in the one case governs the meaning in the other. What St. Paul claims for himself he also claims for every professing Christian — that he, too, has received a Divine "call." This thought with regard to the Christian's (present) position cannot be too often or too strongly urged : like everything which helps to strengthen the sense of connection with and responsibility towards the Divine, it should be constantly pressed. Of multitudes of professing Christians to-day the words of the Prayer Book version of Ps. x. 4 [2] are all too true. "God is not in all their thoughts." That in any position of everyday life any kind of honourable activity may be regarded as a Divine calling[3] is a thought which adds to the sense of the dignity, sacredness, and responsibility of life and work. The pastor may also insist upon the lesson to be learnt from the word "calling" in the Epistle to the Ephesians (iv. 1). The knowledge of what Christ has done for them, and of which the pastor must see that his people cannot plead ignorance, should cause them

---

[1] See Sanday and Headlam, *in loc.* Note how St. Paul took "a creation of the LXX" (against the Hebrew) and "appropriated it to Christian use."

[2] From Vg., "Non est Deus in conspectu ejus"; LXX, is οὐκ ἔστιν ὁ Θεὸς ἐνώπιον αὐτοῦ. The Heb. is different.

[3] See a sermon by R. W. Dale, "Everyday Business a Divine Calling," in *The Laws of Christ for Common Life.*

to regard their life as a Divine "calling." Again, in Rom. xi. 29, the "calling" is connected with privileges received from God. To-day every earnest pastor is confronted with these two difficulties : first, he finds a want of the sense of unity in life ; secondly, he finds a materialistic interpretation of life. On the one hand life is practically regarded as merely a succession of almost unrelated states of consciousness, out of each of which the utmost possible pleasure, or as little as possible inconvenience, must be obtained. On the other hand there is an almost entire absence, except perhaps in the immediate presence or remembrance of death, of anything beyond the things which are seen. Both interpretations tend to a feeling of the irresponsibility of life as a whole, and especially towards the past and the future. The conviction of life as a Divine calling is the true remedy for both these false views of life.

In the salutation in the Epistle to the Colossians to the term ἁγίοις St. Paul adds καὶ πιστοῖς [1] ἀδελφοῖς ἐν Χριστῷ, "to the faithful brethren in Christ." As an appellation of the Christians the term brethren "occurs significantly in the first record of the action of the Church,[2] and then throughout the apostolic writings."[3]

---

[1] Here in its passive sense, "trustworthy, steadfast, unswerving."

[2] Acts i. 15, ἐν μέσῳ τῶν ἀδελφῶν.

[3] Westcott, *Epistles of St. John*, p. 54.

The term is a most suggestive one, and to deal adequately, even from the pastoral point of view, with the practical issues of Christian "brotherhood" would demand more space than I can here afford.

As an idea with a social-religious connotation that of brotherhood is by no means confined to Christianity. It is found in the celebrated Arval[1] brotherhood, and very frequently in connection with the social clubs[2] so common in the early Empire, and between which and the early Christian Ecclesiæ so many parallels have been pointed out. The idea was also in use among the Stoics.[3] For the fulness of its meaning the idea, of course, implies that of a common "Fatherhood," and to the deeper thinkers among the early Christians no doubt the term "brothers" would suggest the idea of a common regeneration to a new and common life derived from an identical source. Upon this implication the Christian teacher to-day must constantly insist, especially as since the end of the eighteenth century the term "brotherhood" has been used with growing frequency of societies which have only the most distant connection with Christianity,

---

[1] See W. W. Capes, *The Age of the Antonines*, p. 151 ff.

[2] About these much which is interesting will be found in Dill, *Roman Society from Nero to Marcus Aurelius*, p. 268 ff. (note especially pp. 279, 280).

[3] *e.g.* Epictetus, *Diss.* i. 13. 3 ; also Marc. Aurelius, *Medit.* vii, 22 (συγγενεῖς).

indeed of some which are actually entirely opposed to Christian ideas.[1]   The absolute failure of many of these societies to achieve in any way the purpose for which they have been formed is an eloquent witness to the fact that the realisation of true "brotherhood" between men demands a deeper foundation than merely a common aim.[2]

History proves that the realisation and *permanence* of true brotherhood depends upon the realisation by the individual members of the moral attributes, in other words of the ethical nature of the common Father.[3]   Harnack, in the *Das Wesen des Christentums*, after speaking of our Lord's teaching upon the Fatherhood of God, proceeds to deal with "The Higher Righteousness."   "In Jesus' view mercy was the quality on which everything turned, and the temper in which it is exercised is the guarantee

---

[1] We have heard of "anarchist" and "nihilist" "brotherhoods."

[2] There is a most instructive chapter (with many references to other works) upon "Fraternity," or rather upon the failures to realise true Fraternity during the last hundred years, in MacCunn's *Ethics of Citizenship*, p. 18 ff.   "Who can say," he asks, "even with the fullest allowance for the animosities which are never likely to be eradicated in the most fraternal of societies, that the development of Democracy in the nineteenth century has ushered in a reign of Fraternity?"

[3] See the chapter on "The Church and the Gospel of Brotherhood" in Shailer Mathew's *The Church and the Changing Order*, where he says so truly, "There has probably been in the history of social agitation no more dynamic thought than the Christian teaching as to the Divine *paternity* and the *consequent* human brotherhood" (p. 97).

that a man's *religious* position is the right one.[1]
How so? Because in exercising this virtue men
are imitating God: 'Be merciful, even as your
Father in heaven is merciful.'"[2] Here Harnack
comes very near to the solution of the problem
of true fraternity, but he seems to stop just short
of it. The real fact is that true brotherhood is
actually just so far possible as human nature
becomes full of the Divine—full of the essential
nature of the One All Father.[3] The Christian,
of course, believes that this essential nature is
obtained only by union with the one perfect
Son in whose essentially filial nature we thereby
share. Thus the realisation of brotherhood among
men implies the realisation of unity of nature of
each, *i.e.* of brotherhood, with Christ. This is
the key to an assertion of Bishop Westcott's[4]
which at first sight seems open to contradiction.
St. Paul went to the root of the matter when in
Rom. viii. 12 ff. he wrote, " Brethren . . . as
many as are led by the Spirit of God, these are
the sons of God. . . . We are children of God,
and, if children, then heirs, heirs of God and

---

[1] Dass die Gesinnung in der sie geübt wird, auch die richtige
religiöse Haltung verbürgt."

[2] *E.T.* (" What is Christianity ? "), p. 75.

[3] Real permanent brotherhood demands large personal self-
sacrifice—the self-sacrifice of Christ and of God.

[4] " There is, as far as it appears, no case where a fellow-man,
as man, is called 'a brother' in the N.T. Such passages as
Matt. v. 22 ff., Luke vi. 41 ff., presuppose a special bond of brotherhood." *Epp. of St. John*, p. 55.

joint heirs with Christ." Our position towards God must be His, and His must be ours, then are we truly "sons," and truly Christ's "brethren," and God's children, and so "brotherhood" is possible. To-day the Christian minister must insist upon this one essential condition of real brotherhood : and while he insists on brotherhood as an ideal, he also makes it clear that this brotherhood can only be maintained by the maintenance of the essential condition. I have no need to point out that we here again meet the same heresy to which I have already referred —the attempt to reconstruct society on a perfect basis apart from the condition of the individual human nature.[1]

In Rom. i. 7 to κλητοῖς ἁγίοις St. Paul prefixes ἀγαπητοῖς Θεοῦ. This designation of those to whom he ministers should be a constant inspiration to the pastor. How can he fail to care for those whom he recognises as "beloved by God"? Here, again, the Pauline and the Johannine theology is at one, for the proof of ἀγαπητοῖς is found in the words "so God loved the world."[2] In this world the pastor who knows his flock will find many lonely souls,

---

[1] Upon the subject of "Brotherhood" there is an instructive article in vol. i. of *The Dictionary of Christ and the Gospels.*

Also see an address upon "Love of the Brethren" in Bishop Westcott's *Christian Aspects of Life*, p. 340 ff.

[2] St. John iii. 16.

who feel themselves to be " dear " to no one. To these the strongest appeal will be that they are " beloved by God." Also the brave Christian teacher will find it necessary again and again to assert the " worth of man." One of the most evil results of the fierce competition of modern industry has been to regard man more and more as an " instrument " and not as an " end." The fact that he is so regarded is burnt deep into the soul of many a worker to-day ; for he knows that as soon as he ceases to be of sufficient value to his employer he will be thrown by him, like a piece of old worn-out machinery, upon the " human scrap-heap." To the employer of labour we must fearlessly assert the value of man. At the same time we must speak to " labour " of the love of God for him. If man is constantly regarded by others as worthless he is at last tempted to regard himself as such, and always with fatal results.

But the Christian, we may believe, is dear to God in a special sense—as " reconciled " to God, as one " accepted in the Beloved." Here again, as always, Christian doctrine is the true key to Christian ethics, both in theory and in practice. Man's redemption in Christ is the proof of the Divine love. But the acceptance and enjoyment of what this implies demands man's faith, and faith always implies obedience. Hence in Col. iii. 12 ff. we have a list of virtues which those beloved (by God) must exhibit in life. There is a true sense in which God loves all men, but for man to retain and enjoy the love of God demands the possession, the cultivation, and the exercise of those moral qualities without which no friendship between God and man, or even between man and man, can subsist.[1]

I cannot close this chapter without at least a brief reference to the words "Grace to you and peace (from God our Father and the Lord Jesus Christ),"[2] which are found in the salutation of every letter of St. Paul to a Church. Much that is valuable will be found upon these words in the various commentaries to the different Epistles.[3] Here I would call attention to these two sentences of Bishop Westcott :—"The words of common courtesy become words of solemn blessing. Christ Himself blesses through the believer." Let us change the one word "believer" into "minister," and we have at once a very solemn exhortation.

We must be channels whereby our people are supplied with "grace" in all the fulness of application of which the word is capable. We must also be a means whereby they enjoy that

---

[1] On the collocation "to all that are in Rome" with "beloved of God" see some helpful thoughts in Bp. Moule's *Epistle to the Romans* (in the *Expositor's Bible*), pp. 20, 21.

[2] The words in brackets vary slightly in the different Epistles.

[3] The best treatment of the words I know is that by Dr. Hort in *The First Epistle of St. Peter*, pp. 25, 26.

"peace" of God which surpasseth every human device to secure tranquillity of heart. The devices employed to compass this tranquillity are indeed many and various to-day.

If we regard the object of our ministry as defined by these words it will be well. If we use them as a measure of self-examination with regard to our efforts on behalf of our people we shall be wise. "Above," it has been said, "are the boundless supplies of grace, and around us are the boundless needs of men. To help to supply these needs from the unsearchable riches of the Christ by Whom comes grace, and 'Who is our peace,' is our task." Like St. Paul, we must make our object clear. Let us make it clear that we recognise that to us has been committed the word of reconciliation, and that, in obedience to the conditions contained in that word, man may be at peace with God, with his fellow-man, and with himself.

Chapter 3

CONCEPTS OF MINISTRY

Οὕτως ἡμᾶς λογιζέσθω ἄνθρωπος . . .—I COR. iv. 1.

Διαιρέσεις δὲ χαρισμάτων εἰσὶν . . . καὶ . . . διακονιῶν . . . καὶ . . . ἐνεργημάτων . . .—I COR. xii. 4–6.

IN the last chapter I pointed out how the salutations to St. Paul's Epistles furnish us with various conceptions, first, of our own relationship to those among whom we minister, and secondly, of the nature and the position of these, when we regard them as the objects of the redemption wrought by Christ. All these conceptions, we saw, may be considered as *ideals* which in the course of our ministerial life we should try to realise.

In this chapter I shall pursue a somewhat similar line of thought. I propose to examine the various *titles* which St. Paul uses to describe the different functions which he performs for the Ecclesia—not only for its members, but also, on its behalf, for those outside it. These various titles will also be found to suggest ideals after which we, in our ministerial work, must strive.

I prefer to regard these titles as describing certain *functions* which St. Paul felt called upon to discharge, rather than as indicating certain "offices" to which he had been appointed, because by carefully maintaining both the word and the idea of "function" we shall keep closer to St. Paul's own idea of the likeness in so many ways of the *Ecclesia* (the body of Christ) to the human body or organism.

The number of these titles is considerable, and this in itself shows how many-sided he regarded the work he was called upon to do, and how various were the different activities connected with it.

We must remember that by the human body as a whole many functions must be performed, and that these functions are actually discharged through various definite organs within the body, each of which should be fitted to discharge its particular function. And just as we should say there are in the body eyes, ears, brain, heart, hands, etc., so St. Paul, after drawing attention (1) to the unity of the physical organism, and (2) to the diversity of functions discharged by its various members, adds, "And God hath set some in the Church, first apostles, secondly prophets, thirdly teachers," etc. etc.[1] Each of these men, the

---

[1] I am tempted to translate "God hath set in the Church men

apostle, the prophet, etc., is then regarded as an "organ" which is ministerial to the body, and also for the work of the body upon its environment. No organism can live upon itself, and the health of the body depends upon its functions as a whole towards its environment being adequately discharged.[1]

No organ must be either neglected or despised,[2] and each organ must be maintained as far as possible in a condition of health—of strong and abundant vitality. The condition of the means of connection direct and indirect between each member and the source of the supply of life, as well as between member and member, are of supreme importance.[3] In the Ecclesia, the body of Christ, the minister discharges certain functions for the body, he is thus in the position of an organ of the body, and must act as such. Of course the analogy between the physical organism and the social body may easily be pushed too far. For instance, in the social body, especially in its early stages of development, one man often has to discharge many functions : this is especially the case with the parochial clergyman to-day,

---

who discharge first the function of the apostle, second that of the prophet . . ."

[1] So no Church can be healthy without extraneous, *i.e.* home or foreign missionary work. "The work of conversion (in the full sense of the term) is the sign of a *stantis aut cadentis ecclesiae.*" *Ecce Homo.*

[2] 1 Cor. xii. 21 ff.   [3] Col. ii. 19.

though the question may certainly at least be asked whether it is for the best for the Church that this should be so, at any rate to so great a degree as is common at the present time. I do not wish to push the analogy too far, but in the physical organism there is such a process as compensation,[1] whereby, should one organ or part of an organ fail to discharge its proper function, another organ will sometimes come to its help ; though the necessity for this compensation is certainly not a proof of the health or efficiency of the body as a whole.

It may be asserted that in his own person St. Paul discharged many functions, *e.g.* those of the apostle, prophet, evangelist, teacher, overseer, etc. This is doubtless true. But before we make St. Paul a precedent for our attempting to perform several different functions we must remember, first, that the social organism which we term the Church has since St. Paul's time developed immensely in complexity. And the rule which states that "with the development of the organism there must proceed differentiation of function" cannot be disregarded. Secondly, we must remember that when we quote St. Paul as discharging the functions of the apostle, prophet, evangelist, teacher, etc., we are not describing him as engaging in entirely different

---

[1] *e.g.* in certain diseases *e.g.* of the heart, the liver, etc.

activities.   As an apostle he may (in the Biblical sense of the term)[1] "prophesy," as well as "do the work of an evangelist" and teach : again, an evangelist may both prophesy and teach.   The greater likeness to what is too often attempted (sometimes unwillingly) by the Christian minister to-day is found in his attempting to combine such entirely different kinds of work as the apostles originally attempted.[2]   But, as we know, even they found that they could not efficiently discharge such a combination.

I must not enter into the difficult question— really one of casuistry—" How far is a Christian minister justified in neglecting to discharge certain functions, supposed to be connected with the pastoral office, in order that he may the more efficiently discharge certain other functions ? " Or, in other words, " How far may the Christian minister be a specialist ? "   The answer to this question involves the answer to another—" How far will his circumstances allow him to specialise ? Can he afford—I do not mean in a monetary sense—to do this ? "   To answer this question we must know both the man and his circumstances, and even then the decision of the conscience cannot be neglected.

---

[1] Fore-telling is, of course, a very small, and certainly not an essential part of the work of the " prophet " of the Bible.   See further in the chapter on " Prophecy."

[2] Acts vi.

I now proceed to consider some of the terms employed by St. Paul to describe his position and his work.

I. APOSTLE (ἀπόστολος)

This some would regard as essentially St. Paul's "official title," the one which marks his rank in the ministry, or his official position in the Church, or towards "the Churches." Certainly in a special sense it does seem to describe his relationship towards these; for in virtue of his apostleship he seems frequently to address them: and, as we have seen, the word stands at the head of every Epistle, except those to the Thessalonians, Philippians, and Philemon.

But there is a more true way of regarding the term, one which seems to be in closer agreement with St. Paul's own method of using it, and one to which we are led by considering the use of certain analogous terms. In his *Christian Ecclesia* [1] Dr. Hort writes : " Much profitless labour has been spent on trying to force the various terms used [2] into meaning so many definite ecclesiastical offices. Not only is the feat impossible, but the attempt carries us away from St. Paul's purpose, which is to show how the different functions are those which God has assigned to the different members

---

[1] P. 157 ff.   [2] In 1 Cor. xii. and in Eph. iv.

of a single body." So far I entirely agree with Dr. Hort. He then proceeds : " In both lists apostles and prophets come first, two forms of altogether exceptional function, those who were able to bear witness of Jesus and the Resurrection by the evidence of their own sight—the Twelve and St. Paul,[1]—and those whose monitions or outpourings were regarded as specially inspired by the Holy Spirit." With this further statement I cannot entirely agree, first, because I do not think that Dr. Hort's qualifications of an apostle are borne out by New Testament usage, secondly because, as they stand, the words "exceptional" and "specially" may be construed to imply "confined to that age." I cannot say that Dr. Hort intended them to mean this, but they do seem open to this construction. Personally I believe that the function of both the apostle and the prophet must be discharged to-day quite as surely as those of the evangelist and teacher.

Otherwise the study of such a term as "apostle" would seem to have little practical bearing upon the everyday work of the ordinary town or country pastor. "But," I shall be asked, "can such a

---

[1] But what of Barnabas ? οἱ ἀπόστολοι Βαρνάβας καὶ Παῦλος (Acts xiv. 14). Also what of Andronicus and Junias ? οἵτινές εἰσιν ἐπίσημοι ἐν τοῖς ἀποστόλοις (Rom. xvi. 7, on which see Sanday and Headlam's note). And surely the words in 2 Cor. viii. 23, ἀπόστολοι ἐκκλησιῶν, help to show that apostleship in the N.T. is regarded as a function ?

man claim apostleship ? " Yes, in a very true sense, I answer, if we are careful to get below the technical or official meaning which has been attached to the term, and if we are content to consider the particular aspect of ministerial work which the term describes. After what Dr. Hort has written in his *Christian Ecclesia* I need do no more than remind my readers that the true idea of the office and work of the apostle is that of the " envoy." The apostle, as Dr. Hort shows,[1] " our Lord sets aside . . . for two great purposes, kept apart in the Greek by the double *ἵνα* : the first, personal nearness to Himself, ' that they should be with Him ' ; the second, ' with a view to sending them forth.' " Briefly, then, we may say that the idea of the " apostle " is that of one near to Christ, yet commissioned by Him to represent Him and His cause, sent on a mission for this purpose,[2] with full personal responsibility, and into whose mission or work the full personality enters. In this way he is distinguished from the *ἄγγελος*, who might be the bearer of a sealed letter, or charged to convey a verbally exact message. Thus the apostle has the responsibility, not only of actually representing Christ, but of applying his commission as skilfully as possible to special needs and circumstances.[3] If we would make our

---

[1] On St. Mark iii. 13–16, *Christian Ecclesia*, pp. 22, 23.

[2] "A *legatus a latere*, from the Lord Himself."

[3] There is an interesting use of *ἀποστολὴν* in Rom. i. 5, viz.

ministry truly "apostolic," in the New Testament sense of the term, we must be careful to combine the sense of Divine commission and equipment with a sense of personal responsibility for employing all our powers to the best of our judgment and ability on Christ's behalf and in furtherance of His purpose.   And we must remember that there is no more important and certainly no more inspiring thought connected with our ministry to-day than its essentially apostolical character. This may be an ideal, but it is an ideal which we should daily try to realise.   The two essential elements of such a ministry,—nearness to Christ, and direct commission from Him to represent Him in and to the world,—when combined, give a sense of security and strength on the one hand, and of tremendous responsibility on the other, with which we cannot afford to dispense.   With these conditions fulfilled our ministry must be an apostolic one ; without them nothing can justify our attempting to dignify it by such a description. The two conditions are written everywhere across the ministry of St. Paul.   His spiritual nearness

---

"grace and a special commission with a view to (ϵis) obedience of faith among all the nations."   Compare 1 Cor. ix. 1, 2, "Have not I a special commission . . . if not to others . . . surely I have to you, for the seal of my special commission are ye in the Lord."   Compare also Gal ii. 8, the spheres of the special commission of the two leaders.   The only other instance of the word in the N.T. is in Acts i. 25, where if $\delta\iota\alpha\kappa\text{ovías}$ represents a function it seems difficult to interpret $\dot{\alpha}\pi\text{o}\sigma\tau\text{o}\lambda\hat{\eta}s$ of official osition.

to Christ (and of Christ to Him),[1] and the consecration of all his powers to Christ's [2] service,
at Christ's call, are everywhere apparent.[3]

II. Servant and Minister (δοῦλος *and* διάκονος) [4]

It will be well for us at first to consider these
two titles, and the functions they imply, together.
For δοῦλος and διάκονος (and their cognate
words) have in common the idea of the *usefulness* of service. Both are employed of those
who are useful to men, if the relationship in
which they stand to those to whom they are
useful is differently conceived. Both are em-

---

[1] *e.g.* Acts xxii. 18, xxiii. 11 ; 2 Cor. xii. 9 ; Phil. iv. 13 ;
2 Tim. iv. 17, etc.

[2] Acts xx. 19 ; Rom. i. 9 ; 2 Tim. iv. 7, etc.

[3] Upon the apostolic ministry of the Church to-day, see an
interesting sermon by Phillips Brooks, " Disciples and Apostles,"
in *Twenty Sermons*, p. 152 ff.

[4] It is quite impossible to surmise the original Greek from the
English versions (A.V. and R.V.). Taking only passages in
which St. Paul speaks of himself : " minister " in both versions
represents ὑπηρέτης in Acts xxvi. 16 ; λειτουργός in Rom. xv. 16 ;
διάκονος in Eph. iii. 7.

ὑπηρέτης is used of St. Paul only in Acts xxvi. 16 and (with
others) in 1 Cor. iv. 1.

λειτουργός occurs in St. Paul, of civil rulers, in Rom. xiii. 6
(ministers of . . . service), of St. Paul himself in Rom. xv. 16
(minister), and of Epaphroditus in Phil. ii. 25 (minister).

διακονεῖν does not occur in the LXX : διακονία (representing
נַעַר or שָׁרַת) occurs in Esth. vi. 3, 5, and in 1 Macc. xi. 58 : διάκονος,
representing the same roots, occurs in Esth. i. 10, ii. 2, vi. 1, 3, 5,
Prov. x. 4, and in 4 Macc. ix. 17.

δοῦλος is common in the LXX., and so is παῖς, for " servant."

ployed of those who are useful to God through their usefulness to men ; and also of those who are, if in different ways, useful to men through their usefulness to God on man's behalf.[1]

I do not think that in the New Testament service to God by Christians (on earth) is ever conceived of as unrelated to man's needs. Certainly by the New Testament teachers true or real service to man is always regarded in its relation to God, or to God through our Lord Jesus Christ. This close blending, if not absolute unity, of the Divine and human purposes of service is one of the most characteristic features of religious life and work. St. Paul has certainly "no sympathy with that kind of religion"—mere profession of desire to serve God, or contentment with merely attending divine worship—"that does not make people practical." At the same time he constantly teaches us that in order to confer permanent benefit on others, the service we render them must proceed from the highest motive and be directed to the highest end.[2]

---

[1] The following words of Ambrose seem worth recalling : "Ergo quia quod utile, id etiam justum : justum est ut serviamus Christo. . . . De hac igitur tractandum est utilitate quae sit plena honestatis, sicut ipsis verbis definivit apostolus dicens : Hoc autem ad utilitatem vestram dico" (i Cor. vii. 35). *De Officiis Ministr.* II. vi.

[2] To-day undoubtedly we do see much excellent philanthropic work being done, from an ethical motive and with ethical results, and which yet appears to be almost if not entirely apart from

This union of Divine and human service or ministry is frequently expressed or implied in the Ordination Services : *e.g.*, the deacons are to "exercise their ministry duly to the honour of God and the edifying of His Church"; one petition in the Litany runs, "that they may duly execute their office to the edifying of Thy Church and the glory of Thy Holy Name"; also the first question to the deacons contains the thought of serving God for (1) the promoting of His glory and (2) the edifying of His people. Then it is important that we should remember that we do not work either for or among isolated individuals, but for citizens and subjects living under a definite order of society, in the midst of which we have received our call, and to which order we have a responsibility ; also that by the very maintenance of this order there is found for us an opportunity whereby God may be glorified.[1] Thus there is also a service of

---

religious convictions. Upon this phenomenon see an admirable paragraph in Illingworth's *Christian Character*, p. 101 f. "The existence of men who lead noble lives, devoted to the service of their fellows, without any conscious reference to God, presents a problem by which many minds are seriously perplexed. . . . These men possess, without knowing it, what really is, if one may use the expression, the most important element in the love of God" (the love of one's neighbour), "and solely in virtue of that possession can live for the service of mankind," etc. etc. The whole paragraph should be studied.

[1] 1 Tim. ii. 1 ff. Note the object, ἵνα ἤρεμον καὶ ἡσύχιον βίον διάγωμεν κ.τ.λ. Friction causes loss of energy and prevents progress. The necessity for self-defence prevents the expenditure of

God through the service of Society, and a service of Society which tends *ad majorem Dei gloriam.*

But when we consider the special connotations with which the two groups of words are employed in the New Testament (as also in Greek literature), we shall find that there is a difference in the relationships implied, also, to some extent, in the nature of the service and in the manner in which it is rendered.

The writers of the New Testament wrote in a world which was permeated with the institution of slavery. Many of their hearers and readers were slaves themselves, all were perfectly familiar with the ideas and customs connected with slavery. To many of our hearers these ideas and customs are more or less unfamiliar. Hence many expressions in the New Testament or referring to slavery are to these either difficult or unintelligible. Thus, except when ministering to a highly educated congregation, the expository preacher to-day must frequently explain to his hearers something of the social conditions and customs of the world in which the apostles worked. Otherwise many passages will fail to have the same force and suggestiveness which they had to their first hearers.[1]

---

energy on higher objects.   Throughout St. Paul's Epistles we have exhortations towards the cultivation of " the peaceful temper " !

[1] *e.g.* I Cor. vii. 22, 23 ; Gal. vi. I, etc. etc.

The radical difference between δοῦλος and διάκονος may be stated thus : — (1) "δοῦλος is opposed to ἐλεύθερος and is correlate to δεσπότης and κύριος, and denotes a *bondman*— one who sustains a permanent servile relation to another." When St. Paul denotes himself δοῦλος Θεοῦ or δοῦλος Χριστοῦ, he does not conceive of such a relationship as terminable.[1] We must show that the same is true to-day, not only of the Christian minister, but of every Christian. At baptism the child is put into the position of a *servus Christi*. This relationship to Christ (with its responsibilities whether discharged or not) is unalterable′ and endures through life. (2) On the other hand, "the idea of διάκονος[2] is that of the servant in his activity for the work," *e.g.* the civil magistrate[3] (whose term of office may be limited) in relation to the maintenance of law and order, or the apostolic preacher[4] who visits a Church for a time in order to preach and teach the gospel.

I have shown in my *Social Teaching of St. Paul*[5] how strongly impressed he seems to have been by the "Servant" passages in the second

---

[1] Rom. vi. 18, 22, 23 ; Gal. vi. 17. (The marks of servitude to Christ are indelible.)

[2] Dr. Hort's treatment of the words διάκονος and διακονία in his *Christian Ecclesia*, p. 202 ff., should be most carefully studied.

[3] Rom. xiii. 4 : note the same persons are called λειτουργοί from another point of view in verse 6.

[4] 1 Cor. iii. 5.

[5] Chap. v., "The Servant of the Lord," p. 58 ff.

part of Isaiah : how it was in words[1] taken from one of those passages that he received his commission as a Christian minister : also how we may, from a historical survey of the literature, assert, that as in the prophet the idea of the Lord's "Servant" narrowed down from the conception of all Israel, as the Servant, to a faithful section of Israel, and lastly to a single representative Individual : so, in the New Testament, we see the converse process at work—the conception of the Lord's Servant broadening out from the Lord Jesus Himself to His immediate disciples, and then, in St. Paul's later Epistles, to the conception where the Church as a whole (and so every member of the same) has a service to render (through the Church) to the world. For the proofs of all these statements I must refer my readers to that book ; why I mention them here is to show that we shall not be exaggerating if we assert that the conception of *service*, whether that of the δοῦλος or the διάκονος, is the most comprehensive of all St. Paul's conceptions of the ministerial or pastoral office. Indeed, we may go a step further and say that the truest conception, not only of the pastoral life, but of the ideal life of every follower of Christ, is that of a life of service. Only we must remember that, as in the human body or organism certain "functions of service" are

---

[1] Acts xxvi. 17, 18, quoted from Isa. xlii. 6, 7.

discharged by certain members Divinely appointed to perform these, so in the Church certain other functions of service must be more particularly discharged by those who have been "called" to occupy certain positions therein.

Dr. Hort has shown that this idea is the true key to the conception of the "ministry" as it is found in the New Testament. It is also the conception of Christian ministerial work most needed to-day. In the opinion of some it may not be the highest conception, but undoubtedly it is the one which appeals most forcibly to the world. The demand upon institutions of all kinds to "prove their usefulness," that is their true helpfulness to man, is to-day being widely made. For the ministers of the Church (in its widest sense) to prove practically that their work does satisfy this test is most important at the present time. No appeal based upon "what we have done in the past" will be regarded as a sufficient plea for exceptional treatment in the present or the future. "It is not by what you have done but by what you are doing we judge, and acquit, or condemn you," is the present answer to that plea. A correct conception of the meaning of St. Paul's words in Rom. xi. 13 [1] would prove useful to many occupying respon-

---

[1] ἐφ᾽ ὅσον μὲν οὖν εἰμὶ ἐγὼ ἐθνῶν ἀπόστολος τὴν διακονίαν μου δοξάζω.

sible positions in the Church at the present time. St. Paul does not speak of "magnifying his office" as the words are too often understood : what he asserts is that by his untiring labours in bringing the light of truth to the heathen, he lifts up and throws a light upon[1] the special work and special object of his own ministry ; he causes it to be respected by showing its world-wide necessity and influence.

In laying such stress upon "service," and all it implies, St. Paul is only following very closely the example of our Lord. We must remember, of course, in considering our Lord's teaching on this subject that we cannot confine ourselves to passages in which He gives *direct* exhortation. Besides such passages we shall find much indirect exhortation to service, for instance in the exhortations He gave on the many occasions when He chose some form of service (whether discharged or undischarged) to represent or illustrate His teaching upon "the Kingdom of Heaven."[2] Why was this ? Was it not because, whatever his position, the recognition in practice by every man (inasmuch as he is a man) of the truth that he is called upon to render some form of service is essential ? This assumes that he wishes to live

---

[1] The idea of glorify always seems to involve the ideas,—first, of that of exaltation, and secondly, that of light thrown upon that which is lifted up.

[2] St. Matt. xiii. 27–28, xviii. 23 ff., xxi. 34 ff., xxii. 2 ff., xxiv. 45 ff., etc. etc.

the life he was meant to live, and that he would live as a citizen of the Kingdom of God? Every man, in virtue of his humanity, has a faculty for service, consequently he has a responsibility for finding an opportunity for the exercise of that faculty.

When we pass from the teaching of our Lord in the Gospels to the teaching of St. Paul in his Epistles, we pass from frequent mention of the *Kingdom* to frequent mention of the *Church*; but between the two conceptions there is this similarity —life or membership in both equally involves service. In our Lord's great saying, "The Son of Man came not to be ministered unto but to minister,"[1] He is not pointing to the purpose of His own life only; by the term He uses of Himself He shows that He is declaring what should be the purpose of every human life in virtue of its humanity. The same truth of the universal obligation to some form of service is implied in St. Paul's teaching, *e.g.* in Rom. xii. 1 ff., where the thought of service is raised to a lofty plane by the metaphor of sacrifice, and by the use of the word λατρείαν;[2] again in 1 Cor. xii. (especially in verse 7, where St. Paul states that to each man is given the manifestation of the

---

[1] St. Mark x. 45, καὶ γὰρ ὁ υἱὸς τοῦ ἀνθρώπου οὐκ ἦλθεν διακονη-θῆναι ἀλλὰ διακονῆσαι.

[2] "The Christian sacrifice implies continued activity . . . it must be a service to God such as befits the reason." Sanday and Headlam, *Romans*; *in loc.*

Spirit (a form of χάρις), πρὸς τὸ συμφέρον. By this endowment an addition is made to a man's power of helpfulness, which is to be used, not only for his own profit, but for the profit of all.[1] A close connection between our Lord's teaching and that of St. Paul may be seen thus :—Our Lord, as we have just noticed, constantly speaks of "the Kingdom," St. Paul frequently of "the Church" : now, if the Church is to be a great instrument in the establishment of the Kingdom, and if member-ship in the Church is to train for and to exemplify citizenship in the Kingdom, then (bearing in mind our Lord's teaching) we can understand how membership in the Church must involve some form of service. For, ideally, life in the Ecclesia is only human life as it should be.[2] But if membership in the Church implies some form of service, then a *position of special responsibility* in the Church must imply the exercise of service to a high degree. Hence it is doubly important that those who are called to discharge a special function in the Ecclesia should remember that the render-ing of service is the one claim to respect, and the only justification for the exercise of authority.[3]

I now proceed to consider St. Paul's use of

---

[1] It will be noticed that the object of πρὸς τὸ συμφέρον is undefined.

[2] Hort, *Christian Ecclesia*, pp. 228, 229. Note especially the words, "The Ecclesia as . . . set forth by St. Paul is realised, as it were, in those monotonous homelinesses of daily living . . ."

[3] St. Matt. xx. 26.

these terms as more particularly descriptive of his own position and work, that is as indicating his conceptions of these.

1. δοῦλος (*and its cognates*)

In Rom. i. 1, St. Paul writes as "a bond-servant of Jesus Christ, a called apostle," etc. Attention has rightly been drawn to the Old Testament use of the "servant of the Lord" as applied to the prophets,[1] or to Moses, Joshua, David, etc., and to worshippers generally. But, while St. Paul's letters are full of ideas borrowed from the Old Testament,[2] and while to him the Christian society was certainly the true Israel,—the society in direct and lawful descent, and the one which showed the true evolution or development from the Israel of the old dispensation,—the word δοῦλος has to him a deeper meaning than any attached to the servant of the Lord in the Old Testament. With St. Paul the meaning is rather, Christ hath *purchased* me for His service. It is for Him and

---

[1] *e.g.* Amos iii. 7 ; Jer. vii. 25 ; Ezra ix. 11 (in each case δοῦλος and in Heb. עֶבֶד). While עֶבֶד is in the Heb. by far the commonest original of our word "servant," the representatives of both in the LXX vary frequently between δοῦλος, παῖς, θεράπων (especially freq. of Moses), etc.

[2] See Sanday and Headlam's note in *Romans*, p. 3. "It is noticeable how quietly St. Paul steps into the place of the prophets and leaders of the Old Covenant, and how quietly he substitutes the name of his own Master in a connection hitherto reserved for that of Jehovah."

His cause I labour.   It is wholly as His property,
as one rendering service to Him, that I address
you.[1]

The only occurrence of δοῦλος in St. Paul's
Epistles as used of himself and his fellow-helpers
in regard to those *to* whom they minister is in
2 Cor. iv. 5, "for we proclaim not ourselves but
Christ Jesus as Lord and ourselves as your bond-
servants for Jesus' sake" (where δούλους is, of
course, most strongly qualified by διὰ Ἰησοῦν).
This passage certainly most clearly asserts St.
Paul's entire self-negation on behalf of the gospel
and of his converts.   He wishes these to understand that there is no true service which he and
his fellow-workers are not prepared to do in
Christ's behalf for them.

This aspect of service needs careful consideration in connection with common experiences of
Christ's ministers to-day.   A study of St. Paul's
language and methods will show us in what sense
we may and may not be the "servants" (δούλους)
of those to whom we minister.   St. Paul's words
about becoming "all things to all men"[2] are
frequently stretched far beyond their legitimate
application.   The earnest effort to put oneself in
the place of another, and to view a matter from

---

[1] "The liberty of the Gospel is the silver side of the same shield
whose side of gold is an unconditional vassalage to the liberating
Lord," etc.   Moule, *Romans* (in *Expositor's Bible*), p. 11.

[2] 1 Cor. ix. 22, 23.

his point of sight—a task so often demanded, yet so difficult to accomplish—is a very different thing from what St. Paul so sternly repudiates when he says, "If I were still trying to please men I should not be a bond-servant of Christ."[1] The slave of men will think only of pleasing men ; the slave of Christ thinks only of pleasing Christ. We can be the servants of men only so far as our service of them is entirely compatible with true service of Christ. His attitude towards Christ must be the primary consideration of every Christian, but particularly so of the Christian in a position of special responsibility. A helpful passage, and one of wider application than appears on the surface, is that where St. Paul says, "Not after the standard ($\kappa\alpha\tau\acute{a}$) of eye-service as men-pleasers, but as bond-servants of Christ doing the will of God, serving heartily ($\dot{\epsilon}\kappa \ \psi\upsilon\chi\hat{\eta}s$) with cheerfulness as to the Lord and not to men."[2] Here we learn that we actually serve Christ through service rendered to those who, in the order of civil society or of the Church, are placed in a position of authority over us. The moment that in our ministerial life or work service of men becomes separable, even in thought, from service of Christ, and still more when such service of men becomes open to the charge of seeking self-advantage, it ceases to be a service which the true $\delta o\hat{\upsilon}\lambda os \ X\rho\iota\sigma\tau o\hat{\upsilon}$ can render.

[1] Gal. i. 10 (Χριστοῦ δοῦλος).   [2] Eph. vi. 6, 7.

The following instances of St. Paul's use of δουλεύειν are interesting :—

Gal. v. 13. "For ye brethren were called with a view to freedom (ἐπ' ἐλευθερίᾳ), only not such freedom (τὴν ἐλευθερίαν) as has for its object an opportunity for fleshly indulgence, but by means of the love (which is characteristic of Christianity) (διὰ τῆς ἀγάπης) be as bond-servants (δουλεύετε) to one another." The object of Christianity is freedom[1]—an essential condition for such a development of character as Christianity presupposes : but this freedom may all too easily be abused and lost.

Phil. ii. 22. "His approvedness ye know; that as a child to a father so with me he did service for (the furtherance of) the gospel." St. Paul is speaking of Timothy with high praise. St. Paul does not say "as a son does service to his father," but in the relationship of a son to a father has he served[2] *with* me. The older minister felt he had to the younger the relation of a father ; the younger realised this position. St. Paul wisely does not speak of Timothy serving

---

[1] There is an interesting parallel between the effects of Christianity and education ; both are destined to produce freedom. But by Christianity the forces liberated are also consecrated to a high purpose. Frequently we may see where there is little education and yet some true Christianity the latter becomes a wonderful substitute for the former ; see Harnack, *The Social Gospel*, pp. 106–111, especially the words, "A truly religious man will always be an educated man, though he may happen to possess little 'culture.'"

[2] Notice that δουλεύειν here is absolute.

him; but of each—one in the position of a
father and the other of a son—serving (Christ)
together for the gospel. Here is a lesson both
to older and younger ministers who serve together
as chief and assistant.

Phil. ii. 6 ff. "Reflect in your minds the
mind of Christ, Who while subsisting with the
essential attributes of God . . . emptied Himself
by taking the essential attributes of a bond-
servant,[1] . . ." *i.e.* set no bounds to His humility.
He "assumed" the characteristic attributes of a
bond-servant. Not in the mere form, but in His
"spirit of service," must Christ be an Example
to us. Here is a warning to all in a position of
social responsibility to-day. Never was it more
common than now (while what is termed "the
democracy" is flattered and being told that it
is "coming to its own") to assume the "guise"
of a servant, to speak servilely, and to do outward acts of service with a secondary motive,
and to do all this without any real desire to
make any Christian self-sacrifice, without any
intention of becoming δοῦλοι for the sake of some

---

[1] On the meaning of μορφή, see Lightfoot, and Vincent *in loc.*
Note also the following comment of Bengel: "In ea Dei forma
extabat filius Dei ab aeterno: neque, quum in carne venit, in ea
esse desiit, sed potius, quod ad humanam naturam attinet, coepit
in illa *extare*." Also the two following comments :—"Service thus
becomes glorious, and manhood is recognised as the appropriate
means for the manifestation of Divine life." "He has emptied
Himself to prove to an unbelieving world the power of real human
goodness." Jordan, *The Philippian Gospel*, pp. 109, 110.

infinitely high purpose. Against this simulation of service we must ever be on our guard, for it prevents all true service (as Christ rendered it) for Christ's sake.

2. διάκονος (*and its cognates*)

We turn now to consider St. Paul's use of this second family of words, and we notice at once how comprehensive to him was the range of possible Christian "ministration" or service, how wide was the view he took of its possible applications.

Because every Christian, whether holding a position of special responsibility or not, must be inspired with the spirit of Christ, and must take Christ for the pattern of his life, he must therefore fulfil the "function" of διακονία;[1] though he may do this in a great variety of ways. The well-known words of our Lord should always be remembered, and should always be applicable to the Christian minister, "For verily the Son of Man came not to be ministered unto, but to minister, and to give His life a ransom for many."[2] With this passage we must combine the words

---

[1] Note carefully Hort, *Christian Ecclesia*, pp. 202–208.

[2] Professor Swete's note on St. Mark x. 45 (*Commentary*, pp. 240, 241) should be carefully studied. All I would venture to add to it is to suggest that καὶ before δοῦναι is epexegetic, and I would translate "even to the giving his life," etc., showing that there was to be no limit to the self-sacrifice of service.

in St. Luke's Gospel (xxii. 26), "I am in the midst of you as he that serveth."[1]

As we study the application of our Lord's spirit and example in the apostolic writings we notice how wide an application is given to these. We notice our Lord's wisdom in leaving wholly undefined the particular directions and methods in which "ministry" was to be rendered to Him or to men on His behalf. It is in the Ecclesia as in the human body, "There are diversities of gifts but the same Spirit; and there are diversities of ministrations (διακονιῶν) and the same Lord; and there are diversities of workings but the same God, who worketh all things in all."[2] It is not that διακονίαι can be either delegated or confined to men holding positions of responsibility, or can be predicated only of men holding a particular kind of position in the Ecclesia. And as I have already shown, there are men who have to occupy more than one kind of position, and who have to discharge more than one function. Indeed, there is no function which can be discharged, there is no work which can be done for Christ, or for men for His sake, which cannot be regarded as a διακονία. The discharge of the function of an apostle was a

---

[1] ὡς ὁ διακονῶν. It should be noticed that both here and in St. Mark x. 45, διακονεῖν is used absolutely. Nothing is said as to the object, or method, or reason of service. The spirit of service is the all-essential matter.

[2] I Cor. xii. 4 f.

διακονία. As Dr. Hort points out,[1] when the apostles appointed the seven deacons, they did not cease to discharge a διακονία, they only sought for opportunity to discharge more effectually the special διακονίαι of preaching, teaching, and prayer.[2] St. Paul's apostleship, the fulfilment of his Divine commission, was one long διακονία[3] which involved a multitude of various διακονίαι, e.g. preaching, distributing alms, etc. Again, viewing his life's work as a whole, it was a ministry with certain qualities or characteristics, e.g. it was a ministry τοῦ Πνεύματος (2 Cor. iii. 8); τῆς δικαιοσύνης (2 Cor. iii. 9); τῆς καταλλαγῆς (2 Cor. v. 18).[4]

There is a use of the word in Eph. iv. 12 which from this point of view deserves special examination. The chapter as a whole "deals with the ground, the growth, and the character of the Christian life";[5] while the more immediate context treats of "the unity and harmonious growth of the Christian body."[5] St. Paul shows that this unity and growth are due to the combination and ministry of all the members. But while a χάρις has been given to every member,[6] at the same time to the body as a whole certain *special* gifts have been given. These gifts are

---

[1] *Christian Ecclesia*, p. 206.
[2] Acts vi. 4 (τῇ διακονίᾳ τοῦ λόγου).   [3] 2 Cor. iv. 1, vi. 3.
[4] It is well for the Christian minister to-day to examine his own ministry in order to see that it possesses these essential qualities.
[5] Westcott, *Ephesians*, p. 56.
[6] ἑνὶ δὲ ἑκάστῳ ἡμῶν ἐδόθη [ἡ] χάρις.

endowed men, who are endowed with the ability to discharge certain special functions, but the use of these endowments has a *nearer*[1] common purpose and also a *further*[1] common purpose, this latter being described in a twofold way. In other words, under Divine influence certain men have given themselves to Christ : He endows these men and "gives them back endowed to the Church " for a special purpose. This purpose is (1) " with a view to the perfecting (or equipment) of the saints," (2) in order that each saint (*i.e.* Christian) may take part in the work,[2] which he, in virtue of both his saintship and his humanity, must do ; that work is the work of " ministry." It is only by the constant addition of men who in their lives satisfy this condition that the Body of the Christ, the Ideal Society, will be built up.

We must notice that St. Paul's idea of the nearer purpose of endowed men exactly coincides with what we know to have been our Lord's method of dealing with those whom He trained for the building up of the Ideal Society. St. Paul regards the Divinely ordered nearer purpose of those ordained to perform special functions[3] in

---

[1] The one, the " equipping," being marked by πρός ; the other, the " work of ministering " and " the building up," etc., by εἰς . . . εἰς. [The work of ministering and the building up of the body of the Christ proceed *simultaneously* : in fact they are inseparable.]

[2] Notice that this work of " ministering " is incumbent upon every professing Christian in virtue of the example of Christ.

[3] The functions of the apostle, evangelist, etc.

and for the body to be the equipment unto perfection of every believer ;[1] with a view to enabling that believer to take part in the work of ministering, so as to make him a useful and active member of the Society. And to what did our Lord mainly devote the years of His ministry on earth but πρὸς τὸν καταρτισμὸν[2] of those who, in obedience to His call, had dedicated themselves to Him and His purpose? The wisdom of His method was proved by its success—the rapid growth of the Christian society in its earliest days.

But this work of κατάρτισις demands very considerable qualifications. And often it is from the lack of these qualifications that the work is so badly done. He that would equip others must himself be equipped to a very high degree of efficiency. I do not wish to press the point unduly, but all the functions suggested by the words apostles, prophets, evangelists, pastors, and teachers, if they are to be adequately discharged, demand a very considerable *intellectual*[3] equipment. Far too much has been made of the absence of intellectual equipment in the first Christian teachers : their writings, which certainly are not the productions of illiterate men, prove

---

[1] τῶν ἁγίων.

[2] See Latham's *Pastor Pastorum,* A. B. Bruce's *Training of the Twelve,* Kregel Publications, 1979.

[3] By laying stress on this intellectual endowment, I would not for a moment minimise the importance of another kind of equipment equally or even more important—the "moral-spiritual."

this. When Christ gave to His Church such men as the one who could write this Epistle, or the Gospel and Epistles of St. John, or the Epistle to the Hebrews, or St. Luke's Gospel and the Acts, He gave men who possessed not only very considerable intellectual powers, but who knew how to use those powers. It will be well for Christian pastors and teachers to think of the equipment demanded to-day of those who are appointed to equip the men who are to practise medicine, or law, or who are to take part in scientific work. What then must be the equipment of the Christian minister who is called to equip other Christians to be really [1] useful members of a society charged with the loftiest and most comprehensive purposes! I must not consider at length the verses which follow, but they are full of implications of the high standard required for the adequate Christian life. I may, however, notice the three aspects of Christian progress mentioned in verse 13 :—" The first is intellectual, where faith and knowledge combine to create unity in the soul, the object of both being the Son of God. The second is personal maturity." (Surely the perfection of all that true manhood should imply.) " The third is the conformity of

---

[1] The minister of every parish or congregation should be able to train men and women to become efficient Sunday-school teachers or workers among the poor. To do this adequately demands a considerable intellectual equipment.

each member to the standard of Christ "[1]—the highest of all standards.

In its obedience to St. Paul's principles for training citizens the State is to-day far wiser than the Church. The demand of the world to-day is for *efficiency*, which is not very different from "capability to perform an ἔργον διακονίας for the community." The State has learnt by bitter experience the costliness of the "unemployable"—who cannot perform such an ἔργον. Hence the immense sum spent on education and training of all kinds and the demand for efficient teachers. Until the Church learns the absolute necessity of its ministers being qualified for the task of equipping men, especially in character and conduct, to become useful members of the σῶμα τοῦ Χριστοῦ—the social Christ—we shall not witness the building up of this society, which it is our final purpose to achieve.

There is another thought which this passage suggests. St. Paul in the word ἔδωκεν no doubt refers to the gift, at some definite time, of these men for their special work, just as he was given to the Church at his conversion, when he gave himself to Christ. But those who study St. Paul carefully will agree that his personal endowment was far richer when he wrote this Epistle than when he wrote the First Epistle to the Thessalonians. Can we say of all ministers that their

[1] Westcott, *Ephesians*, p. 63.

personal endowment, after ten or twenty years
in the ministry, is always so much richer than it
was when they were ordained ? Are they more
intellectually equipped to train others ? If, in
one sense, Christ gives us to the Church once for
all, in another sense He constantly gives us, *i.e.*
as each new call or opportunity [1] for work comes
before us.[2] Do we see the necessity for making
ourselves [His gift] as fit as possible an instrument for doing the work He would have done ?

There is an application of διακονία and of
διακονεῖσθαι in 2 Cor. viii. and ix. which, from
its practical bearing upon a field of ministerial
responsibility much debated at the present time,
demands careful examination. These chapters
deal with the collection which St. Paul had for
some time been urging should be made for the
poor Christians in Jerusalem. Incidentally they
furnish some very valuable advice as to the
grounds upon which a Christian minister should
appeal for liberal giving, and as to the *methods* he
should employ in the management—the collection
and distribution—of " public " money, or of money
given for charitable objects.

---

[1] In Acts xiii. 2 we read, " Separate to Me Barnabas and
Saul for the [special] work (εἰς τὸ ἔργον ὅ) to which I have called
them." What had not St. Paul learnt since the day of Damascus !
There are some very fruitful thoughts in the chapter " A Three
Years' Travail," in *The Fifth Gospel*, pp. 56 ff.

[2]   " What if the truth broke on me from above
         As once and oft-times ? "

To-day we hear widely spread complaints of the want of generosity in professing Christians.   May not this arise from a want of clear teaching, such as St. Paul here gives, upon the reason why the Christian, in virtue of his profession of Christianity, is bound to be a generous giver ? [1] Again, when we give, or refuse to give, we are apt to confine our attention to the effects of our giving or refusing upon the *objects* of the appeal. St. Paul shows how inadequate is such a view. A particular object may not appeal to us, but to refuse to give in a particular case is very different from that general want of liberality which is so common to-day.

St. Paul regards liberality as a proof of the presence of the grace of God.[2]   Should there be a want of liberality, the reason will probably be that an essential primary condition has not been satisfied.[3] He then points out the probable effects of our generosity upon others.[4]   He shows that the effect of generosity will not be impoverishment of ourselves, but God will cause us to abound if not in material wealth (which is, however, St. Paul's primary meaning) yet in that wealth which God deems best for us.

I would add two other thoughts which these chapters suggest to the working minister :—First, by his own clear and urgent exhortation [5] St. Paul

---

[1] 2 Cor. viii. 9, ix. 7.   [2] viii. 1.
[3] viii. 5.   [4] viii. 24, ix. 6 ff.   [5] viii. 16.

teaches us the necessity of urging this duty (however unpleasant it may be to do so) upon our congregations. Secondly, he shows the need of scrupulous care that everything connected with the collection or distribution of money shall be above suspicion.[1] The lesson[2] of the chapters may be expressed thus :—God's grace in the Christian must produce grace in conduct,[3] which will take the form of ministering to the needs of others. This ministry is exemplified in the life of Christ, Who was full of the Divine grace. The reference to our Lord is valuable because it shows how we must give much more than money. He gave Himself, and the giving of self is the foundation of all true liberality.

Before leaving this subject of ministry there are two passages in this same Epistle to which I would draw attention.

In chap. iii. 1 ff. St. Paul repudiates the idea that either he or Timothy are " beginning again to commend themselves," or that they require such " letters of commendation "[4] as seem to have been in use in the early Church. His converts, those to whom he writes, were the

---

[1] 2 Cor. viii. 19 ff.

[2] There are some admirable remarks upon this by Chrysostom in the 6th Book of the *De Sacerdotio*.

[3] See a sermon by Dr. Dale, " The Grace of Christ a Law of Conduct," in *The Laws of Christ for Common Life*.

[4] The Epistle to Philemon is a συστατικὴ ἐπιστολή. For references to such letters in both profane and sacred literature see Meyer's note (*E.T.*) *in loc.*

letter which he has to show, a letter both *to* them and *from* them : a letter to them because they could read the change produced by Christianity in their own hearts, a letter from them because others could read the change in their conduct. "Ye are being manifested to be an epistle of Christ—a letter composed, that is dictated, by Christ, but 'ministered,'[1] that is written at Christ's dictation, by us. We are the amanuenses of Christ who, by the power of the Spirit of a living God, must try to write on the hearts[2] and minds of men what Christ dictates to us." In this writing the Spirit of the living God is the instrument[3] used by the apostles ; hence their ministry is a ministry of the Spirit. Thus one object of our ministry is so to write the message of Christ upon the hearts of men, that all, themselves included, may read it. It is well to remember that just as the fertility of the seed depends in great measure upon the nature and condition of the soil,[4] so the legibility of this writing will depend on the nature and condition of the heart upon which the message is written. Thus in our ministry we have to prepare men's hearts, or to induce men to prepare their own hearts, to receive the message of Christ.[5]

In chap. iii. 7–9 the substantive διακονία

---

[1] διακονηθεῖσα.   [2] Cp. Jer. xxxi. 33.

[3] Men are generally regarded as the instruments of the Spirit, but the converse is equally true.   [4] St. Matt. xiii. 4 ff.

[5] The lessons of the parable of the "Sower" and of modern psychology are in this identical. See further on p. 153.

occurs four times in three consecutive verses. The passage deals with the intrinsic and also relative glory of the Christian ministry, which is termed ἡ διακονία τοῦ πνεύματος, and ἡ διακονία τῆς διακοσύνης, in contrast to the Mosaic ministry, which was ἡ διακονία τοῦ θανατοῦ, and ἡ διακονία τῆς κατακρίσεως.

The explanations given by Meyer of these four genitives are interesting if not, perhaps, entirely satisfactory.

(1) "The ministry *dedicated to* the Holy Spirit, *i.e.* forming the medium of His operation (the teaching ministry of the gospel)." This is another instance of what I have several times drawn attention to, that the Christian minister is to be the instrument through which the Holy Spirit works.

(2) "The ministry which is *the medium* of righteousness, for it is the office of "gospel teaching" to preach the faith in Jesus Christ by which we have righteousness before God."

In both these cases I think Meyer fails to notice the ministry of *example* and of personal influence, in addition to the ministry merely of teaching. Our life, our daily conduct, no less than what we say, is a *medium* or channel whereby the Spirit and righteousness are imparted. We may remember the clause in the Litany, "that both by their preaching and *living* they may set forth," etc.

(3) "The ministry *conducing* to the rule of death . . . the ministry of Moses which he accomplished by bringing down the tables of the law from Sinai to the people."

We must be careful in our ministry that we are not guilty of a similar action, that is of setting forth a law, even the law of Christ, without also ministering to the people that whereby they may accomplish what God requires of them. We must remember St. Paul's words in Gal. iii. 5, "He then that supplieth bountifully [1] to you the Spirit and worketh powers among you"—Is the origin of this "works of law," or "obedience of faith"? The law had no power whereby the requisite change could be effected.

(4) "The ministry which is the *medium* of condemnation." Our ministry will necessarily include a measure of condemnation, but this must not be its characteristic feature, else it will be failing to effect its true purpose.

There is one other suggestive thought in these verses which must not be forgotten—the effect upon the face of Moses of his communing with God, of his being in the near presence of God. This is described as "the glory of his countenance." We learn, too, of the transient nature of that glory, also of his desire to hide that transiency, which was a sign of the transiency of the ministry in which he was engaged. Our ministry is meant

---

[1] ἐπιχορηγῶν. The A.V. "ministereth" is misleading.

to be permanent, and that which glorifies it is, again, the reflection of the Divine upon it. This reflection in our case is meant, like the ministry itself, to be permanent. Hence the importance of our constantly seeking and maintaining a close communion with God, through which alone we may be able so to do His will—perform our διακονία towards Him—that our speech and life are alike reflections of His purpose and means by which that purpose is made known to men.

III. HERALD (κῆρυξ)

This title I shall here treat very briefly, for a consideration of the work of the Christian minister as a herald, as one who "heralds" the gospel, will naturally come under consideration in a chapter upon St. Paul's preaching.[1]

The title is actually used by St. Paul of himself only twice, viz. in 1 Tim. ii. 7 and 2 Tim. i. 11. In both passages St. Paul speaks of his having been appointed[2] a herald, an apostle, and a teacher with special reference to the Gentiles. In both passages the three words occur in the same order, and doubtless describe different aspects or factors of his missionary preaching.[3]

---

[1] See p. 306 ff.

[2] ἐτέθην : the apostle's ministry was not self-chosen ; cf. 1 Cor. xii. 18, ὁ Θεὸς ἔθετο τὰ μέλη . . . ἐν τῷ σώματι καθὼς ἠθέλησεν.

[3] The only other instance of κῆρυξ in the N.T. is in 2 Pet. ii. 5 (of Noah), but κήρυγμα occurs eight times ; in 1 Cor. ii. 4 it signifies

Naturally "herald," the description of one who performs the necessary *preliminary* function, comes first. When the work of the herald is combined with that of the apostle — the man Divinely commissioned, and that of the teacher— the one who explains and shows how to do—we have a very comprehensive description of the work of the missionary preacher.

The office of the herald is to make an announcement, to proclaim, to declare. At the commencement of His ministry our Lord is described as "heralding (or proclaiming)[1] the gospel of God and saying the appointed time is fulfilled and the kingdom of God is at hand : repent and believe in the gospel."[2] To "herald" evidently means to set forth the contents and conditions of the gospel, for the words "believe in" certainly imply that these were made fully clear. The Christian minister to-day must be careful to perform this office. The missionary to the heathen is not likely to forget it ; but those who work at home among professing Christians in a so-called Christian country are far too apt to assume that the contents of the message and the conditions of God's offer of salvation are clearly known by all. Doubtless much of our preaching and teaching to-day is ineffective through this

---

the facts of the gospel. κηρύσσειν frequently occurs (more than sixty times). Note Rom. x. 14, χωρὶς κηρύσσοντος, "without a preacher."

[1] κηρύσσων.   [2] St. Mark i. 14.

assumption, one which investigation into the real state of the case proves to be far from justified.

IV. PROPHET

In 1 Cor. xiv. 6, St. Paul asks, "What shall I profit you unless I speak to you either by way of revelation, or of knowledge, or of prophesying, or of teaching?" In the 1st verse of the same chapter St. Paul bids the Corinthians to desire with special earnestness "to prophesy." In the 3rd verse he asserts that "he that prophesieth speaketh unto men edification, and exhortation (or encouragement), and consolation," also that "he that prophesieth edifieth the Church." These passages are sufficient to show that St. Paul set an exceptionally high value upon the function of prophesying, and also that he exercised the gift. As this subject is of exceptional importance, first in connection with St. Paul's own work, secondly in connection with ministerial work generally in the apostolic and succeeding ages, and thirdly in connection with the work of the Christian ministry to-day, I have made "prophecy" the subject of a separate chapter.

V. PREACHER

As I have also made St. Paul's preaching the subject of a special chapter, I need not say more about it here than to remind my readers that in the Acts and in his Epistles the words "preach" and "preacher," as found in both the Authorised and Revised Versions, represent more than one word in the original Greek. In some places the word "preach" may represent κηρύσσειν, and "preacher" represent κῆρυξ. In other passages "preach" may represent a part of the meaning of the word εὐαγγελίζεσθαι, as in Rom. i. 15, 1 Cor. i. 17, Gal. i. 9. In Rom. xv. 19 it represents a part of πληροῦν; in Gal. iii. 8, a part of προευαγγελίζεσθαι; in 1 Cor. ix. 14 (in the A.V.), a part of καταγγέλλειν.

St. Paul was before everything else a preacher. In the course of his missionary labours he was constantly preaching. As a preacher in our sense of the term he was sometimes a herald, sometimes an evangelist, sometimes a prophet, sometimes a teacher. His preaching included the discharge of all these various functions. So it is with the Christian preacher to-day. In the same sermon each of these different works may need to be fulfilled.

VI. TEACHER (διδάσκαλος)

An adequate treatment of St. Paul as a teacher —an inquiry into the methods and contents of his teaching—would require a volume to itself. Here I can only hope to give the chief thoughts which a study of his teaching suggests.

Only twice,[1] as I have already noticed, does St. Paul speak of himself as a teacher, only once [2] is he definitely called a teacher by another. In 1 Cor. iv. 17, Col. i. 28, and in Acts xx. 20 he speaks of himself as teaching; in Acts xv. 35, xviii. 11, xxi. 21, 28, and in xxviii. 31 he is described by others as teaching.

It is difficult to treat St. Paul's discharge of the function of teaching by itself, for with him as with the Christian minister to-day this work is not isolated. As apostle, as herald, as evangelist, and as prophet, he would constantly be teaching.

Regarded more narrowly, we may say that the teacher's work is twofold. First, to try to enforce discipline in life—to obtain and to maintain the conditions without which it is not possible to gain the attention of those he would teach to the ideas he would place before them; secondly, to set forth, explain, and gain admission for these ideas. This is probably why the functions of "pastor" and "teacher" are so closely joined in Eph. iv. 11,[3] and why "pastor" precedes teacher; for teaching is impossible without some measure of discipline.

Fortunately we are learning how important it is for the teacher to be also a disciplinarian : though in this latter capacity the younger clergy

---

[1] 1 Tim. ii. 7 and 2 Tim. i. 11.   [2] Acts xiii. 1.

[3] τοὺς δὲ ποιμένας καὶ διδασκάλους. The other words are joined simply by δέ.

are still often grievously wanting. More than thirty years of constant experience in large day and Sunday schools, and much work in them in conjunction with many of my younger brethren, are my reasons for these statements. What proportion of men at their ordination, or even when they obtain a parish of their own, could be described in any way as διδακτικοί? How many men after years of ministerial life still continue to be quite unable to teach? And yet what work is more important? I need not refer to our Lord, for as the " Prince of teachers," as the One from whom, more than any other who ever lived, we may learn what teaching is, He has been the subject of many volumes. We may not perhaps blame the recently ordained severely if they are not experts in teaching, but we must blame the system which places men in a certain position without in any way ensuring that they have received at least some instruction or training in one of the most important duties attached to that position. We must especially blame the man who years after ordination is still unable to teach, for by study and practice he might have trained himself to do this. I believe it is, at least partly, because men find themselves to be such inefficient teachers that many of them, instead of making themselves efficient, actually cease entirely from teaching. It is not, as a rule, that men do not know enough, at any rate when they are ordained ;

though many a man, from ceasing to study, loses that *freshness* of knowledge which is essential for successful teaching. But they have never been taught how to obtain the conditions in which they can teach, and how to obtain an entrance into the minds of their scholars for the knowledge they wish to impart.

There is every reason to suppose that in the future far greater responsibility for teaching will devolve upon the clergy.[1] The giving of religious instruction will more and more rest with them. And as efficiency increases in secular education those whom we teach will be more and more able to appreciate (or to despise) the religious teaching which is offered to them.

But the clergy have not only to teach, they have to train others to teach. They ought to be capable of giving adequate instruction upon both the science and art of teaching, because the efficiency of the great multitude of almost wholly untrained Sunday-school teachers depends upon the efficiency of the clergy to train them.

The fact that our Lord tells us that one of the offices of the Holy Spirit is to teach [2] should, for two reasons, impress us with the importance of being able to teach, first because it shows us the sacredness of the calling of the religious

---

[1] Through the gradual abolition of all denominational, if not religious, teaching in day schools.

[2] St. John xiv. 26. διδάξει.

teacher, and secondly because it proves to us the sacredness of that which we have to teach. I have already laid stress upon how St. Paul again and again shows us that the various offices of the Holy Spirit[1] are performed through men who, by Him, are filled with the ability to discharge these offices. In this way the Spirit through the Church carries on the work of Christ. Hence our teaching must be regarded as nothing less than the carrying on of the teaching work of Christ through the power of the Holy Spirit.

In 1 Cor. ii. 6 ff., St. Paul speaks of what he imparted to his hearers, and then states that these truths were revealed to him through the Spirit ($\delta\iota\grave{a}$ $\tau o\hat{v}$ $\pi\nu\epsilon\acute{v}\mu\alpha\tau o\varsigma$), for the Spirit searcheth the depths (the *mysteria interiora*) of God.[2] In gaining Divine or Spiritual knowledge the presence of the Holy Spirit within the teacher is essential. This knowledge we must possess, and must impart in words which the Spirit teacheth ($\lambda\acute{o}\gamma o\iota\varsigma$ . . . $\grave{\epsilon}\nu$ $\delta\iota\delta\alpha\kappa\tauo\hat{\iota}\varsigma$ $\pi\nu\epsilon\acute{v}\mu\alpha\tau o\varsigma$): "applying spiritual methods to explain spiritual truths."[3] St. Paul then proceeds : "For the natural ($\psi\nu\chi\iota\kappa\grave{o}\varsigma$) man does not receive the things of the Spirit of God, for they are $\mu\omega\rho\acute{\iota}\alpha$ to him," etc. The

---

[1] 1 Cor. xii. 4 ff.

[2] This I understand of the Holy Spirit aiding the consecrated human faculty to do the same.

[3] Lightfoot *in loc.*

argument here used by St. Paul might have been used by a modern psychologist, who would say, "Before a pupil can be expected to assimilate or understand an idea the teacher must be careful to see that he has something to understand or assimilate *with*." Here is a valuable hint to preachers, especially to uneducated congregations. The foregoing is only one of many instances in which St. Paul seems to have anticipated the results of modern scientific investigation.[1]

The lesson to the religious teacher should be clear. He must seek and obtain the presence and help of God's Holy Spirit—the Spirit of wisdom,[2] of understanding, and of knowledge,[3] and the subjects of his teaching must be τὰ βάθη τοῦ Θεοῦ. The grammar, history, geography, and antiquities of the Bible are not these : and it is so easy to forget that knowledge *about* the Bible is not "religious" knowledge. Above all, the Christian teacher must be careful to prepare *men*, by helping to impart to them a spiritual nature so that they may be fit to receive spiritual teaching.

The following references to teaching by St. Paul are worthy of careful attention :—

In Rom. ii. 21, St. Paul, imbued with the spirit

---

[1] See further in my *Social Teaching of St. Paul*, pp. 92 ff. and 154 ff.

[2] On the meaning of "wisdom" see chapter on " Wisdom," p. 356.

[3] See Professor G. A. Smith on Isa. xi. 2 ff., in his *Isaiah*, vol. i. p. 187 (*Expositor's Bible*), where he writes : " The Spirits of the Lord mentioned by Isaiah are prevailingly intellectual."

of the true teacher, asks indignantly, "Thou who teachest another, teachest thou not thyself?" The passage deals with the boasting of the Jews about their superiority in the possession of knowledge of God, and of revelation from God. The description of the Jewish teacher is striking. He is one who is confident that he perceives God's will; he is confident also in his trained judgment, in his highly educated taste, of his capability, among good things,[1] of choosing the best, of his sufficiency as a guide to the blind, a light to those in darkness, a corrector to those lacking sense or judgment, as a teacher of the immature, etc. Having drawn this picture of entire self-satisfaction, St. Paul pertinently asks, "Thou therefore that teachest another, teacheth thou not thyself?" This passage by itself is sufficient to prove that St. Paul was a great teacher. We must notice first his full description, from the true teacher's point of view, of what the teacher must try to do: secondly, his strong implicit rebuke of the folly of underestimating the attainments or capacity of those to be taught[2]—a fatal error, yet one commonly made in practice: lastly, St. Paul lays his finger

---

[1] "Non modo prae malis bona sed in bonis optima." Bengel on Phil. i. 10, *New Testament Commentary*, p. 427. Kregel Publications, 1981.

[2] There are some excellent warnings against this in Blunt's *Duties of the Parish Priest*, pp. 149 ff. If these warnings were needed in 1856, when that excellent book was published, they are much more needed to-day.

upon what is probably the most common of all causes of failure on the teacher's part, namely, self-satisfaction with his own capabilities, and therefore no effort to improve these. The picture is, of course, practically identical with that of the Pharisees in the Gospels, upon whose unfitness for their position, and consequent harmfulness to the higher life of the people, our Lord speaks so strongly.

In Eph. iv. 20 ff. we see how closely St. Paul connected Christian conduct with Christian teaching :—"But ye did not so learn the Christ, if at least it was He whom ye heard, and it was in fellowship [1] with Him ye were further taught, even as there is [essentially] truth in Jesus,[2] that ye put away the old man, having regard to your former manner of life, according to the lusts of deceit, and that ye be renewed in the spirit of your mind, and that ye put on the new man," etc.

Upon this passage these three notes of Bishop Westcott's should be carefully remembered :—(1) On ἐδιδάχθητε in verse 21. "Ye were further taught, as ye were then enabled to receive further instruction"; implying that *continuous* instruction was then the experience of the Christian convert. (2) On verse 23. "Two things are required for the

---

[1] Verse 21, the ἐν αὐτῷ : "in Him" (probably as the sphere of instruction).

[2] Who is the Truth ; and who came to bear witness to the Truth. Cf. also St. John i. 14, πλήρης ἀθηθείας.

positive formation of the Christian character—
the continuous and progressive renewal of our
highest faculty" (intellectual), "and the decisive
acceptance of the new man" (practical). (3) "The
spirit by which man holds communion with God
has a place in his higher reason. The spirit,
when quickened, furnishes new principles to the
νοῦς, by which it is delivered from ματαιότης."
We must remember that "ideas" are motive
powers which are conveyed into a man by
teaching. We must also remember that *spiritual*
ideas (the source of which is God's Holy Spirit
—the Teacher) conveyed by teaching into a
man become the power of the Holy Spirit in
the life whereby conduct is changed. We may
also say that for a healthy progressive life we
need a constant fresh supply of the highest
mental stimulus[1] in the form of spiritual teaching.
Doctrine or teaching is the inspiration or motive
power, it is also the controlling or regulative
power, of conduct.

In Col. ii. 6 ff., St. Paul speaks of what must be
the result of Christian teaching. Bishop Lightfoot
paraphrases this passage thus: "Let your conviction and conduct be in perfect accordance with
the doctrines and precepts of the gospel, as it was
taught to you." For several reasons this passage
is an interesting one. Its meaning seems to be:
As ye received (from your teachers) the Christ,

---

[1] ἀνανεοῦσθαι, the present tense pointing to a continuous process.

even Jesus the Lord (in contrast to the false teaching being disseminated in Colossæ), walk in Him, having been rooted (once for all) and being continuously built up (by constant teaching)[1] in Him, and being more and more stablished as to your faith, even as ye were taught (by Epaphras) . . .

Here again we see the necessity of constant true teaching, first as a safeguard against false teaching, for the mind is as a field in which weeds will grow if it is not fully sown with the Word of God; secondly, as a means whereby we are constantly being "built up," like a building to which additions in height and breadth are always being made.

Another valuable passage is that in 2 Thess. ii. 13, " Because from the beginning God chose you to salvation by sanctification of spirit and belief in truth." The passage is difficult for two reasons: first, is ἐν instrumental or does it refer to the sphere in which two processes are proceeding? Second, is πνεύματος here the human spirit or the Holy Spirit? The answers are really not material, for if ἐν refer to the sphere it must be the sphere in which the two forces referred to are acting. If we take πνεύματος of the human spirit,[2] it is that spirit under the influence of the

---

[1] "*gewurzelt* (Ursprung, daher *Perf.*); *aufgebaut* (Entwicklung, daher *Præs.*)." Von Soden *in loc.*

[2] So Findlay.

Divine. The importance of the passage consists
in the close combination of the two forces producing two processes, also because sanctification
is shown to precede increase of true knowledge.
We must in a measure convert before we can
teach ; at the same time growth in sanctification
and in true knowledge must proceed simultaneously.

Many other passages from St. Paul's writings
on this subject might be quoted, but these will be
sufficient to show how very high an importance
St. Paul attached to the ministry of teaching.

VII. AMBASSADOR

In 2 Cor. v. 20, St. Paul speaks of himself and
his fellow-ministers as ambassadors on behalf of
Christ.[1] In Eph. vi. 20 he speaks of himself as
an ambassador on behalf of the revealing of the
mystery of the gospel in a chain.[2] Once he
appeals to Philemon as Παῦλος πρεσβύτης,[3] where
Lightfoot states that "πρεσβύτης may have been
written indifferently for πρεσβευτής in Paul's
time"; he adds that, "the main reason for
adopting this reading is the parallel passage in
Ephesians,[4] which suggests it very strongly."

---

[1] ὑπὲρ Χριστοῦ οὖν πρεσβεύομεν. The word πρεσβεία occurs in
Luke xiv. 32 and xix. 14.

[2] ἐν ἁλύσει.   [3] Philem. 9.   [4] vi. 20.

The term as applied to the Christian minister is a very suggestive one. In 2 Cor. v. 20 the idea is that of an ambassador to subjects estranged from, if not actually inimical to, their lawful sovereign. The language is somewhat difficult and the metaphors must not be too closely pressed ; but there does seem to be a reference to our position in relation to each of the three Persons in the Holy Trinity. It is Christ we represent, as though the Holy Spirit were doing His special work[1] through us—the removal of sin which separates and causes enmity between man and God : "We beseech you on behalf of Christ, be ye reconciled to God." One great part of our work must be to go, in the power of the Holy Spirit, after those in a "far country" and bring them home reconciled to their Father. In this sense St. Paul may have found Philemon, who seems in a twofold sense to have been in a far country, and certainly far from God.

The importance and dignity of the ambassadorial office must be remembered. As Christ's ambassadors we represent Him and carry out His purpose. In reconciling men estranged from God we make the possibilities of the "At-one-ment" into actualities. But, like St. Paul, we are often "ambassadors in chains"—in the chains of un-

---

[1] $\pi a \rho a \kappa a \lambda o \hat{v} \nu \tau o s$, the work of the $\pi a \rho \acute{a} \kappa \lambda \eta \tau o s$. The frequent rendering of $\pi a \rho a \kappa a \lambda \epsilon \hat{\iota} \nu$ by " comfort " in the R.V. is, of course, much to be regretted.

toward circumstances. Like him we may be confined in one place, and inclined to think we could do much more good elsewhere. But had St. Paul not been a prisoner the Church might have been to-day without four of his letters—some of her most precious heirlooms. The following words from Bishop Lightfoot's *Ordination Addresses* [1] upon the ambassadorial function of the minister of Christ may well be remembered : "What ideas are involved in this image of an ambassador ? We may sum up the conception, I think, in three words, *commission, representation, diplomacy*. The ambassador, before acting, receives a commission from the power for whom he acts. The ambassador, while acting, acts not only as an agent but as a representative of his sovereign. Lastly, the ambassador's duty is not merely to deliver a definite message, to carry out a definite policy : but he is obliged to watch opportunities, to study characters, to cast about for expedients, so that he may place it before his hearers in its most attractive form. He is a diplomatist."

VIII. Steward (οἰκονόμος)

There is no idea connected with the Christian ministry more important or more fruitful than that of stewardship, because it covers all that the

[1] P. 47.

word *responsibility* suggests. Directly and indirectly, explicitly and implicitly,[1] the immense responsibility of life, of endowments and possessions of all kinds, of position and of service, is clearly impressed upon us throughout the New Testament. And what is expected of Christians generally[2] in regard to this is expected to a much greater degree of Christian ministers.

Unfortunately we have in connection with οἰκονόμος and its cognate words again a want of uniformity in translation in both our Authorised and Revised Versions. This tends to prevent our noticing that connection between one passage and another which helps to elucidate the meaning of both.

The idea of the ministry as a stewardship is clearly brought out in the Ordination Service for Priests in the following words : " That you have in remembrance into how high a Dignity, and to how weighty an Office and Charge ye are called, that is to say, to be Messengers, Watchmen, and Stewards[3] of the Lord ; to teach and to premonish, to feed and provide for the Lord's family," etc. The idea is also very present in these words : " Have always therefore printed in your remembrance how great a treasure is committed to your

---

[1] *e.g.* St. Matt. xxiv. 45, cp. St. Matt. xiii. 52.

[2] I Pet. iv. 10, καλοὶ οἰκονόμοι (which suggests the manner of the performance of stewardship).

[3] " Nuntii, speculatores, et dispensatores."

charge. . . . And if it shall happen the same Church, or any Member thereof, to take any hurt or hindrance by reason of your negligence, ye know the greatness of the fault," etc.   And again, in the actual sentence of Ordination, we have, " Be thou a faithful Dispenser of the Word of God and of His Holy Sacraments." [1]

Before considering St. Paul's conceptions of the οἰκονόμος and of οἰκονομία, it will be well to notice some of the qualities which our Lord regards as on the one hand essential to, and on the other hand as incompatible with, the due discharge of stewardship. In St. Luke xvi. 8 the unjust steward is commended as having acted, φρονίμως (*i.e.* prudently, intelligently), "with a shrewd adjustment of means to ends," and also with foresight.   It is interesting to notice that in the LXX of Gen. xli. 39, when Pharaoh says to Joseph, "Thou shalt be over my house," he gives as one of his reasons, οὐκ ἔστιν ἄνθρωπος φρονιμώτερος καὶ συνετώτερός σου.[2]   In St. Luke xii. 42 the steward is set over the household,[3] in order to give a measured portion [4] of food at the right time.   Here we have suggested responsibility as to the nature, amount, and season of

---

[1] " Esto etiam fidelis verbi Dei et sanctorum ejus sacramentorum Dispensator."

[2] אֵין־נָבוֹן וְחָכָם כָּמוֹךָ in Hebrew.

[3] ἐπὶ τῆς θεραπείας.   Cp. θεραπεία of Pharaoh's household in Gen. xlv. 16.

[4] [τὸ] σιτομέτριον.

dispensing. The faithful steward will act in his master's absence just as he would in his presence. On the other hand, the unfaithful steward is cruel and oppressive ; he thinks of his own enjoyment even to excess. His punishment shall be a terrible one,[1] and his portion in death is μετὰ τῶν ἀπίστων.[2]

From St. Luke xvi. 1 it is clear that the steward must not be open to accusations, or at least that he should be able to refute such as may be brought against him. Further, with a steward wastefulness is a crime ; our health, our time, our influence, our opportunities of service are among the τὰ ὑπάρχοντα τοῦ Θεοῦ. Again, the steward must be prepared at any time to give the [necessary][3] account of his stewardship. There are charges which, if not disproved, render continuance in stewardship impossible. We must notice the comprehensive description in verse 8, τὸν οἰκονόμον τῆς ἀδικίας, for justice is the fullest recognition in practice of the completest claims of others—master and fellow-servants—upon us. There is a most important exhortation for ministers in our Lord's personal comment in verse 8[4] (which should be carefully compared with xii. 42). For both "in due season" and

---

[1] διχοτομήσει αὐτόν.

[2] Note the connection with πιστός in verse 42.

[3] τὸν λόγον in verse 2.

[4] εἰς τὴν γενεὰν τὴν ἑαυτῶν ; in xii. 42 we have τοῦ διδόναι ἐν καιρῷ.

"towards their own generation" assume an intelligent perception of the actual state of things at present, and also what is required to supply the needs of those whose nature and circumstances are similar to our own.

I now pass to St. Paul's teaching on stewardship,[1] and I naturally first turn to the opening verses of 1 Cor. iv., where he claims the title of steward for himself and his fellow-ministers. We must remember the context. He has been rebuking the errors of the Corinthians concerning the Christian teachers and their office, and has shown that when one party claimed himself for their leader, and another party Apollos for their's, both were under a wrong conception. All things— including all that Paul or Apollos or Cephas could teach them—were their's, and they were Christ's, and Christ was God's. St. Paul then proceeds :[2]—This is the right view, the view which reasonable and thoughtful men will take of us. They will regard us[3] as humble helpers of Christ, even[4] as stewards of Divine mysteries—

[1] A comparison of this with that of our Lord proves the truth of Professor Shailer Mathew's words, "Any man who seeks to get back to Christ will find . . . that in every step he takes toward the Master he will find ahead of him the guiding footsteps of this same Paul. No man ever understood Jesus as did the Apostle to the Gentiles." *The Church and the Changing Order*, p. 84.

[2] οὕτως is probably prospective, but what St. Paul has just written is evidently still in his mind. Having refuted the false conception of the ministry, he proceeds to set forth the true.

[3] λογιζέσθω.

[4] I regard the καί as epexegetical, "who are stewards."

that is as men to whom a stewardship in reference to these mysteries has been committed. Christ came unfolding the Divine mysteries ; in this work we must assist Him ; while we are engaged in it He must be in us. We are thus His instruments to whom He has committed the function of stewardship, with all the tasks and responsibilities inherent in it.

In considering the various responsibilities of the steward, that of dispensing must be emphasised. But before we can dispense we must have wherewith to dispense. So I would plead for a careful remembrance of another part of the steward's duty, that of furnishing himself, from his Master's possessions, with what those dependent upon him need. Here, again, I would refer to Rom. xii. 1 ff.,[1] where τὰ σώματα may certainly include a well furnished and well disciplined mind. It is surely only reasonable that those who (in answer to Christ's call) offer themselves for this office of stewardship should furnish themselves, out of the inexplorable wealth of the Christ,[2] with all that is necessary for those dependent upon them. And this will imply a θυσίαν ζῶσαν, and not the offering of that which has had life in the past— as learning or knowledge of the Scriptures gathered in the years preparatory to ordination,

---

[1] παραστῆσαι τὰ σώματα ὑμῶν θυσίαν ζῶσαν.
[2] Eph. iii. 8, ἀνεξιχνίαστον, from ἐξιχνιάζω, to track out (Vg. *investigabiles*).

but which has not any vital connection with present experience.[1]   We must be living teachers, able to dispense living knowledge.   As Bishop Westcott says,[2] " The Apostle is careful to show that his teaching is not the repetition of a form of words once given to him, and to be simply received by his disciples.   It had cost him thought and it claimed thought."

The word " mystery," as used by St. Paul, demands care.   The following definition of Bishop Westcott's is useful :[3]—" The Divine counsel now revealed which was the expression *of His will*. The fact of a revelation is always implied in the word 'mystery' in the New Testament."   Then, from the words, " Be thou a faithful Dispenser of the Word of God and of His holy Sacraments," in the Ordination Service, when read in connection with the Vulgate[4] of 1 Cor. iv. 1, it is easy to understand too little as well as too much.   For towards Christ in regard to the sacraments the minister has a very important stewardship to fulfil.   He must see that they are so dispensed by himself that their true meaning is clearly understood by those to whom he ministers them. This   stewardship   is   not   discharged   by   a

---

[1] It is only by continuous present study that knowledge acquired in the past still lives.

[2] *Ephesians*, p. 45.   [3] *Ephesians*, p. 13.

[4] The οἰκονόμους μυστηρίων Θεοῦ of 1 Cor. iv. 1 is in the Vulgate *dispensatores mysteriorum Dei*.   In Eph. iii. 9, ἡ οἰκονομία τοῦ μυστηρίου is in the Vulgate *dispensatio sacramenti*.

mechanical administration ; which, from constant use, is all too easily apt to creep in. But that we have a stewardship in regard to the sacraments does not imply that by the word μυστήρια St. Paul meant what we mean by "sacraments."

The meaning of verse 2[1] is probably, "The whole duty of a steward is comprised in his being found faithful," that is according to Christ's standard of faithfulness ; for to Christ's teaching upon stewardship the words may be supposed to refer.

The only other occurrence of οἰκονόμος in St. Paul's Epistles of one discharging a Christian function[2] is in Tit. i. 7. "It is necessary for a bishop (one having oversight) to be blameless as God's steward, not self-willed, etc. Both the words ἀνέγκλητον and αὐθάδη should be noticed. Against him it must be impossible to substantiate accusations ; again, he must be neither arrogant nor over-complacent. The two adjectives seem to express the two requirements of faithfulness. The steward must be absolutely trustworthy ; he must faithfully discharge his responsibility to his master, hence he must not be over-complacent to his master's servants ; he must discharge his responsibility towards them, hence he must not be arrogant.

---

[1] ὧδε λοιπὸν ζητεῖται κ.τ.λ. On the various interpretations of these words see the Commentaries on the Epistle.

[2] οἰκονόμος in Rom. xvi. 23 and in Gal. iv. 2 is used in a purely technical sense. The Vulgate in the first is *arcarius civitatis*, in the second *actor*.

The substantive οἰκονομία occurs six times in St. Paul's Epistles.   Each instance is instructive :—

1 Cor. ix. 17.[1]   St. Paul is speaking of the right of the Christian preacher to maintenance, and also of his own preaching of the gospel gratuitously. Yet he takes no credit to himself for doing this. He must preach the gospel for οἰκονομίαν πεπίστευμαι, "I have a stewardship entrusted to me, which I must faithfully discharge."   With this saying we may compare that to the elders at Miletus, where looking back upon his Ephesian ministry St. Paul asserts,[2] "I am pure from the blood of all men, for I shrank not from declaring unto you the whole counsel of God."   It is thus that he has discharged the stewardship committed unto him.   Bishop Lightfoot's translation[3] of this passage should be noticed : "I am God's slave entrusted with an important office : and a rigorous account will be required of me"; and he draws attention to the fact that St. Paul conceives of his position here as one analogous to that of the "steward" in St. Luke xii. 42 ff., where the steward is the *dispensator*[4] or slave employed to give the other slaves of the household their proper rations.   This is a work in

---

[1] This is the only instance of οἰκονομία in St. Paul without a genitive following.

[2] Acts xx. 26, 27.   On this see further on pp. 208 ff.

[3] On Eph. i. 10 in *Notes on Epistles of St. Paul*, pp. 319 ff.

[4] So the Vg., probably correctly, as against *villicus* in Luke xvi. 1 ff.

which the Christian minister may fulfil the calling of a δοῦλος Χριστοῦ.

Eph. i. 10. Here I would take Dr. Armitage Robinson's rendering: "Having made known unto us the mystery of His will, according to His good pleasure, which He hath purposed in Him for dispensation (εἰς οἰκονομίαν)[1] in the fulness of the times." Here, also, the thought of stewardship is underlying: the fulness of the times, or rather, seasons (τῶν καιρῶν) means the period which commenced with the Incarnation: during this season, in the manifestation of Christ, God's will is made known: in this process of "dispensation" Christ is the chief Agent, but Christ's ministers share the work with Him: as such they have a responsibility towards Him, Who, inasmuch as He associates them with Himself, has conferred upon them a stewardship towards those to whom they minister, in regard to the manifestation of Him. Dr. A. Robinson says: "Dispensation is here used in its wider sense . . . of carrying into effect a design." Of this "carrying into effect" Christ's ministers are entrusted with a share; therein lies their responsibility, consequently their stewardship.[2]

---

[1] This is the only occurrence of οἰκονομία in the N.T. in which the R.V. does not give "stewardship" either in the text or the margin. J.A. Robinson, *Ephesians*, Kregel Publications. 1978. pp. 30-32.

[2] Lightfoot's note *in loc.* (*Epistles of St. Paul*) should be consulted.

Eph. iii. 2. "If ye heard of the stewardship (the responsibility of administering) the grace of God[1] which was given to me for (towards) you." The idea here is the same as in 1 Cor. ix. 17, viz. a faithful dealing with "the wealth of the Divine treasury" so freely given by God for the benefit of men. We may compare St. Paul's expressed desire and purpose in Rom. i. 11, "That I may impart to you some spiritual gift." Have we been careful to supply ourselves with such gifts from this same Source? Are we equally fit and equally ready to bestow such gifts upon those towards whom we have a stewardship?

Eph. iii. 9. "And to make clear what is the [Divine] arrangement[2] (*Verwaltung*) of the mystery . . . that now through the Church" (and therefore especially through its representative teachers) "might be made known," etc. Here, again, the thought of responsibility, and so of stewardship, is implied; but the responsibility is not directly towards the mystery itself being revealed, but towards the making clear, and so justifying, the method of God—the method of administration of the mystery which God has chosen. Through the ages, the Apostle can see, there has run a Divine "purpose," there has

---

[1] "Das Haushalteramt der Gnade." Von Soden.

[2] The οἰκονομία is the expression of the will of the οἰκοδεσπότης as well as the rule by which the οἰκονόμος has to work.

also been a Divine method:[1] as a teacher in
the Church, St. Paul has both to explain this
purpose and justify this method. Here there
seems to be suggested to the Christian teacher
an additional responsibility. When St. Paul
is engaged in justifying the ways of God to men,
he does this not as an individual, but as a member
of a society which is [Divinely] charged with
this task. While we recognise that frequently
the authority of the Church has been claimed
for that to which the words "the truth" can
hardly be applied, we must be careful that our
explanation of "God's ways towards man" is
no mere irresponsible expression[2] of private
opinion; for when we speak, we cannot help
speaking as members of a society charged to
make manifest a definite philosophy of God
and history.

Col. i. 25. "Of which ($\dot{\eta}$ ἐκκλησία) I was made
a minister according to the stewardship in the
house of God which was given me for your
benefit to fulfil the word of God, even the
mystery . . ." The whole passage from which
these words are taken should be deeply engraven

---

[1] Which, though apparently manifold, is yet one, $\dot{\eta}$ πολυποίκιλος
σοφία.

[2] One is naturally tempted to quote 2 Pet. i. 20. But that
passage probably means, "Prophecy is not exhausted by one
interpretation to which it is, as it were, tied." See Mayor
in loc.

upon the mind of every minister of Christ. Both
διάκονος and ἡ ἐκκλησία are explained by κατὰ τὴν
οἰκονομίαν ; and πληρῶσαι[1] (as von Soden says) is
Aufgabe der οἰκονομία. Again, τὸν λόγον τοῦ Θεοῦ
is " the gospel " in its fullest sense. Then we must
connect the discharge of Christian stewardship with
the thought of suffering[2] which is so prominent
in the preceding verse. " Stewardship means
service, "[3] and service implies faithful stewardship, which often can only be discharged at the
cost of much personal suffering. And we must
not forget δοθεῖσάν, for "every gift from the great
Householder to His stewards involves the obligation to impart it." The possessions are His, if
entrusted to us, to be given through us to His
other servants. The special practical lesson from
this particular occurrence of οἰκονομία is I think
that expressed in πλησῶσαι τὸν λόγον τοῦ Θεοῦ.[4]
How many ministers of Christ realise what these
words imply? How many try to put into
practice St. Paul's purpose? No application
which is *confined* to preaching is adequate. Christ
Himself is ὁ λόγος.

1 Tim. i. 4. " Not to give heed to fables and
endless genealogies inasmuch as they promote

---

[1] " πληρῶσαι=etwas vollziehen, ausrichten, durchführen, ein
Auftrag (*commission*) erfüllen." Von Soden.

[2] " Now I rejoice in my sufferings on your behalf," etc.

[3] Dr. Maclaren, *Colossians* (in the *Expositor's Bible*), p. 124.

[4] We must remember St. John i. 14.

questionings rather than the dispensation of God which is in (the sphere of) faith." Here the οἰκονομία is God's plan or arrangement of His household.[1] As stewards of God it is our duty to use our time and our abilities in loyal obedience in the promotion of His ordering, rather than to spend these in idle speculations. This passage adds yet another to the many applications given to us by St. Paul of the idea of the stewardship of God's ministers.

Putting together these various instances of the use of οἰκονομία by St. Paul, we see that in each the thought of a deep sense of *responsibility*— the chief qualification for faithful stewardship —is implied. Where οἰκονομία means a Divine arrangement we learn that our duty is to enter intelligently into that arrangement, to work loyally according to it, and, by teaching and conduct, to commend it to our people. Where it means "the office of stewardship" (*e.g.* towards the gospel, or towards men, on behalf of Christ) we must so faithfully discharge the office that Christ's servants — towards whom we are responsible—are through us supplied with all that is needful for their highest welfare.

Et ad haec quis tam idoneus?

---

[1] "Die von Gott gesetzte Hausordnung oder die in derKirche (seinem Hause, iii. 15) geltende Heilsordnung." B. Weiss *in loc.*

IX. Worker unto the Kingdom of God.

After mentioning the names of certain of his companions, St. Paul adds in Col. iv. 11, οὗτοι μόνοι συνεργοὶ εἰς τὴν βασιλείαν τοῦ Θεοῦ. The term "fellow-worker" seems to have been a favourite one with St. Paul,[1] by which to unite with himself and indicate one or more of those who were associated with him in promoting the cause of Christ. The term is richly suggestive. St. Paul seems very rarely to have been a solitary worker. No one knew better that in work union is strength, and that two working together will often accomplish far more than twice as much as each man would if working alone. Then in St. Paul's use of the term there is generally a gracious humility and generosity. Undoubtedly in every case where it is used he was the leader, and by far the most important as well as the most efficacious member of the partnership. But he loves to place others beside himself. The general and the captain and the private are all fellow-soldiers in the same army : the architect and the overseer and the labourer engaged in the building of a house are all fellow-workers

---

[1] συνεργός occurs in St. Paul 11 or 12 times (for the reading in 1 Thess. iii. 2 is doubtful), viz. Rom. xvi. 3, 9, 21 ; 1 Cor. iii. 9 ; 2 Cor. i. 24, viii. 23 ; Phil. ii. 25, iv. 3 ; Col. iv. 11 ; Philem. 1, and 24. There is also an interesting use in 3 John 8, συνεργοὶ γινώμεθα τῇ ἀληθείᾳ. The verb συνεργεῖν occurs in St. Paul in Rom. viii. 28 ; 1 Cor. xvi. 16 ; 2 Cor. vi. 1.

towards its "edification." Unless the victory or the completion of the work is to be delayed, the help of each is essential. And St. Paul does not think of his συνεργοί as working *for him*, or assisting him; he and they are together working for God, indeed with God.[1] Differences of relative importance vanish when there is a comparison of each with the infinite. Could this truth be remembered, much friction and jealousy in associated work for Christ would vanish. One passage in which the word συνεργοί occurs may detain us for a moment. In 2 Cor. i. 24 we find συνεργοί ἐσμεν τῆς χαρᾶς ὑμῶν. Here Christian ministers are fellow-workers with their people in promoting the true joy of these. The ministers promote this by helping their people to cultivate what will ensure this joy, that is the strengthening of their faith. These few words contain a valuable lesson—to see that the charge sometimes made against religion, that it makes people gloomy or unhappy, is entirely untrue. St. Paul knew that *gaudium Domini est fortitud‚ nostra*.[2]

But the point upon which I would here lay stress is the Christian minister (in association with others) as a worker *towards the Kingdom of God*. For this is an aspect of his work of special importance at the present time, for it suggests the *social* work of the ministry and of

---

[1] I Cor. iii. 9.   [2] Neh. viii. 10.

the Church.   The ministers of Christ must to-day take the lead as συνεργοί towards the realisation or establishment of the ideal or perfect state, the state or sphere in which God's will is done.[1] This definition, of course, applies to the Kingdom whether regarded as belonging to this age or the age to come.

St. Paul's conception of "the Kingdom,"[2] and his whole teaching in regard to it, should be made the subject of special study.   We must notice that to St. Paul the Kingdom is *ethical* in character, the sins which prevent entrance into it and life within it are clearly stated :[3] also that it is in a sense "timeless," like the Divine life, whether in Christ Himself or in those "in Christ."   The passing of the present age does not affect it essentially.   That upon which it is founded, the materials out of which it is built, the laws which govern it, the life lived in it, the sustenance of its citizens—are all independent of time.   If we take the fourteen instances of the mention of the Kingdom by St. Paul we shall find that in every one, except the two in 2 Timothy,[4]

---

[1] The two clauses in the Lord's Prayer must be read together.

[2] Some useful thoughts may be found in A. B. Bruce's *St. Paul's Conception of Christianity*, pp. 362 ff.

[3] Gal. v. 19–21 ; Eph. v. 5.

[4] This may be regarded as true even of these two, if we remember the timelessness of the conception ; St. Paul will simply pass through martyrdom to the full enjoyment of citizenship in the Kingdom.

the satisfaction of a distinct ethical condition is implied.[1]

As an inspiration to the social worker, the importance and power of the teaching, whether of our Lord or St. Paul, upon the Kingdom cannot be exaggerated. The social worker to-day surveys a kingdom which lies within the sphere of the Evil One[2] in which his authority and power are alike great. Yet the Kingdom of God also exists,[3] though without limits of time and place. This Kingdom the social worker must see ; of its nature and conditions he must have a clear conception, through the powers of moral and spiritual vision. The Kingdom is an ideal or pattern towards which he works : he works towards the day when the kingdoms of this world shall be like to it. The laws of this Kingdom are the eternal laws (or conditions) of human welfare ; for everything that is essential to this Kingdom, like the Kingdom itself, already exists. Of it the Christian is already a citizen. The object of the Church, and so of the ministers of the Church, is the extension, victory, and abiding supremacy of this Kingdom. The Church

---

[1] Compare the ethical conditions laid down by the earlier O.T. prophets for the establishment of the Messianic reign.

[2] 1 John v. 19 (see Westcott's note *in loc.*).

[3] Phil. iii. 20, ὑπάρχει. The following is a complete list of occurrences of βασιλεία in St. Paul :—Rom. xiv. 17 ; 1 Cor. iv. 20, vi. 9, 10, xv. 24, 50 ; Gal. v. 21 ; Eph. v. 5 ; Col. i. 13, iv. 11 ; 1 Thess. ii. 12 ; 2 Thess. i. 5 ; 2 Tim. iv. 1, 18. It also occurs in Acts (in connection with St. Paul) in xiv. 22, xix. 8, xx. 25, xxviii. 23, 31.

must proclaim its nearness and conditions,[1] and the ministers of the Church must be fellow-workers with God in Christ in delivering men from the power of darkness and in translating them into it. We have come to see that the so-called "social problem" is an ethical one. St. Paul saw this long ago, and constantly said so. The problem is not one of "eating and drinking" but one of character. Therefore it can only be solved by an ethical or moralising power. This power is that of the Holy Spirit, one in essence,[2] but capable of many manifestations, and of being transmitted and utilised in many various ways. This ethical power of the Holy Spirit it is our task to supply.

X. Soldier

Twice St. Paul applies the title of συστρατιώτης to himself—once in conjunction with Epaphroditus (Phil. ii. 25), and once with Archippus (Philem. 2), who probably exercised some ministerial function[3] in the Church. That St. Paul regarded both his own work and the Christian life generally as a

---

[1] ἤγγικεν ἡ βασιλεία τοῦ Θεοῦ· μετανοεῖτε καὶ πιστεύετε ἐν τῷ εὐαγγελίῳ, St. Mark i. 15.

[2] The analogy with the essential unity of physical energy in the universe must not be overlooked. This energy, too, manifests itself in various forms, and is capable of utilisation in almost an infinite variety of ways.

[3] Lightfoot, *Colossians*, p. 42, also on Col. iv. 17, Βλέπε τὴν διακονίαν ἣν παρέλαβες ἐν Κυρίῳ.

warfare we have abundant evidence. Again and again he uses metaphors drawn from the life of the soldier to illustrate not only his own position and work (that of the Christian minister—of the officer in Christ's army) but that of the ordinary Christian man. In 1 Cor. ix. 7, where he is claiming the right of the minister of Christ to live from the gospel, he adduces not only the examples of the vine-dresser and the shepherd, but, before these, of the soldier.[1] Here the Apostle asks, " Does one ever serve as a soldier at his own expense ? " In 1 Cor. xiv. 8 he asks, " If the trumpet sound an uncertain note, who will rouse himself to the war ? " Here there may be a reference to prophecy as a rousing and " heartening " power in the Christian warfare. In 2 Cor. vi. 7 he asserts that he and his fellow-ministers commend themselves by means of weapons[2] of (God's) righteousness on the right hand and on the left. In 2 Cor. x. 3, 4, St. Paul states that they do not war according to an earthly method, and that the weapons of his campaign were not fleshly but mighty for God to the destruction of strongholds.[3] In Eph. vi. 11 ff.

---

[1] See T. C. Edwards *in loc.*, who thinks the three pictures may represent the minister (1) warring against evil, (2) as a missionary planting Churches or doing the work of conversion, (3) exercising pastoral oversight.

[2] ὅπλα has no exact English equivalent ; it includes both " weapons " and " armour."

[3] " Indifferentism " was certainly not a principle with St. Paul.

we have the familiar picture of the completely armed Christian soldier, every detail of whose "panoply" should serve as a standard or mirror for self-examination, especially for officers in the Christian army. In 1 Tim. i. 18 the work in which Timothy must be engaged is described as "warring the good[1] warfare in the strength of certain exhortations and encouragements he has received." Lastly, in 2 Tim. ii. 3, 4, St. Paul writes : "Take your share of hardships as a soldier of Jesus Christ *sans peur et sans reproche* (καλός). No one serving as a soldier entangles himself with the affairs of this life."

Do we as ministers of Christ keep sufficiently before us the *militant* aspect of our life and work —the conception of these as a warfare?[2] It is not a pleasant conception except, perhaps, to the ecclesiastical controversialist. But in its deepest sense it is one to which we have been pledged from the time of our baptism. And we must remember, from the conditions of modern life, that unless we are careful to go beneath the surface of things it is not one which is likely to be forced upon us. A well-known spiritual teacher has recorded how once, when preaching to a fashionable congregation, he was struck by

---

[1] There is no connection in which we need to remember more carefully the meaning of καλός than in everything connected with the militant side of Christianity.

[2] The silence of our Ordination Services on this aspect of the ministerial life is at least curious.

the anomaly of a number of smartly dressed people (most of whom were probably very well satisfied with themselves and their surroundings) singing "Onward Christian soldiers, marching as to war"!

But every earnest Christian minister who knows his people, and who knows the moral conditions under which many of them live and the temptations to which they are exposed, knows the need of constant warfare against the powers of evil on their behalf. He has constantly to fight and he has to encourage them to fight against moral evil. He must try to remove the sources of temptation— the strongholds of the enemy. He must see that those under his care are as well equipped as possible (and the condition is a comprehensive one) for the warfare in which they ought to be, if they actually are not, engaged. He must also see that the weapons with which they fight are not altogether antiquated and hence useless, either for attack or defence, against the modern weapons of the enemy. The fashion to-day, and therefore the danger, is to make terms with our foes. We, like Israel of old, are tempted to settle down with the enemy's fortresses still untaken in the land.

We have to face the dangers from "undermining" as well as from direct open attack. For there are foes, often unnoticed, which are slowly eating out the moral strength of our people.

This seems to be especially true of the moral dangers to which the so-called upper classes of society are subject. But in each sphere of pastoral labour and with the different *strata* of society the particular form which the forces of evil assume will vary. Our first duty is to gain a knowledge of these in the sphere committed to our charge, to gain as clear and as exact as possible an estimate of the nature and strength of the enemies of righteousness in our neighbourhood. And how little, as a rule, do those in one class of society know of the peculiar temptations which are attacking those in another class! Then we must resolutely and unceasingly attack these foes with all the forces of righteousness at our command. We must fight against the temptation to speak of evils as "inevitable," or of saying "peace" when there *should be* no peace. Here, as elsewhere, perception and effort, knowledge and power—the endowments of God's grace—must be both cultivated and employed.

XI. Husbandman

The actual word γεωργός occurs in St. Paul's writings only in 2 Tim. ii. 6, and there only in an illustration, but the application to the Christian minister (for the charge in verse 1 to Timothy is personal)[1] is quite clear. St. Paul tells Timothy

---

[1] Σὺ οὖν, τέκνον μου.

to be strengthened in the grace which is in Christ
Jesus, in the sphere in which is all spiritual
strength. This need of strength is illustrated by
three examples—those of the soldier, the athlete,
and the husbandman. The soldier must endure
hardness, the athlete must submit to discipline
in preparation and be strictly obedient to the
rules of the contest,[1] the husbandman must bear
hard and long continued labour.[2] The Christian
minister must be a "labouring man." But it
is in I Cor. iii. 6 ff., where St. Paul compares
the work of himself and Apollos to certain
different operations performed by the γεωργός,
that the suggestiveness of the application of the
title of "Husbandman" to the Christian minister
is most clearly seen. St. Paul is combating false
conceptions of the ministerial office. In the place
of these he would put true conceptions. These
he illustrates from the work, first of the husbandman, secondly of the skilled "master builder."
The first I will consider now : the second shall
be the subject of the next section.

Verses 6–9 are full of suggestive thoughts. St.
Paul writes : "I planted, Apollos watered, but

---

[1] νομίμως is interesting in connection with modern psychological
study : it suggests that the formation of character (moral strength)
is dependent, as we know it to be, upon obedience to certain definite
fixed (Divine) laws.

[2] Pres. tense, τὸν κοπιῶντα γεωργὸν. κοπιᾶν and κόπος are
favourite words with St. Paul : the first occurs fourteen times and the
second eleven times in his Epistles. The special connotation of the
word is that of wearying and exhausting labour.

God makes to grow.   So then neither is he that
planteth of importance, nor he that watereth, but
God Who makes to grow : he that planteth and
he that watereth are (essentially) one, but each
will receive his own reward in proportion to his
own toil, for we are God's fellow-labourers : ye
are God's tilled land. . . ."[1]

God's ministers perform different functions, each
of which may be equally useful : at the same time
all their toil, without the help and blessing of God,
unless they are συνεργοί with God, and unless
He is a συνεργός with them, will be in vain.
And compared with His share in the work, theirs,
however necessary, is infinitesimal.[2]

Again, though they perform different functions,
there is among or between them an absolute
unity of purpose.   This unity is in the Divine
Mind.

Yet the individual service (different according
to the personal endowment and the need governed
by circumstances) and the responsibility to God
for rendering this service must be remembered.
And each shall for this receive his own reward
according to his wearying and exhausting toil.
Lastly, St. Paul says, "ye are God's tilled land,"
land which is capable of yielding a harvest as

---

[1] Cp. St. Matt. xiii. 38, ὁ δὲ ἀγρός ἐστιν ὁ κόσμος.   The field is
conterminous with the habitable earth.

[2] Bengel's note : "διάκονοι, *ministri*.   Humile verbum, eoque
aptum."

contrasted with land which is incapable of this. The parallels with this passage in the Gospels are many. It is interesting to notice that the only places in which γεωργός is used in the Synoptists [1] is in the three parallel accounts of the parable of the Wicked Husbandmen, where the γεωργοί are evidently the spiritual or religious rulers of the Jews. The essential lesson of the parable is the difference between so working as to recognise that we are only *stewards*, or so working as if we regarded ourselves as *owners*. The first implies the desire to serve God, the second to enrich ourselves. In not seeing this essential difference lay the error of the Corinthians as regarded the work of the Christian teachers. The Corinthians had regarded these teachers as ends, as those to whom a final allegiance could be rendered. By doing this the Corinthians were tempting these ministers of God so to regard themselves. Actually, as St. Paul shows, he and his fellow-ministers were exactly what the wicked husbandmen refused to recognise themselves to be—δοῦλοι of the Owner, working for Him and rendering to Him the fruit of their labours.

In the Θεοῦ γεώργιον two fields of labour seem to be noticed—that among the unconverted and that among the converted. " I planted among

---

[1] St. Matt. xxi. 33 ff. ; St. Mark xii. 1 ff. ; St. Luke xx. 9 ff. The only other instance of γεωργός in the Gospels is in St. John xv. 1, where in the simile of the Vine and the Branches God is termed ὁ γεωργός.

those who had not as yet accepted Christ, Apollos followed me and instructed them in the faith." Both works have to be done by the minister of Christ to-day, for both are still necessary. Few possibly do both works equally well. But both, if well done, need much hard labour.

The analogies between the labour of the minister of Christ and the labour of the husband-man which at once suggest themselves are many. Both deal with that which has life. Neither can impart life, but both have to foster life and to train to right and useful growth. The purpose of both consists in all that is covered by the words "culture," or "cultivation," i.e. unto a rich and fruitful productiveness. For each there is a work which must be done in due season. The work of both needs patience,[1] and both must know how to bear disappointment. Both have to struggle against, indeed both must try to destroy, growths[2] foreign and inimical to the growth they would foster. For both unremitting care is necessary, and both if they would achieve success must work in strictest obedience to law, the husbandman according to the laws of nature, the minister according to the laws of revelation. It is because of their knowledge of these laws that they work in faith; and this faith, if true, will issue in obedience. Lastly, both must leave the final issue to God.

---

[1] Jas. v. 7. N.B. μακροθυμῶν ἐπ' αὐτῷ.   [2] St. Matt. xiii. 25.

XII. The Skilled Master Builder
(ὡς σοφὸς ἀρχιτέκτων)

This is another very suggestive title which St.
Paul applies to himself, and by which he describes
a certain conception of his work. As I have
already noticed, it occurs in the same context as
that in which we find Θεοῦ γεώργιον of his field of
labour, and, like it, is an attempt to substitute in
the minds of his readers a true, for a false conception, of the ministerial office. To the words
Θεοῦ γεώργιον in 1 Cor. iii. 9 he adds Θεοῦ
οἰκοδομή ἐστε, and then, starting from this
word οἰκοδομή, he continues, "According to the
grace of God given to me, ὡς σοφὸς ἀρχιτέκτων, I
laid a foundation . . ." The word occurs only
here in the New Testament, but it is found at
least three times in the LXX :—(1) In Isa. iii. 3 [1]
(also preceded by σοφός), among the list of
those whom God will remove from Judah and
Jerusalem, and who are evidently regarded as
highly useful to the community. (2) In Sirach
xxxviii. 27 it is coupled with τέκτων in a passage
which contains a remarkable number of expressions, which if we regard the minister as a skilled
workman are applicable for self-examination and
self-consecration.[2] (3) It occurs in 2 Macc. ii. 29,

---

[1] The Heb. and LXX differ slightly. The Heb. for σοφὸν ἀρχι-
τέκτονα is חֲכַם חֲרָשִׁים, either skilled in "magic arts" or handicraft (?).

[2] e.g. verse 27, "He will set his heart to preserve likeness in his

where, as here, it is used figuratively of "a clerk of the works" in connection with the building of a house.

By St. Paul the word is evidently used in this sense, for God is the "architect" or designer of the building whose erection St. Paul is called upon to oversee. We must not forget the words which precede this title. It is according to (κατά) the "grace of God" that St. Paul does this work. God has granted to him, as He will grant to every true worker for Him, who will do his best to qualify himself, a special endowment for the special work to which God has called him. St. Paul's work in this case was that of laying a foundation, whether of a Christian Church or of various Christian lives. The word σοφός might suggest boastfulness : it really means that a skilful master builder will see that the foundation of his building is good. By St. Paul this condition is certainly fulfilled, for the foundation he has laid is "Jesus Christ." We must notice the full title, implying that the foundation of a life must be no imperfect or mutilated creed. That "Jesus is the Christ" was, we know, essentially the foundation of St. Paul's own belief, it was the inspiration of all his post-conversion life. St. Paul at least

---

portraiture, and will be wakeful to finish his work"; verse 28, "He will set his heart upon perfecting his works," etc. ; verse 33, Useful work, sometimes without honour among men ; verse 34, Yet of true value.

suggests [1] that the master builder is not responsible for the plan, the outline, and nature of the superstructure.   That, too, is fixed.   He is, however, responsible for the nature of the materials used, and for the way in which the work is done. The intrinsic worth of the materials may vary from the exceedingly precious to the practically worthless.[2]   To see that the material is the best possible is a great responsibility to the master builder.   I need not pursue the passage itself any further, but may pass to its applications and suggestions, which for the working minister to-day are many.

First, we must see that the foundation which we lay, or upon which we are called to build, is the One Foundation—the only foundation upon which a satisfactory and permanent structure can be erected.   The Universal Church is an οἰκοδομή Θεοῦ, so is every local Ecclesia, so also is every individual Christian life, because "edifying" is possible for all these.   The minister must see that the foundation of every οἰκοδομή for which he is specially responsible, in relation to which he is specially the ἀρχιτέκτων, is "Jesus Christ": he must see that He, and He alone, is the foundation of every life, social and individual, he seeks to build up.

Also with regard to the *materials* (here a word

---

[1] Verse 12.   Note the definite article, ἐπὶ τὸν θεμέλιον.
[2] Verse 12.

of wide application) of which both the Ecclesia and the "people committed to his charge" are being formed, his responsibility is also great. The whole subject of religious "syncretism" is deeply interesting, whether we study it on the large scale,[1] with regard to the whole history of the Church from the first, or on the smaller scale of the present or the local. A clearer knowledge of the subject in the past would have prevented, and in the present might still prevent, many a bitter and unedifying controversy. Many of those who in the past were called upon to perform the function of an ἀρχιτέκτων were too lax in "passing" materials for building. The office of one who has to perform the task for which the New Testament term is δοκιμάζειν [2] is a responsible and an anxious one.

To us the difficulty of decision is much increased by the greater complexity of modern life. In earlier days there was more sharpness and clearness in the lines which could be drawn between the Christian and the unchristian, between that which is capable of being sanctified to the Master's use and that which is not. The question comes

---

[1] Much that is instructive will be found in Harnack's *Ausbreitung* (*E.T.* vol. i. pp. 391 ff.). Also in Soltau's *Das Fortleben des Heidenthums in der altchristlichen Kirche*. (This latter book should be read with caution, and one must deprecate the *tone* in which much of it is written.)

[2] The word is common (17 times) in St. Paul. The following instances are interesting : Rom. xiv. 22, μακάριος ὁ μὴ κρίνων ἑαυτὸν ἐν ᾧ δοκιμάζει.; 1 Cor. xi. 28, δοκιμαζέτω δὲ ἄνθρωπος ἑαυτόν, καὶ οὕτως κ.τ.λ.; 2 Cor. viii. 22, τὸν ἀδελφὸν ἡμῶν ὃν ἐδοκιμάσαμεν, etc.

before the working minister in this form, " What may I employ or permit to be employed in the building of the Church, for which I am the ἀρχιτέκτων ? What is and what is not compatible with true Christianity ? " The minister desires to " edify," but his material may be scanty, and much even of that may be of very imperfect quality. On the one hand the stricter members of his flock counsel rejection, while those who pride themselves upon being more liberal-minded counsel acceptance. In his own ears there sound two voices. First, " What things have been done in thy name, O Christianity ! " Secondly, " To reject this or to refuse that may be to reject some natural gift, or pleasure, or custom, harmless in itself, which needs only to be rescued from present associations and to be sanctified to a higher use in order for it to become actually useful for building." Then, not infrequently, he finds that the acceptance of some materials involves the rejection of others : they will not be joined together in the same building.

With the minister as ἀρχιτέκτων lies to-day all that is included in that very comprehensive term " organisation,"—a task for which men seem to be so differently endowed, but which cannot be entirely disregarded by any. Organisation, to the minister of Christ, implies the choice, and the equipment of the right men and women, also the placing of these in various positions for the different kinds of work to be done. He is also to some extent responsible for seeing that these perform the functions which have been allotted to them. One of the tasks of the foreman is to get work out of those who work under his direction. To do this he must constantly teach, train, inspire, encourage them. His eye and his judgment, but, above all, his heart and his sympathy must be everywhere. As he thinks of all this he may well ask with St. Paul, "Who is sufficient for these things?" With all that God has supplied or will supply him he must carefully equip himself. Then, and only then, can he answer this question in the spirit and words of St. Paul :—*Sufficit tibi gratia mea : nam virtus in infirmitate perficitur.*

ΔΙΩ΄ΚΩ

I cannot close this long chapter without adding one more description which St. Paul gives of himself—not only as a Christian minister but as a Christian man. This description is contained in a sentence, which must never be forgotten by the worker for Christ :—

οὐχ ὅτι ἤδη ἔλαβον ἢ ἤδη τετελείωμαι, διώκω δὲ εἰ καὶ καταλάβω, ἐφ᾽ ᾧ καὶ κατελήμφθην ὑπὸ Χριστοῦ ['Ιησοῦ].[1]

These words are of universal application, so far as our "selves" and our work is concerned. Luther said, "He who *is* a Christian is no Christian, but he who is becoming such." We

---

[1] Phil. iii. 12.

may say, He who *is* a Christian minister is no
true minister of Christ. Well has a great
Christian teacher reminded us of the "inevitable
incompleteness of all true knowledge" and of the
"inevitable incompleteness of all true work." The
"finished" soul is necessarily the finite soul. God
"is," the beasts "are," the true man, and the true
minister of Christ "ever seeks to be." The task
of constantly adding to our apprehension and
possession of truth, of ever becoming more
holy, of becoming more efficient and of greater
and wider usefulness, is "laid upon us" by a
Divine necessity. In the ministry contentment
with ourselves or our achievements is fatal.
"There is," it has been well said, "a sweet
exhilaration in healthy movement." We must
remember that the moment we are tempted to
regard spiritual, or moral, or intellectual achievements as permanent possessions, they begin to
slip away from us. St. Paul's description of
himself is a perfect picture of the "strenuous life,"
and to that life we are pledged. We have to
continue to be "really alive all round and all
the time."

For living the strenuous life there are two
essential conditions—self-discipline and a supply
of Divine strength constantly renewed. Divine
grace and human effort must be combined. St.
Paul's words, "Work out thoroughly to the
bottom your own salvation, for it is God who

is energetic in you both with regard to the willing and the doing in the fulfilment of His benevolent purpose," [1] are specially applicable to the minister of Christ.

We must never grow weary in the pursuit of truth and righteousness : we must never feel tired of constantly attempting to adjust ourselves and our message to ever changing conditions and so to ever new demands. We must maintain quickness of perception, clearness and soundness of judgment, responsiveness of feeling, hopefulness of spirit, and, above all, a sympathy which ever grows, not only wider, but deeper.

---

[1] Phil. ii. 12, 13.

Chapter 4

THE ADDRESS TO THE
EPHESIAN ELDERS AT MILETUS

A Pastor's Charge to Pastors

προσέχετε ἑαυτοῖς καὶ παντὶ τῷ ποιμνίῳ ἐν ᾧ ὑμᾶς τὸ πνεῦμα τὸ ἅγιον ἔθετο ἐπισκόπους.—ACTS xx. 28.

ἢ οὐκ ἀκούεις τί φησι τοῖς πρεσβυτέροις Ἐφεσίων τὸ τοῦ Χριστοῦ σκεῦος τὸ ἐκλεκτόν.—CHRYSOSTOM, *De Sacerdot.* iv. 8.

In any attempt to describe St. Paul's conception of the Ministerial or Pastoral Office his address to the elders at Miletus demands very careful treatment. I shall not enter at length into the question of the genuineness of the speech.[1] The similarity of both its teaching and its language (vocabulary and mode of expression) to the teaching and language of St. Paul's letters,[2] and especially, as we might expect, to those of the Pastoral Epistles, must strike every careful reader.

---

[1] Recently, in his *Luke the Physician* (*E.T.* pp. 138, 139), Harnack has spoken most strongly in favour of its genuineness.

[2] A very striking list of the similarities between this address and the Epistle to the Ephesians is given in Westcott's *Ephesians*, p. xlix. Harnack says : "This whole discourse calls to mind the Epistles to the Thessalonians."

But the similarities of language are not at all those we should expect to find if the speech was the work of a clever forger, that is of one who, with St. Paul's letters before him, composed the speech for the occasion which seemed to demand it.   In that case we should have had identical expressions consisting of several consecutive words.   What we actually find is a distinctly Pauline vocabulary and a body of Pauline doctrine, but hardly an instance of what may be termed a quotation.   To regard it as a clever compilation makes a far greater demand upon our credulity than does a belief in its genuineness.

The wealth of teaching connected with pastoral work which the address contains, when we consider its brevity, is extraordinary.   If ever the salient points were seized in a brief report (and we must regard the speech before us as no more than this) we may well believe they have been seized here.   Let me say at once that this speech may be extremely useful to the working pastor, as a mirror for self-examination, as a standard whereby he may test his own aims and conduct.

In reading it we must remember that St. Paul knew intimately [1] the Church to whose responsible officers it was addressed.   Here, as always, insight was the true key to foresight. [2]   It was

---

[1] Verses 20, 25, 31.

[2] This power in our Lord, seen in His insight into the real con-

because St. Paul knew so well the actual conditions at Ephesus that he could warn so clearly and so usefully with regard to the future. The true pastor is a *watchman*,[1] as well as a prophet; indeed, because he is a watchman he can be a prophet. He sees the origins of possibilities of dangers within, he detects the first signs of the approach of these from outside. If the Church is to influence and guide the world she must in insight be superior to, and in foresight in advance of, the world. Intense and minute study of actual conditions is essential for insight: loftiness and breadth of vision must be added for foresight. The true statesman, it has been said, is not content to be abreast of his time, he will be in advance of it. We must not be satisfied with meeting the movements of those who would oppose us, we must "head" them.

For one reason the speech is of peculiar importance. Apart from the Pastoral Epistles, it contains the only extant advice of St. Paul addressed directly to those holding an office or position of special responsibility in the Church. In St. Paul's Epistles (other than the Pastorals) he deals only implicitly and indirectly with the duties of those who have to exercise a special

---

ditions in Jerusalem—the temper of its ecclesiastical rulers and people—accounts for His tears and prophecy over the city (St. Luke xix. 41 ff.).

[1] Ordination Service for Priests.

function in the Ecclesia. Here a body of such men is directly addressed upon the responsibilities which their position involves.

In the speech, as so often in St. Paul's utterances, it is difficult to discover any formal arrangement, or even any logical sequence of thought. That the contents should be largely autobiographical, drawn from personal experience, and that the choice of these should appear to be, to a great extent, governed by feeling and emotion, are evidences in favour of Pauline authorship.

It seems possible to gather the main contents under three heads :—

1. References to his own ministry in the past,[1] especially as it was known to his hearers from their personal experience of his labours during the three years he was working in Ephesus and the neighbourhood :—

Vv. 18–21, 25, 27, 31, 33–35.

2. A forecast of the immediate future :—

(*a*) As regards himself, vv. 22–24.

(*b*) As regards his hearers,[2] vv. 25, 29, 30.

3. Short and earnest exhortations as to their attitude towards themselves and towards the Church in which they had responsibility :—

Vv. 28, 31, 32,[3] 35.

---

[1] Cp. 1 Cor. iv. 16, xi. 1 ; 1 Thess. i. 5 ff., etc.

[2] This includes a forecast of conditions he saw about to arise in Ephesus.

[3] In the form of a prayer.

The only way in which to deal adequately with a passage so full of both teaching and suggestiveness, and at the same time so compressed in its language, will be to consider it word by word.

Verses 18, 19. " Ye yourselves know that from the first day I set foot in Asia what my conduct (πῶς) was with you all the time, rendering service to the Lord with all humility and tears and trials which befell me from the deliberate plottings of the Jews." St. Paul commences his address with an appeal to their personal knowledge of his conduct as a bond-service[1] to the Lord, which is in entire accordance with his appeals elsewhere.   Experience shows the power of this method of appeal, and above all of the necessity of our so living that such an appeal can be fearlessly made.   The powers of personal example and of personal self-sacrifice are certainly by far the strongest of all influences upon others.   The personal, as I have shown elsewhere, is the channel of the spiritual and the moral, and the supply of these will depend upon the nature of the medium.[2]   St. Paul's chief anxiety for the Church in Ephesus arises from the inevitable weakening of its defences through the necessary

---

[1] Note the early position of δουλεύων : cp. the early position of δοῦλος in Rom. i. 1 ; Gal. i. 10 ; Phil. i. 1 ; Tit. i. 1.

[2] The traditional saying of our Lord's—" Be ye approved money-changers."

withdrawal of his own personality. And it must not be forgotten that the power of personal example is generally proportionate to its cost, for self-sacrifice alone is fruitful. The conditions under which his own service had been rendered, and the difficulties under which he had laboured, St. Paul gathers up under three heads : first, "humility" ;[1] secondly, "tears"; thirdly, "trials from the plottings of the Jews."[2] The constant self-discipline of humility, sorrow for sin and its results, and frequent opposition (sometimes amounting to almost persecution) are still among the conditions amid which the minister of Christ must often render service to his Master.

(1) It is not always easy for one who often, from force of circumstances (*e.g.* in a working-class parish or in a country village), is in a very real sense *the persona* of the place to exercise humility ; but the cultivation of this virtue is essential for *ministerial* work, and failure in influence is only too often due chiefly to its absence. In Eph. iv. 2, St. Paul places it first among the virtues which must characterise the Christian calling. In Phil. ii. 3 it is stated to be the essential spirit of the Incarnate Christ.

(2) Sorrow for sin and for the results of sin is another condition in which the minister of

---

[1] ταπεινοφοσύνη, a Pauline word ; in N.T. here, five times in St. Paul, and in 1 Pet. v. 5.

[2] ἐπιβουλαῖς, Acts ix. 24, xx. 3, xxiii. 30, all of the Jews.

Christ must live and serve : it is the counterpart to joy in the Lord, joy in increase of righteousness : it also arises from "the love of souls," for sin harms and destroys these.[1]

(3) The word πειρασμῶν[2] here is almost a euphemism to describe St. Paul's experiences at the hands of those who everywhere dogged his footsteps and sought to take his life.   It describes rather the aspect in which he wished to view the troubles which they caused him, than the nature of the troubles themselves.   Service of Christ is a warfare in which, of necessity, many wounds must be received.   Well is it for us if we can regard these wounds as "trials" from a Divine source for some good purpose :[3] this is especially difficult when we are conscious of what ἐπιβουλή really signifies, that is "will in action directed against us."   The moral effect upon ourselves of opposition so directed against us needs to be very carefully watched.

Verse 20.   St. Paul continues to appeal to their experience, but he now passes from his personal life to his ministerial work.   ["Ye yourselves know] how that I shrank from declaring to you

---

[1] See further in the chapter on "The Love of Souls," pp. 221 ff.

[2] The use of the word in 1 Cor. x. 13 (and in 1 Pet. i. 6) makes its meaning clear.

[3]
> "Tunsionibus, pressuris
> Expoliti lapides
> Suis coaptantur locis
> Per manum artificis."

nothing of the things profitable to you, and teaching you publicly and from house to house, testifying both to Jews and to Greeks repentance toward God, and faith toward our Lord Jesus Christ." These words contain a wonderfully condensed summary of the chief activities of St. Paul's ministry. He "announced"[1] and he taught (publicly and privately), and in both he gave his testimony. We must notice that both words (ἀναγγεῖλαι καὶ διδάξαι) speak of the positiveness of the message. This, as we know from many passages in his Epistles, was St. Paul's method. His description of his work in Col. i. 28 as a proclamation (καταγγέλλομεν), and as teaching every man, offers a close parallel. He tells the Corinthians that he preached Christ crucified;[2] that his speech and his preaching[3] were not in persuasive words of wisdom but in demonstration of the Spirit and of power. He tells the Galatians that before their eyes he had placarded (προεγράφη) Christ crucified.[4] Then he asks them whether he had become their enemy because he tells them the truth.[5] In verse 27 of this same chapter St. Paul repeats

---

[1] ἀναγγέλλειν in St. John xvi. 13, 14, 15, is used of the work of the Holy Spirit, another proof that the Christian minister has to do the Spirit's work. In St. John xvi. 25 it is used of Christ.

[2] I Cor. i. 23, κηρύσσομεν, do the work of a herald.

[3] I Cor. ii. 4, τὸ κήρυγμά μου, "The contents of my proclamation."

[4] Gal. iii. 1.   [5] Gal. iv. 16.

the words, "I shrank not from announcing," or "proclaiming," and then defines the subject of his proclamation as "the whole counsel of God." By these words I understand the entire revelation of God's counsel with reference to action.[1] The point I would here press is St. Paul's emphasis upon the need of proclaiming *all* that is profitable for his hearers, that is the whole of God's counsel. St. Paul could have saved himself much had he been content to proclaim only what was palatable to his hearers, had he indeed withheld just that part of God's purpose which was especially distasteful to them. The temptation to the preacher to omit the unpalatable, especially if its proclamation is likely to have unpleasant consequences to himself, is often stronger than he cares to admit even in his own heart. St. Paul seems to have feared that after his departure only a part of the message might be given in the Church in Ephesus; this would be the source of the danger described in verse 30 (ἄνδρες λαλοῦντες διεστραμμένα).

Proclamation and teaching must go together. It is not by argument, by exposure of the untruthfulness of other messages, by disputation, it is by proclamation, that the preacher must seek to win men to Christ. It is more than possible

---

[1] Westcott on Eph. i. 11. On the need of preaching the whole truth, see Maclaren, *Colossians*, p. 141 f. A partial or one-sided proclamation of truth is a very fruitful source of heresy.

to confuse (and weary) our hearers by placing before them several interpretations or messages, and then by exposing the untruthfulness or weakness of all but one, to seek to bring them to believe this.   Such a method may have its place in the lecture-room, it is altogether unsuitable for the pulpit.   Both the announcing and the teaching are described by διαμαρτυρόμενος [1] as "a solemn affirming."   The object of this solemn affirmation is "the [2] repentance towards God and faith in the Lord Jesus"—a changed attitude towards God as the result of further knowledge, and an attitude of trust (issuing in obedience) towards the Lord Jesus.   To produce this attitude—that of the justified—must still be the object of our preaching.

Verses 22, 23.   "And now behold I go bound in the spirit to Jerusalem, not knowing what shall happen to me there; except that the Holy Spirit solemnly testifieth unto me in every city, saying that bonds and afflictions await me."   Here we have a break [3] in the speech.   St. Paul

---

[1] διαμαρτύρεσθαι is the ordinary LXX word for solemn testimony, Deut. iv. 26, viii. 19, etc.   A study of this word, which occurs nine times in the Acts, out of fifteen in the N.T., is interesting.   The only occurrence in St. Paul outside the Pastoral Epistles is in 1 Thess. iv. 6, where it means "earnestly protested."

[2] Under one article, as if almost a single idea.   Bengel's note is : "Summa eorum, quæ utilia sunt, summa doctrinæ Christianæ, summa consilii divini, Poenitentia et Fides."

[3] Marked by καὶ νῦν ἰδοὺ; compare verse 25.

turns from the past to the immediate future
(almost the present). In verse 22 I understand
"spirit" of the human spirit upon which and
through which the "Holy Spirit" acts, which
He sanctifies and governs. The verse is full
of suggestiveness, and the parallel with the last
journey of our Lord to Jerusalem is very
striking.[1] From a combination of St. Matt.
xvi. 21, ὅτι δεῖ αὐτὸν εἰς Ἱεροσόλυμα ἀπελθεῖν, with
St. Luke ix. 51, καὶ αὐτὸς τὸ πρόσωπον ἐστήρισεν
τοῦ πορεύεσθαι εἰς Ἱερουσαλήμ, we get the complementary picture of the Divine necessity and the
human determination (yet under the guidance
and strength of a Higher Power). The Divine
Spirit works upon and with the human spirit,
and the "Lord is the Spirit,"[2] and the "Acts"
is in a very true sense "the Gospel of the
Holy Spirit." The Spirit is ever behind the
apostolic workers. Like St. Paul we may not
know what may befall us, but the disciple must
be prepared to "fill up that which is lacking in
the sufferings of the Christ for His body's
sake"[3]—the Church. Bengel[4] rightly draws
attention to the effect upon others of St. Paul's
devotion of purpose.

---

[1] Phillips Brooks has finely said, "Every true life has its
Jerusalem towards which it is constantly going up." This "going
up" must be in the company of Christ.

[2] 2 Cor. iii. 17.   [3] Col. i. 24.

[4] "Omnium intererat scire, et omnes proficiebant, videntes
obedientiam Pauli."

Verse 24. " But I do not make my life a
matter of computation in comparison with com-
pleting the course [1] marked out for me, even [2]
the ministry [3] which I received [4] from the Lord
Jesus, to testify solemnly the good news of the
grace of God." The words at once remind us
of our Lord's saying, [5] "Whosoever would save
his life shall lose it ; and whosoever shall lose
his life for My sake and the gospel's " (the two
purposes are one) " shall save it." The good
news of the grace of God is the good news
that God has in Jesus Christ redeemed the
world. This must still be the message of the
minister of Christ to-day. The conception of ἡ
χάρις τοῦ Θεοῦ is thoroughly Pauline, and the
" priority of God " is one of the many points of
likeness between the Pauline and the Johannine
theology. I cannot leave this verse without
remarking a similarity between our Lord and
St. Paul in · their use of a short and simple
description of their whole life's purpose or
work, often consisting of no more than a single
word. It is a sign of that unity of purpose

---

[1] δρόμος, elsewhere only in Acts xiii. 25 (of the Baptist), and in
2 Tim. iv. 7 of St. Paul himself. In all three cases the nearness
of the end seems to be suggested.

[2] καί here is epexegetic, viz. " even."

[3] Note the comprehensive sense of τὴν διακονίαν.

[4] For no man taketh this ministry unto himself.

[5] " Doubtless with special reference to the grace by which
Gentiles were admitted into covenant with God." Hort, *Christian
Ecclesia*, p. 103.

in a life by which every activity or expenditure of energy can be referred to a single aim. Our Lord is "the Truth," He came "to bear witness to the Truth." To St. Paul his life is τὸν δρόμον μου; it is equally "the ministry received from the Lord Jesus."

Verse 25. "And now behold I know that no longer shall ye see my face, (even) all of you among whom I passed (through) heralding the Kingdom." The first half of the verse gives the reason for the solemn warnings about to follow; the second half contains another comprehensive definition or description of St. Paul's work, viz. κηρύσσων τὴν βασιλείαν. The parallel with the description of our Lord's work in St. Mark i. 14, 15 is very close, and the fulfilment of the prophecy or exhortation in St. Matt. xxiv. 14 is exact. As I have already suggested, "the heralding of the Kingdom" is the form of announcement most needed from the pulpit to-day. The laws of the Kingdom of God, and that welfare depends upon obedience to those laws, is perhaps the most necessary of all messages for the present. We must convince men of the nearness of the Kingdom (ἤγγικεν), of the possibility of enjoying its benefits. Before leaving this verse two points should be noticed: First, the vividness of the picture suggested by διῆλθον, "among whom I passed through." We must impress people with the temporariness of opportunities. They must be taught the responsibility of feeling and acting *now*. Secondly, the unselfishness of St. Paul. He is not thinking of himself, so he does not say, "I shall see *your* face no longer"; he is thinking of them, and so says, "Ye shall no longer see my face." In the life of the minister to-day the temptation to think of circumstances, even of people, as they affect himself, is strong. But a self-centred "ministry" is a contradiction in terms.

Verse 26. "Wherefore I testify to you to-day that I am pure from the blood of all men." These few words contain both a solemn warning and a high ideal for every minister of Christ. We must remember the passage in the Ordination Service, "If it shall happen the same Church, or any Member thereof, to take any hurt or hindrance by reason of your negligence, . . . consider with yourselves the end of your Ministry towards the children of God . . . and see that ye never cease your labour . . . until you have done all that lieth in you . . . to bring such as are or shall be committed to your charge unto that agreement in the faith and knowledge of God, and perfect-ness of age in Christ, that there be no place left among you, either for error in religion, or for viciousness in life. . . . And seeing that you cannot by any other means compass the doing of so weighty a work, pertaining to the salvation of man but with doctrine and exhortation taken out of the holy Scriptures . . . consider how studious ye ought to be in reading and learning the Scriptures," etc.

We must so work and teach that, like St. Paul, at the close of a ministry, we may say, " I am pure from the blood of all."[1] The reason why St. Paul can say this is given in the next verse.

Verse 27. " For[2] I have not failed to announce (or declare) the whole counsel of God to you." To St. Paul the declaration of the whole gospel is one test of a faithful ministry. No part of the " Divine counsel," so far as it can be known, must be omitted, suppressed, or explained away. These words have an important application to study as well as to teaching and preaching : for the " counsel of God " has to be *learnt* before it can be expressed. The connection between knowledge and life—between truth and life—is very close ; indeed, salvation depends on knowledge and life upon truth. Because Christ is the Way He is the Truth, and because He is the Truth He is the Life. " This is life eternal that they may know Thee." Only those who have been long in the ministry can realise how strong are two temptations : first, to cease to learn and so to cease to be able to teach ; and secondly, to lay special stress on particular parts or aspects of God's counsel — those fragments or aspects

---

[1] " Hæc cura debet esse valedicentis." Bengel.

[2] " Ergo qui subduxit, quæ annunciare debuerat, non est purus a sanguine auditorum." Bengel.

which more than others appeal to ourselves. Yet unless we give the "whole counsel" we may fail to give to our hearers what they most need for salvation and life. We are ambassadors for Christ, and therefore to conceal or ignore any part of the message with which He has entrusted us is to be unfaithful to Him whom we represent. The words which we should speak are meant to be the channels of spirit and of life. Unless such words are spoken, the channels by which they are supplied may be cut off. And "the whole counsel of God"—God's will as revealed in action—includes His judgment upon disobedience —"tribulation and wrath and anguish . . . upon every soul that doeth evil." We must reveal God as a God of judgment. We can do this even more fully than could St. Paul, for we have a wider knowledge of an inexorable law. Both the "will" of God and the "counsel" of God should mean to us far more than they could mean to the Apostle, for the revelation of God vouchsafed to us is far more full than that vouchsafed to him. His pleading for a "revelation of the whole" is specially binding upon us.

Verse 28. "Take heed to yourselves and to the whole flock in which the Holy Spirit has appointed you to exercise overseership, to act as shepherds [1]

---

[1] ποιμαίνειν in the religious sense is found in Matt. ii. 6 (from Mic. v. 2 and Ezek. xxxiv. 23 f.); John xxi. 16; 1 Pet. v. 2; Jude 12; Rev. ii. 27, vii. 17, xii. 5, xix. 15.

to the Ecclesia of God, which He acquired by means of the blood of His Own.[1] This verse contains a great wealth both of exhortation[2] and of inspiration for all who are called to exercise the pastoral function in any kind of position or capacity. We must remember that the analogies St. Paul uses, the ideals to which he appeals, and upon which his exhortations are based, had their roots in the Old Testament, and that the functions of the Shepherd were claimed by our Lord for His own work, and by Him directly delegated to those who should carry on that work.

St. Paul's first exhortation is, "Take heed[3] to yourselves." St. Paul knew that personal religion —communion with the Divine,—personal watchfulness, and personal culture must be the first care

---

$\pi o \iota \mu \acute{\eta} \nu$ (18 times in N.T.), directly of our Lord in Matt. xxvi. 31 (from Zech. xiii. 7); Mark xiv. 27 (parallel to last); John x. 11, 14, 16; Heb. xiii. 20; 1 Pet. ii. 25.

$\pi o \acute{\iota} \mu \nu \eta$ in a religious sense is found in Matt. xxvi. 31; also in John x. 16.

$\pi o \acute{\iota} \mu \nu \iota o \nu$ always in a religious sense. Luke xii. 32; 1 Pet. v. 2, 3.

The following passages will be found very helpful. Hort, *Christian Ecclesia*, pp. 98 ff.; Bigg's note on 1 Pet. v. 2 (pp. 187 f.); Westcott's note on Heb. xiii. 20; Swete's note on Rev. ii. 27; also Westcott's notes on John x. 14–16.

[1] This is probably the true reading. *See* Hort, *Christian Ecclesia*, p. 102.

[2] The references to shepherd and flock in our Ordination Services are perhaps hardly so frequent or so full as might have been expected.

[3] The difference between $\pi \rho o \sigma \acute{\epsilon} \chi \epsilon \tau \epsilon$ (here) and $\acute{\epsilon} \pi \epsilon \chi \epsilon$ in 1 Tim. iv. 16 is very slight: it is that between "Turn thine attention towards" and "Let thine attention rest upon." The Vg. translates both by *attendite, attende*; Luther, by *hab acht*.

of those who would influence others for good. In our zeal for others, in seeking to fulfil our commission towards them, self - culture in its most comprehensive sense may all too easily be neglected.[1]   Doing depends on being ; and there is a dangerous side to self-forgetfulness.   St. Paul's second exhortation is, "Take heed to the whole flock."   The conception of the [local] *Ecclesia* as a flock in which the Holy Spirit sets us to have oversight is again full of applications.   The origin of the expression[2] and the bearing of this verse upon the constitution of the Early Church have been so fully dealt with in Hort's *Christian Ecclesia* that I shall not dwell upon these here.   When we speak of the need of remembering the *pastoral* nature of the ministerial office we must be clear as to what the pastoral function implies.   Dr. Hort says : "The precise form which the work of these elders was to take is not clearly expressed." While "the side of shepherding most expressed by ποιμαίνειν is government and guiding," he thinks that, especially in virtue of verse 31, "this watching does seem to involve teaching[3] . . . the practical form taken by the Apostle's vigilance must be in some way carried on by themselves." And, as Dr. Hort adds, "it is hard to see how

---

[1] Cf. Song of Solomon, i. 6.   [2] Ps. lxxiii. (lxxiv.) 2.

[3] *Christian Ecclesia*, p. 101.   The close connection of "pastors" and "teachers" in Eph. iv. 11 should be remembered.

the work of tending and protection could be performed without teaching."

We must notice how by two thoughts St. Paul insists upon the immense responsibility of those having oversight. First, the origin of the appointment (however humanly mediated) is Divine ; second, the value of the flock is reckoned in terms of "the blood of God's Own."[1] It was the constant presence of such ideas that caused and enabled St. Paul to "glorify his ministry." As Dr. Maclaren says, "the incidental introduction" of this reference to the purchase of the Church by the Divine blood "implies the Ephesians' familiarity with it. It had been made a prominent part of St. Paul's preaching. It contains, in brief, the Apostle's whole doctrine of the purpose and the effect of the death of Christ."[2]

I hope I shall not be considered fanciful if I see in St. Paul's change of συναγωγή into ἐκκλησία (the body of free and responsible citizens) a hint to the elders (balancing the other side of the exhortation) that they had to "shepherd" a body of men with the "rights" of free citizens.[3] The Church is a democracy (in the true sense of the word) ; it is not a mob of irresponsible people

---

[1] "Hic ergo grex est pretiosissimus." Bengel.

[2] *Bible Class Lessons*, "Acts," p. 250.

[3] The LXX of Ps. lxxiii. (lxxiv.) 2 runs, Μνήσθητι τῆς συναγωγῆς σου ἧς ἐκτήσω ἀπ᾽ ἀρχῆς. We notice the change of ἐκτήσω into περιποιήσατο, "made a special possession for Himself." See Hort's note on 1 Pet. ii. 9 (p. 127).

governed by irresponsible rulers.   In a very real sense the pastor to-day must be prepared to purchase souls with his own blood.   This is one way in which he has to "fill up that which is lacking of the sufferings of (the) Christ."[1]   As Bishop Westcott says, "His 'blood' is the vital energy by which he fulfils his work."[2]   The pastor must be prepared to expend this in large measure.

Verses 29, 30.   "I know that there shall enter in to you, after my departure, grievous wolves not sparing the flock, and from among (ἐξ) yourselves there shall arise men uttering distorted things to lead away the disciples after themselves."   Here, again, we see how "insight is the key to foresight."   St. Paul speaks with the confidence begotten of full knowledge : and this knowledge is the product of a keen insight into actual conditions.   In virtue of this insight St. Paul foresees the two directions from which evil will come : First, agents destructive towards his hearers, and who will not spare the flock, will enter the fold ; second, even out of his present audience (the listening elders) men will arise speaking distorted things in order to draw away the disciples after themselves (not to draw men to Christ).   Both dangers are present to-

---

[1] Col. i. 24.

[2] On Heb. xiii. 20, where he quotes the following striking words of Herveius : " Pascit autem non solum verbo doctrinæ sed corpore et sanguine suo."

day, and the true pastor, who has insight, will watch and warn against both.

The first danger comes from enemies of Christianity whose purpose is destruction in order to enrich themselves. The number and the strength of these is always great, and the more missionary or aggressive Christianity becomes, the greater is their virulence. We know the trouble which the fear of interference with vested interests produced in Ephesus.[1] To-day vested interests in various strongholds of iniquity are fighting bitterly on the side of evil, and therefore against the cause of Christ. The second danger comes from those who preach a distorted message. We have seen how the origin of most heresies is distorted truth, and the object of those who preach thus is generally to gain a following for themselves rather than for Christ. Then history shows that a distorted or incomplete form of faith, which implies an incomplete doctrine both of God and man, is generally followed by a wrong treatment of man, arising, of course, from this incomplete conception of man's nature and destiny. Thus even from the wholly practical and human point of view a true faith is essential to the highest and completest human progress. Not only Church history, but the histories of various nations will supply many proofs of the truth of this assertion.[2]

---

[1] Acts xix. 23 ff.

[2] An example of this is seen in the position of woman, and in

Verse 31. "Wherefore watch,[1] remembering that for three years night and day I ceased not with tears admonishing each one." The antidote to both the above dangers is constant watchfulness. This injunction, one frequently given by our Lord,[2] may be regarded here as having reference to both the external and internal dangers. We must see that our people do not become a prey. We must also watch our own teaching that no partiality, no want of proportion leads to heresy. St. Paul here again refers to his own example, repeating very much what he had said in verse 20, except that now he substitutes "admonishing" for "announcing and teaching," and "each one" for "publicly and from house to house." The task of admonishing[3] is one of the most important that falls to the lot of the preacher and teacher. In the language of psychology it is to bring a subject into the centre of the field of consciousness and strive to retain it there. To be aware of, and to watch a danger is essential, if we would avoid or repel it. The serious nature of the danger, from its possible terrible consequences,

---

the prevalence of slavery, in Mohammedan countries. Foreign missionary literature is full of examples of the same truth.

[1] Bengel's note is γρηγορεῖτε, *vigilate*, Verbum pastorale.

[2] *e.g.* St. Matt. xxiv. 42, xxv. 13, xxvi. 38, 41, etc. The word is Pauline : 1 Cor. xvi. 13 ; Col. iv. 2 ; 1 Thess. v. 6, 10.

[3] The words νουθετεῖν and νουθεσία are with the exception of this instance found in the N.T. only in St. Paul's Epistles. The German *an das Herz legen* gives the exact meaning, to fix the mind upon the mind of another that he may be on the alert.

is indicated by the repeated " with tears." The true father—and the pastor has to be a father to his flock—educates his children " by the discipline and admonition (νουθεσία)[1] of the Lord." We must not pass over the final words of the verse, ἕνα ἕκαστον, the "admonition" must be applied individually.[2] The temptations of men are so different. Many of St. Paul's converts were doubtless very imperfectly Christianised, as are numbers of so-called Christians to-day. Among our hearers are many τῶν ἀσθενούντων ; in various, and very different ways, these need help.

Verse 32. "And now I commend you to the Lord[3] and to the word of His grace [which] is able to build you up and to give you the inheritance among all who are sanctified." Here we have, for the last time, a division[4] in the speech. The verse is really a creed, an expression of faith, almost in the form of a prayer. St. Paul is on the point of concluding his address : he looks upon the elders : he must leave them, but he cannot leave them to themselves. They are not strong enough to stand alone ; so he commits them to [the Lord] and to the word of His grace.

---

[1] Eph. vi. 4. Bengel's note on ἐν παιδείᾳ καὶ νουθεσίᾳ is, " harum altera occurrit ruditati, altera oblivioni et levitati."

[2] τοῖς κατ' ἄνδρα κατὰ ὁμοήθειαν Θεοῦ λάλει. Ignat. ad Polyc. i.

[3] The authority for τῷ Θεῷ seems much stronger, viz. ℵ A C D E L P, etc., but for τῷ Κυρίῳ we have B 33, 68, sah. cop., and the alteration of Κυρίῳ to Θεῷ is much more probable than the opposite.

[4] Marked by the καὶ . . . νῦν.

Do the words which follow refer to the Lord, or to the word of His grace? God is certainly able both to build them up and to give them the inheritance; but if τῷ δυναμένῳ refers to God, why the addition of "the word of His grace"? It seems best in the face of this difficulty to regard the Revised Version as correct, and to consider these last words as describing the instrument which God will use, the channel through which His power will be conveyed.[1] "Edification" as an object is thoroughly Pauline; and that the message of God is powerfully instrumental towards realising this object is asserted in such passages as, "He that prophesieth speaketh unto men edification . . . he that prophesieth edifieth the Church."[2] The thought in the second phrase, "to give you the inheritance among all that are sanctified" (especially when we remember that this privilege is at least mediated through the word of His grace), reminds us of the passage in the Epistle to the Ephesians which runs, "That the God of our Lord Jesus Christ, the Father of glory may grant to you a spirit of wisdom and revelation in the [full] knowledge[3]

---

[1] The nature of the heresies which St. Paul feared may have determined the form of the description of the instrument.

[2] 1 Cor. xiv. 3, 4.

[3] In face of the controversy as to the meaning of ἐπίγνωσις (Armitage Robinson, *Ephesians*, p. 248 ff.), the following note of Bp. Westcott's is valuable: "Ἐπίγνωσις has always a moral value, and in the N.T. is used exclusively in reference to facts of the religious order, and specially in reference to the knowledge which

of Him, having the eyes of your heart enlightened with a view to your knowing what is the hope of His calling, what the wealth of the glory of His inheritance in the saints, and what the surpassing greatness of His power towards us who believe," etc.[1] "The primal *source* here is God; the mediatorial *instrument* is the spirit of wisdom and revelation in the knowledge of Him; the *end* is to know the wealth of the glory of His inheritance in the saints."   As "ministers of the Word" we must learn from St. Paul the double power of the Word : first, to edification ; secondly, towards obtaining a place among the redeemed.

Verses 33–35. " I coveted the silver or gold or raiment of no one. Ye yourselves know that these hands ministered to the needs of myself and of those who were with me. I have showed you that so toiling hard it is necessary to support the weak, and to remember the words of the Lord Jesus, that He said, It is more blessed to give than to receive."

In these concluding sentences we have a sudden transition to the personal and to the material. Once more St. Paul points to his own life of hardship and self-sacrifice. His work has been one of wearying toil, and it has been entirely

---

we are enabled to gain of God and of His purpose for man's salvation"
(*Ephesians,* p. 23), Kregel Publications, 1979.
[1] Eph. i. 17–19.

disinterested.   He has given freely, and has taken nothing.   The power and influence of such conduct, of such a personal example, are extremely great. The least suspicion of seeking after self-advantage is fatal to the highest ministerial influence.   St. Paul had especially in mind those as yet un-confirmed in the faith.   These might find a stumbling-block in one who even seemed to be teaching for gain.   These, as yet weak brethren, have constantly to be remembered in our work. In more than one place in St. Paul's Epistles they are the subject of his special solicitude.   The thought of the need of self-sacrifice for their sake gives a wide application to this traditional saying of our Lord's.   When the ministry has remembered the great principle enshrined in these words it has been mighty for good; when it has forgotten that principle it has, at least as a power for Christ, failed.

Chapter 5

THE LOVE OF SOULS

ἀδελφοί μου ἀγαπητοὶ καὶ ἐπιπόθητοι, χαρὰ καὶ στέφανός μου.
—PHIL. iv. 1.

ζηλῶ γὰρ ὑμᾶς Θεοῦ ζήλῳ.—2 COR. xi. 2.

To justify a man entering the Christian ministry, and to enable him to persevere in its work, two conditions must be fulfilled—first, the conviction of a "call" from God, secondly a love for man, and therefore a desire to serve man.[1] Without the first his ministry will want the all-important qualities of inspiration and confidence; without the second it will lack the very reason for its existence.

This "love for man" may be differently described, and in itself it may be said to be a complex feeling. It has been termed "the love of souls," and the definition is a useful one, because it indicates that in "man" we must not forget individual men, women, and children. From experience we know that this particular form of forgetfulness is actually far easier than at first sight might seem possible. The love for

---

[1] These must not be too sharply divided : the first may come through the second.

man has also been described as "the enthusiasm of humanity," which means "a love for the ideal of man."[1] The true pastor will combine a love for the ideal of human nature with a love for the actual men, women, and children to whom he is a neighbour,[2] that is, all whom he may know, with whom he may in any wise come into contact, and whom he may influence for good.

An intelligent love for a person will wish the best for them, it will therefore wish for them the ideal nature issuing in the ideal life. To the Christian minister there can be but one ideal nature and one ideal life—the nature and the life of Christ.[3] Hence the ideal nature and life are the nature and life of Christ realised in every man. A love for men must be a love for what they may be. It does not think primarily of what they are.

But true love never exists apart from hate ; and the stronger the love the stronger will the hatred be.[4] The Divine hate, like the Divine love, is

---

[1] *Ecce Homo*, chap. xiv.

[2] Instead of "Who is my neighbour?" we must ask, "To whom can I be a neighbour?"

[3] Here we must remember "The letter killeth, but the spirit giveth life."

[4]　　　"And would'st thou reach, rash scholar mine,
　　　　　Love's high unruffled state ?
　　　　Awake, thine easy dreams resign :
　　　　　First learn thee how to hate.
　　　　Hatred of sin, and Zeal and holy Fear,
　　　　　Lead up the Holy Hill :
　　　　Track them till Charity appear
　　　　　A self-denial still."
　　　　　　　　J. H. N. in the *Lyra Apostolica*.

infinite. If we have an ideal which we would see realised, we shall passionately hate all which prevents its realisation. The essential characteristic of Christ is His sinlessness. Hence our ideal for man must include his sinlessness, therefore in the Christian minister together with a love for man there must go a hatred of sin.

In our Lord's ministry the threefold combination of the sense of a mission from God, of a love for man, and of a hatred of sin, is constantly before us. The following references will suffice to prove this :—

First, His Divine mission : God is τὸν ἀποστεί-λας με ;[1] our Lord's works are τὰ ἔργα ἃ δέδωκέν μοι ὁ πατὴρ ἵνα τελειώσω αὐτά.[2] Our Lord desires that men should recognise the Divine source of His mission[3] (notice the four times repeated ὅτι σύ με ἀπέστειλας in chap. xvii.) :[4] and, finally, the great commission to the Church.[5]

Secondly, our Lord's love for man. It must be remembered that, naturally, our Lord *says* little of this. The proof of it lies in His life—His actions, His teaching and healing, His self-sacrifice and His death. It is interesting in this connection to remember that the word σπλαγχνίζεσθαι in the New Testament is, with

---

[1] St. Matt. x. 40 ; St. Mark ix. 37 ; St. Luke ix. 48, x. 16.

[2] St. John v. 36. The perfect tense emphasises the permanence of the mission of Christ, and so of our own mission.

[3] St. John xi. 42.   [4] Verses 8, 21, 23, 25.

[5] St. John xx. 21 (where see Westcott's note).

two exceptions,[1] used only either of our Lord,[2] to our Lord (as an appeal),[3] by our Lord of Himself,[4] or of a feeling to be cultivated.[5] We must also remember the similes of the Good Shepherd, the Lost Sheep, and the Good Samaritan—all of which reveal the inmost heart both of Jesus and the gospel.

Thirdly, our Lord's hatred of sin. This is particularly seen in His hatred of what prevents moral and spiritual growth, and so prevents the realisation of the ideal of man : it is seen in His denunciation of those who cause offences (which prevent progress),[6] and especially in His frequent denunciation of the Pharisees,[7] who, by their self-satisfaction and self-righteousness, prevented moral and spiritual progress, and so the realisation of the true ideal.

When we turn to St. Paul we find the same sense of a Divine call, the same love of souls, the same hatred of sin and of all that prevents the realisation of the Divine ideal of man. The situations in which he found himself placed, the enemies he had to combat, the rebukes and exhortations he uttered, are very similar to our

---

[1] St. Luke x. 33 (of the Good Samaritan), xv. 20 (of the Father of the Prodigal Son).

[2] St. Matt. ix. 36,, xiv. 14, xx. 34 ; St. Mark i. 41, vi. 34 ; St. Luke vii. 13.

[3] St. Mark ix. 22.   [4] St. Matt. xv. 32 ; St. Mark viii. 2.

[5] St. Matt. xviii. 27.

[6] St. Matt. xviii. 6 ff. ; St. Mark ix. 42 ff. ; St. Luke xvii. 2.

[7] *e.g.* St. Matt. xxiii. 13, 15, 24, 28, 34.

Lord's. To take only two instances, we may compare his exhortation to the Galatians against the Judaistic teachers, " With freedom did Christ set us free ; stand fast, therefore," etc.[1] (a freedom essential for the true development of man), with our Lord's denunciation of the Pharisees who bound upon men heavy burdens. Again, we may compare his saying about things "which are not of any value against the indulgence of the flesh "[2] (addressed to the Gnostic teachers of Colossæ) with our Lord's charge against the Pharisees of being within full of excess and of all uncleanness.[3]

With St. Paul's conception of his Divine call I have already dealt. So I pass at once to his "love of souls." We must remember that by himself his Divine call is very closely connected with the service of man, and especially in the way of freeing man from the bondage of ignorance and sin. His call was followed by his commission,[4] which included these words, " to open their eyes . . . that they may turn from the power of Satan unto God, that they may receive remission ($\mathring{a}\phi\epsilon\sigma\iota\nu$) of sins . . ."[5] What does this mean but to give men the power of freedom from the authority ($\tau\mathring{\eta}s$ $\mathring{\epsilon}\xi o\nu\sigma\acute{\iota}as$) of sin, which had obtained authority over them ? With this we may compare our Lord's account of His own

---

[1] Gal. v. i.   [2] Col. ii. 23.   [3] St. Matt. xxiii. 25, 27.
[4] $\mathring{a}\pi o\sigma\tau\acute{\epsilon}\lambda\lambda\omega$.   [5] Acts xxvi. 18.

mission, where we have the same combination of giving of sight and giving of freedom—" He hath sent Me to proclaim release to the captives and recovering of sight to the blind." [1]

Thus we may say that, from the first, St. Paul felt a call to the highest form of philanthropic work—to perform the best possible service for man. In a pregnant sentence he tells us how he regarded this commission. To the whole world, to humanity, he says, ὀφειλέτης εἰμί,[2] for he owed them the gospel which had been entrusted to him for them. This was a debt in payment of which his life was spent, though even then he felt he could not pay it in full. His words, " Owe nothing to anyone," εἰ μὴ τὸ ἀλλήλους ἀγαπᾶν, show this.[3] " Love is to be a perpetual and inexhaustible debt . . . always due." But as we read these various sentences, even the last, thoughts like these might suggest themselves :—St. Paul is speaking only of the discharge of a *duty*. He is convinced of Christ's Divinity, and that Christ has given him a commission which includes, not only the preaching of the gospel and bringing men into subjection to it—making them orthodox Christians, but also the service of men generally. Thus in his preaching and in his ministerial or pastoral work St. Paul is only obeying a command which he

---

[1] St. Luke iv. 18.   [2] Rom. i. 14.
[3] Rom. xiii. 8 (Bishop Moule *in loc.* in the *Expositor's Bible*).

regards as Divine and therefore dare not disobey. But all this is very different from that spontaneous philanthropy which is the true "enthusiasm of humanity," and the true "love of souls" as such, and which moreover is the special characteristic of Christ, as St. Paul himself again and again asserts;[1] indeed, we may go further, and say it is the special quality of God.[2]

I draw attention to this because, both from our study of history and from our personal experience, we are sometimes tempted to see in the work of so-called Christian pastors and teachers two primary motives both of which appear to be stronger than "the love of souls": first, the desire to make others orthodox;[3] secondly, the determination to perform every duty of their profession most punctiliously. Both these motives are valuable and praiseworthy in their place; but neither are so Christ-like, and therefore so Christian, as a pure love of souls. Where this last exists, even without a creed which is wholly orthodox in every particular, there is sometimes more essential Christianity, more of Christ's own spirit, than where, without a real enthusiasm for humanity, we see either

---

[1] Eph. iii. 17, v. 2 ; cp. Gal. ii. 20 ; 2 Cor. viii. 9.

[2] Rom. v. 8 ; Eph. ii. 4 ; cp. St. John iii. 16.

[3] The danger lies in making orthodoxy (right opinion) an end, and not a means, though a most important one. Right conduct, the issue of right character, must, to be permanent, be founded on right principles, *i.e.* on right conceptions of God, man, and duty.

untiring and thoroughly well - meant efforts to bring men to intellectual conformity, or ceaseless devotion to what is, quite conscientiously, regarded as "duty." But as St. Paul knew, and as his own practice teaches us, there is no appeal to the human heart like the conviction of pure and spontaneous and (if I may, *more Germanico*, coin "an extended adjective") special-ecclesiastical-interest-forgetting love. This appeal of love may be made in our conduct, inspired by a heart full (if unconsciously so) of the Divine love ; or it may be made by telling the "simple" gospel story of Christ crucified, for all time the perfect revelation of infinite love, at once human and Divine.

I lay stress upon the need of the cultivation of the "love of souls" because to-day, as perhaps never since the first centuries of her existence, the Church and the ministry are on their trial before the world. They are, as I have said, the subject of constant and not always kindly criticism. Ministers of Christ are not only in a position of responsibility, they are also in a position of privilege. Men are quite able to recognise the pure spirit of Christ, and they demand of us, as St. Paul in his Galatian letter implies that men demanded of him,[1] that the minister's motive shall be absolutely pure and disinterested. Men profess to be able to distinguish between ministers who are looking after

---

[1] See Ramsay's *Galatians*, pp. 256 ff.

their own interests, who are zealous in strengthening an ecclesiastical institution, and those who are only anxious to serve their fellow-men. The ministry has been charged with being "a huge trades-union," whose chief anxieties are the protection of its privileges, and the maintenance or increase of the incomes of its members.[1] We must show that such an accusation is false. We can only do this by our conduct being so patently and consistently "other-seeking" that it must be admitted to be inspired by a purely altruistic motive.

At the same time, even when the effort to save souls is actually inspired by nothing else than a pure love of souls, methods have to be pursued which are open to the charge of indirectness, even to that of pursuing quite secondary objects. As St. Paul more than once states quite plainly, those who live for others have to live.[2] And when many are working together for a common object they naturally form some kind of an institution or society : such an institution—a "constituent" or "purposive" society[3]—is an instrument for a purpose, and therefore nothing which will conduce to the efficiency of the institution can be disregarded. Then, as every philanthropic worker knows, while the saving of

---

[1] From an article in the *Clarion*.

[2] 1 Cor. ix. 14 ; Gal. vi. 6 ; 2 Thess. iii. 9.

[3] See Giddings' *Inductive Sociology*, p. 199.

men or the transformation of character must be our primary aim, we cannot disregard the circumstances under which men live ; for character and environment act and react upon each other.[1] Also while change of conduct is our ultimate purpose, we must remember that conduct is governed by ideas, and ideas have to be disseminated before they can be assimilated ; hence teaching is a most important factor in the saving of souls. Even the pursuit of what may be regarded as purely secular philanthropy involves a multitude of activities, intellectual as well as "practical," which at first sight are open to a charge of more than indirectness, indeed to the careless observer they may seem to have little or nothing to do with the object professed.

Thus in proving that St. Paul was deeply inspired by the love of souls and the enthusiasm of humanity, we must be careful to show that, while doctrines which he taught and methods he pursued may at first sight seem very indirectly connected with these, a deeper study of both these doctrines and methods will prove that they were very really calculated to further his chief purpose, indeed were essential, if that purpose should be accomplished.[2]

---

[1] Of course one danger to-day is to attribute all social evils to "circumstances," and to imagine that upon improved circumstances improved conduct would necessarily follow—a dangerous "half-truth."

[2] As we explain this we must show that our own teaching and

The "love of souls," we have seen, implies that we would have all men become what we believe a desire for their highest welfare and most perfect happiness wishes for them. Here are men and women and children for whom we desire the best : we see what they are, we must also be clear about what we would have them become. On this point St. Paul has absolutely no doubt : " My little children, of whom I am again in travail until Christ be formed in you."[1] To understand these pathetic words we must recall the circumstances under which they were written, namely, the threatened apostasy of his Galatian converts. They reveal the true pastor's difficulties and disappointments[2] as well as his purpose : they utter his anxiety as well as his object. The very word τεκνία is deeply suggestive. It expresses both the tenderness of the Apostle's heart and the weakness of his converts' characters ; yet it implies the possibility of growth which they really possessed : it is a word both of affection and gentle reproach. In regard to these to whom he is speaking the whole work of spiritual "motherhood" will have to be repeated, for they seem to some extent to have already lapsed.[3] Every feeling which inspires the mother must

---

conduct—based upon N.T. principles—has the same end in view. But we must be careful that our teaching and conduct are such as to bear this explanation.

[1] Gal. iv. 19.   [2] Note πάλιν . . . μέχρις οὗ.

[3] Such lapses are, alas ! all too common in pastoral experience.

inspire the true pastor ; every labour performed by her must be undertaken by the pastor on behalf of those most immature but yet potential Christians who form the great majority of every flock.   The words μέχρις οὗ reveal the Apostle's faith, and without such faith, issuing in constant, unremitting labour, the task of both pastor and philanthropist will be vain.   Infinite patience also will be required.[1]   With this passage we may compare the one in 1 Cor. iv. 14 and 15, where St. Paul compares his relation to his converts with that of a father to his children,[2] and where again, in the choice of the very words employed, we have many a valuable suggestion for our own conduct.   " Not as one making you ashamed do I write these things, but as one warning my beloved children : for though ye have thousands of instructors in Christ ye have not many fathers, for in Christ Jesus through the gospel I begat you."   In the word παιδαγωγούς[3] there is again a reference to immaturity, and at the same time an assertion that no παιδαγωγός, even in the Roman sense of the word,[4] can take the place of a father—a truth which needs to be learnt

---

[1] " Non desistendum a nitendo."   Bengel *in loc.*

[2] How true again is Bengel's comment : " Spiritualis paternitas singularem necessitudinem et affectionem conjunctam habet, præ omni alia propinquitatem " !

[3] On the meaning of παιδαγωγός here, and generally, see Ramsay's *Galatians*, pp. 381 ff.

[4] The Roman *paidagogos* seems to have assisted in teaching the child.

to-day by both ministers and parents. In both these passages St. Paul has laid stress on the immaturity of his converts; in Eph. iv. 13 he states the ideal into which this immaturity must be developed, "until we (Christians) all as a body attain unto the unity of the faith and of the knowledge of the Son of God, unto a fully developed man,[1] unto a standard of maturity of (measured by) the fulness of the Christ." Here we have "an effective call to unceasing endeavour,"[2] a description of three aspects of Christian progress — intellectual, in personal maturity, and in the conformity of each to the standard of Christ, for "the perfection of each Christian is determined by his true relation to Christ."[3] To raise those for whom he works to this standard must be the object of unceasing effort on the part of the minister of Christ. In 2 Cor. xi. 2, St. Paul's affection for his converts is revealed by its comparison with another human relationship: he cares for his Corinthian flock ($\dot{v}\mu\hat{a}s$) as a father who is greatly jealous[4] for the purity of his daughter's character. St. Paul would have the Ecclesia[5] of Corinth fit to be united with Christ in the closest conceivable of all human bonds.

---

[1] εἰς ἄνδρα τέλειον.

[2] μέχρι in verse 13 ; cp. μέχρις οὗ in Gal. iv. 19.

[3] Westcott *in loc.*   [4] " Zelo magno et sancto."   Bengel.

[5] "Non singulatim sed conjunctim." Bengel, whose notes on this passage should be read.

St. Paul's love of souls is revealed in all his Epistles, and not least in that to the Galatians, which has been termed the "sternest" of all his letters.   I have already quoted one passage from this Epistle : to this I would add the appeals in iv. 12 ff. and in vi. 1 ff., in both of which he addresses his readers as "brothers," the ex-hortations in v. 1 and vi. 2, the warning in v. 13, 15, where again he speaks as a brother to brothers.   In the question in v. 7, "Who did hinder you?" he seems to show the solicitude of a father.

But it is in his letter to the Philippian Christians, and in his second letter to the Corinthians, that we seem to come nearest to the affectionate pastoral heart of St. Paul.   In the first of these we have such expressions as, "I have you in my heart," or rather, "from the fact that you are always in my heart";[1] "God is my witness how I yearn upon you all in the heart of Christ Jesus";[2] having the desire to depart . . . yet to abide in the flesh is more needful for your sake";[3] "fulfil ye my joy";[4] "my brethren be-loved and longed for";[5] "my God shall supply every need of yours."[6]   Each of these ex-pressions breathes the very breath of love.   The

---

[1] i. 7, διὰ τὸ ἔχειν με ἐν τῇ καρδίᾳ ὑμᾶς.   St. Paul would have them assume this.

[2] i. 8.   [3] i. 24.   [4] ii. 2.

[5] iv. 1.   [6] iv. 19.

Second Epistle to the Corinthians is equally full of proof of St. Paul's affection : "If we be afflicted it is for your encouragement";[1] "If I make you sorry, who then is he that maketh me glad?"[2] "My joy is the joy of you all";[3] "Our mouth is opened unto you, O Corinthians, our heart is enlarged";[4] "Open your hearts to us";[5] "I will gladly spend and be spent for your souls."[6] In other Epistles we find similar evidence of the same spirit."[7]

We must remember that this love of St. Paul's for those for whom he works is that of an intelligent father, or mother, or brother. We are told of the "blindness" of love. But "it is not love but passion which is blind." If true love ever is blind, it is so in reference to what those who have it not regard as impossibilities in those they profess to love. It is not blind to defects, and it is quite clear about its aims for those who are loved. It also knows what is possible for them, and it knows upon what the realisation of these possibilities depends. To St. Paul men and women can only become what they may be through their reception and assimilation of all that is meant by the "grace of Christ." "The true enthusiasm of humanity is inspired by the Christian faith. This faith in the power of grace and

---

[1] i. 6. [2] ii. 2. [3] ii. 3.
[4] vi. 11. [5] vii. 2. [6] xii. 15.
[7] *e.g.* 1 Thess. ii. 7, 8, 19, iii. 8 ; Rom. ix. 1 ff., etc.

in the possibility of spiritual growth is a great
stimulus to interest in men."[1]   Therefore, as we
have seen, while St. Paul loves he teaches, and
he "forms"; at the cost of personal self-sacrifice
he provides the materials, the guidance, the circumstances for growth; he also admonishes and
warns, and, when necessary, he rebukes with
sternness.

To do this last service of love wisely, that is
skilfully, is perhaps the most difficult of all the
tasks which falls to the lot of the pastor; but it
cannot be shirked.   Upon *how* to rebuke we may
learn much from St. Paul.   At the same time we
must remember that his extant writings (except
the Epistle to Philemon and possibly the Pastoral
Epistles) are *public* documents to be read in
public.   And even from his reticence in the
Epistles to the Corinthians we can see that St.
Paul would have echoed our Lord's admonition,
"If thy brother sin against thee, go, show him
his fault between thee and him, alone; if
he hear thee, thou hast gained thy brother."[2]
When occasion demanded, St. Paul, like our Lord,
could rebuke with severity.[3]   But St. Paul saw

---

[1] Jordan, *The Philippian Gospel*, p. 54.

[2] St. Matt. xviii. 15.   1 Tim. v. 20, τοὺς ἁμαρτάνοντας κ.τ.λ., does
not contradict this.   Those sinning are presbyters, men holding a
position of responsibility.   Timothy would then act as the representative of the Church, as the guardian of its discipline.   πάντων
means "all the presbyters."

[3] 1 Cor. v. 1 ff., vi. 1 ff.

the danger of unmeasured rebuke. He recognised that the Christian rebukes, not simply to punish, but to reform ; not to harm, but to save. St. Paul's object, which must also be ours, was to separate the sin from the sinner,[1] to destroy the first while he saved the second.[2] His advice to Timothy must be remembered : " Reprove (bring home to the conscience), rebuke, exhort, and do all, and not only the last, ἐν πάσῃ μακροθυμίᾳ for ἡ ἀγάπη μακροθυμεῖ."[3]

One of our greatest temptations is not to rebuke at all. But this is a distinct dereliction of an obvious duty.[4] No authority from St. Paul can be quoted for such a treatment either of sin or of the sinner. He is far too conscious of the destructiveness of sin, of its tendency to rapid growth, and of its infectiousness—" A little leaven leaveneth the whole lump."[5] One way in which we may often administer a rebuke with effect is indicated in 2 Thess. iii. 14,[6] τοῦτον σημειοῦσθε (show your disapprobation of him), μὴ συναναμίγνυσθαι αὐτῷ (so as not to mix freely with him). The one of whose conduct we disapprove is not to be entirely

---

[1] Note the primary meaning of ἄφεσις.   [2] 2 Cor. ii. 6, 7.

[3] 2 Tim. iv. 2. ἔλεξον, "ein Appell an das Bewusstsein." Von Soden.

[4]   " We bid wrong be done
      When evil deeds have their permissive pass,
      And not the punishment."

[5] Gal. v. 9. Leaven as a symbol of evil. From ζύμη, our English "zymotic" for a class of disease.

[6] Every word should be noticed.

shunned, but the *manner* of our intercourse with him must not be that which we pursue with the blameless ; ἵνα ἐντραπῇ, so that he may feel ashamed ; καὶ μὴ ὡς ἐχθρὸν ἡγεῖσθε, upon which Bengel's comment is, " Ubique cavetur ne in extrema incidiamus " ; ἀλλὰ νουθετεῖτε ὡς ἀδελφόν, this last duty must not be forgotten.   Because if we treat a person differently from what we treat others, he should know the reason of our conduct.[1]

A second temptation in rebuking others is to think only of the offence, of the wrong done, and to forget the particular nature or circumstances (*e.g.* temptations) of the wrong-doer in question. The success of one physician over another in effecting a cure is not always due to a superior scientific knowledge of the nature and usual course or action of the disease.   It is often rather due to greater insight into the nature and character of the patient.   If the study of character and of the idiosyncrasies of human nature is essential to the physician of the body, it is still more essential to those who would act as physicians of souls.[2]   That St. Paul was a keen and careful student of character, and that he knew well that "medicamentum, quod hunc

---

[1] " Scire debet, cur id fiat," says Bengel.

[2] The greater attention being paid by the medical profession to the study of psychology should be an example to the clergy. Cp. Chrysostom (*De Sacerd.* ii. 4), " διὰ τοῦτο πολλῆς δεῖ τῆς συνέσεως τῷ ποιμένι καὶ μυρίων ὀφθαλμῶν, πρὸς τὸ περισκοπεῖν πάντοθεν τὴν τῆς ψυχῆς ἕξιν."

morbum imminuit, alteri vires jungit,"[1] we have
many proofs. For example, his exhortation in
I Thess. v. 14, "Admonish the disorderly, encourage the faint-hearted, support the weak," and
also his whole treatment of the strong and weak
brethren in Rom. xiv. and xv., are proofs of this.

There is one other temptation to the minister
which I must notice, viz. to consider actions to
be seriously wrong because they are unpleasant to
him, or cause him serious personal inconvenience,
or pecuniary loss, or even because they wound
his personal pride. He is even apt to measure
their wickedness by the degree of their personal
unpleasantness. The apparent magnitude of
objects, especially of mental objects, and even of
sins and "offences," varies according to their
nearness or distance from ourselves. There is
much to be learnt from St. Paul's words, οὐκ ἐμὲ
λελύπηκεν, in 2 Cor. ii. 5. Thus the true pastor,
who loves souls, who is inspired by the spirit of
the *Paster Bonus*, will neither be blind to the sins
of his flock, nor will he fail to rebuke these when
he sees that rebuke is necessary. But in this,
as in all other efforts on their behalf, his method
will be governed by this golden rule of St. Paul,
Omnia ad aedificationem fiant.

But a true love of souls will do more than

---

[1] Greg. *Regul. Pastoral.* Pars. iii. Prolog. The whole of the
third part of Gregory's manual is an amplification of this exhortation.

rebuke blemishes, it will warn against dangers
and seek to remove these;[1] it will also teach, so
that life may enjoy increased means and opportunities for development.

With the pastor's efforts to warn and to teach
I have already dealt. Here I need only add that
no true pastor will be content with a mere general
admonition, such as that given in a sermon. He
will, from his knowledge of his flock, know where
from time to time a word of personal warning,
one given in a kindly and sympathetic spirit, is
necessary. Here, too, as in public admonition, he
will do it ἐν πάσῃ σοφίᾳ.

The chief point to remember is that in all our
efforts to help and to save souls, from " the love
of souls," we must keep our object and purpose
absolutely clear. That object is to help men to
grow into the likeness of Christ—to realise Christ
in their lives, and this, we must impress upon
them, can only be done by the putting away of
sin.[2] Hence sin is the deadly enemy of the true
Christian pastor; and sin may be viewed under
many aspects, for it takes many forms.[3]

---

[1] " The Church has been too content to do ambulance work. The
office of the Good Samaritan is thoroughly Christian, but we must
do all we can to make the road from Jericho to Jerusalem more
safe for the traveller." Shailer Mathews, *The Church and the
Changing Order*.

[2] Heb. ix. 26. By us, as by Christ, this can only be accomplished at the cost of personal self-sacrifice, which we can only
make " in Him."

[3] After giving (on p. 231) a list of terms for sin, Trench (*N.T.*

This is not a treatise upon either the ethics or the doctrine (the theology) of St. Paul. It is outside the range of my purpose to deal, except indirectly, with these, and they cannot be separated except as phenomena and explanation. I cannot therefore enter upon a study of St. Paul's doctrine of "sin," or "salvation," or "redemption," or "reconciliation," or "justification," or "sanctification," or "grace." But the pastor who would learn how to combat sin will not be ignorant of any of these, for a knowledge of each doctrine, and skill in the application of each, is a valuable weapon in the hand of the Christian warrior. When St. Paul attacked sin he did so "with a very definite theology at his back." The Christian teacher, like the officer in the army, needs to-day a "scientific training": he must know the nature of the weapons of his warfare, and he must be trained to use them skilfully. In one sense these weapons are the same to-day as they have been in all the ages of the Christian warfare.[1] But in another sense they have changed and developed, as have the weapons and the tactics of the enemy, from age to age.[2] Here we can see an analogy with the development of the weapons used in physical warfare and with

---

Synonyms) remarks : "A mournfully numerous group of words which it would be only too easy to make larger still."

[1] Eph. vi. 10 ff.

[2] To the student of history many of our present enemies are "old foes with a new face."

the weapons used by the physician and surgeon in their warfare against disease. What we have to remember is that the love of souls implies not only the reality of sin but the warfare against sin. It is forgetfulness of these two truths which makes much of our so-called philanthropy so ineffective.

A careful study of the 1st chapter of St. Paul's Epistle to the Romans will show us that to St. Paul the love of souls (those "in Rome" are "Beloved of God" and "called to be saints") is quite unthinkable apart from a warfare against the dangers from sin which encompass men living in the world. St. Paul's object is to produce in men that "obedience" which proceeds from faith in Christ. This obedience is at once the condition of the righteous or ideal life, and a synonym for that life. St. Paul longs to visit the Christians in Rome; he wants to help them; he is ready to preach the gospel to them, for the gospel is the Divinely appointed power unto salvation (moral safety or safety from sin[1]), because therein a Divine righteousness is being revealed. At once St. Paul, in his letter, turns to the other side of experience—"the wrath of God is also now being revealed"—as clear as the daylight to those who

---

[1] "The fundamental idea contained in σωτηρία is the removal of dangers menacing to life, and the consequent placing of life in conditions favourable to free and healthy expansion." In the N.T. σωτηρία "covers the whole range of the Messianic deliverance." Sanday and Headlam, *Romans*, pp. 23, 24.

will see—"against every kind and instance of ἀσέβεια against God and of ἀδικία against man, against men who hinder the Truth from doing its appointed work."[1]

If, then, our hearts are filled as was St. Paul's with a true love of souls, with an earnest desire to see men and women what they may become, and if we are convinced that only through faith in Christ, leading to obedience to Christ, and issuing in union with Christ, can they become so, then we must not only proclaim God's wrath upon sin, we must in word and in deed fight against sin with all our powers.

Suppose we could remove from our parishes the drink, the impurity, the dishonesty, the oppression, the idleness, and other evils which are simply and solely the results of sin ; in other words, suppose we could remove the evils *which are not inevitable*, we should then hardly recognise the places in which we live.[2] Conditions which at present are a veritable hell, and lives which actually now seem to be literally living in hell, and upon which "the wrath of God" seems to have "come to the uttermost,"[3] would both be transformed.

---

[1] "Men held down the truth in unrighteousness, they restrained it from having free course in their hearts and in the world, because of the painful moral obligations which it involves."

[2] To help to bring about these changes must be the reason for the clergy taking part in work which has for its object the improvement of the conditions of the people.

[3] 1 Thess. ii. 16.

Are we, from our "love of souls," as careful as St. Paul was to state both sides of the Divine revelation? Is our warfare against sin as earnest as our teaching about righteousness? When we see rich and influential men making fortunes out of the means and the promotion of sin, are we brave enough to speak to them of "the wrath of God"? When sin, with all its attendant misery, enters our own homes, we are indeed wroth with those who have caused its entrance there. Are we equally inimical to what is around us destroying the souls committed to our pastoral care? Dare we speak to-day in the strain and with the accent with which St. Paul wrote in the 2nd chapter of the Epistle to the Romans? Dare we speak to men who promote sin of their "treasuring up for themselves wrath in the day of wrath and revelation of the righteous judgment of God"?

Truly, in his love for souls, in his hatred of sin, and in his warfare against all that is destructive of the souls for whom Christ died, St. Paul is (if we will only learn from him) a wonderful inspiration and example.

Chapter 6

THE MOTIVE POWER OF MINISTRY

μείνατε ἐν τῇ ἀγάπῃ τῇ ἐμῇ.—JOHN xv. 9.

αὕτη ἐστὶν ἡ ἐντολὴ ἡ ἐμὴ ἵνα ἀγαπᾶτε ἀλλήλους καθὼς ἠγάπησα ὑμᾶς.—JOHN xv. 12.

Si volumus commendare nos Deo, caritatem habeamus.— AMBROSE, *De Off. Ministr.* ii. 27.

THERE are certain chapters in St. Paul's Epistles which acquire a clearer and deeper meaning when we read them in the light of his pastoral spirit [1] and as the result of his ministerial experience. Such a chapter is this 13th of First Corinthians.

The chapter must be studied in close connection with those which immediately precede and follow it—the 12th and the 14th—for these three chapters have one subject, the endowment of the Church and its members.

In the 12th chapter, whilst the unity of the

---

[1] The spirit which has been defined as " the love of souls," or as " the enthusiasm of humanity." See the previous chapter on " The Love of Souls," p. 221 ff.

Ecclesia is constantly asserted, the prevailing thought is of the *diversities* (διαιρέσεις), first of gifts or endowments (χαρίσματα), secondly of services (διακονίαι), thirdly of effectual operations (ἐνεργήματα). But the highest endowments may be so utilised, and the most earnest service of various kinds may be so pursued, as to have a selfish object; while the more effectual our operations the greater is often the danger of their ministering to personal pride. The possessor of some fine endowment in a high degree may cultivate that endowment as an end in itself. We know what the pursuit of art simply for "art's sake" means. Ceaseless activity in any kind of service may actually become a fetish, and in itself a cause of self-esteem;[1] while effectiveness may be exercised in opposition to Christ as well as on His behalf. Again, there are such things as rivalries of gifts, and between methods or forms of service. We have all seen the undue depreciation of one, the unwise exaltation of another. Indeed, the history of the troubles of the Church from its earliest days is a painful commentary upon the exercise of the gifts and activities described in this 12th chapter, regardless of one essential condition.

The final words of that chapter demand attention. St. Paul asserts that although the

---

[1] Preachers will boast of the *number* of the sermons they have preached, pastors of the *number* of calls they have paid!

lowest gifts have their place in the Church, and whilst opportunity may be found for exercising them, it is our duty to aim at possessing the highest.[1] Then, again, whilst every personal endowment is a "gift" of God, we must remember that our own effort is necessary, if we would fully participate in the higher endowments. We are also responsible for the right use of all. Finally St. Paul adds, "And I proceed to show you a way beyond all comparison [2] the best." By "way" I think St. Paul means a determining and impelling and controlling principle and motive. What he is demanding is the Christianising, that is the highest moralising of the gifts by their being motived, inspired, and consecrated by LOVE.

It is not necessary to dwell upon the meaning of ἀγάπη.[3] The chief point to remember is that here love is not regarded as a "gift" to be *compared* with other gifts, it is rather a spirit, or temper,[4] in which all gifts are to be used or exercised. St. Paul constantly speaks of the Christian as a man or woman "in Christ,"[5] or as one in whom Christ dwells. If love is a synonym

---

[1] Possibly St. Stephen may be cited as an example.

[2] καθ᾽ ὑπερβολὴν ὁδόν.

[3] See especially Sanday and Headlam, *Romans*, pp. 376, 377. Note that "love is the correlative in the moral world to what faith is in the religious life."

[4] Christianity itself has been defined as a certain "temper."

[5] Upon this expression, so common in St. Paul, and whose meaning is so vital for understanding his teaching, see Deissmann's *Die neutestamentliche Formel " in Christo Jesu."*

for the spirit and motive of Christ, when we say that all these gifts have to be exercised and used *with*, or *in*, love, we mean that they have to be exercised "in Christ." Just as to be "in Christ" infinitely moralises the whole life, so to exercise a gift "in love" infinitely moralises its use and exercise.

Verse 1. "If I speak with the tongues of men, even of angels, and have not love, I have become (mere) sounding brass or a clanging cymbal."

St. Paul's first application of his great principle refers to the use of "tongues"—a gift of ecstatic, and probably highly emotional utterance, and evidently very highly prized by the Corinthians. St. Paul at once refuses to consider the gift apart from the personality through which it is exercised. If that personality is not motived by love the speaker has become a mere instrument of sound without moral (or spiritual) character. Two applications at once suggest themselves : first, to what is termed *popular* preaching, however eloquent and clever, which does not proceed from a Christianised heart, which is not inspired by the love of souls, and whose object is not the salvation or edification of men ; secondly, to the emotional singing of hymns whose words, if studied carefully apart from the music, are seen to be either heresy or nonsense, if they do not come perilously near to blasphemy.

Verse 2. "Even if I have [the gift of] prophecy

and know all the mysteries and the whole of knowledge, even if I have such complete faith as [to be able] to remove mountains and have not love, I am nothing."

St. Paul here passes on to the higher gifts: first, of prophecy, revelation, and knowledge (the powers of interpretation and exhortation depending on spiritual insight and large possessions of knowledge); secondly, of faith, which may be regarded as conferring personal ability or influence to so great a degree as to enable one "to accomplish the apparently impossible."[1] The world may bestow great praise upon me and my achievements, but, in the judgment of God, by Whom alone true appraisement is possible, I am without significance, I am of no value, if the all-important spirit and motive and purpose be wanting. The need of moralising, of consecrating to Christ's service the highest powers and possessions of the intellect, as well as all that personal influence can mean, is a lesson which this age must learn. That such spiritual[2] endowments as prophecy and faith can be misused should cause the minister of Christ deep reflection. Yet St. Paul is only asserting what our Lord taught in the Sermon on the Mount.[3] There our Lord implies that we may both prophesy and do mighty works (by the power of faith) actually "in His Name,"

---

[1] Meyer *in loc.*   [2] Chap. xii. 9 and 10.

[3] St. Matt. vii. 21, 22.

without doing the will of God. To do that will as He did it we must be inspired by His spirit of love.

Verse 3. "Even if I 'dole out in food' the whole of my substance, even if I sacrifice my body, that I may boast,[1] and have not love, I am in no way profited."[2]

Now St. Paul passes to a counterfeit of love. Actions which externally seem to be the very mirror of what Christ did may be of no profit to us. The history of Christendom will supply many an example and proof of the truth which St. Paul here states. We may dole out all we possess, we may even sacrifice our physical life ; what are termed "charity" and asceticism may be pursued actually without limit, yet, if our motive be wrong, if the personality through which these are accomplished be unmoralised by love, the doer shall be "without profit." The warning in these words of St. Paul is capable of wide application for the ministerial life. "Charity" and asceticism are practically indispensable character-making instruments, and by continual practice we may train ourselves to the exercise of both to a high degree ; but the moment they have reference to self as their *ultimate* purpose, they cease to be

---

[1] Westcott and Hort with ℵ A B read ἵνα καυχήσωμαι (so marg. of R.V.) : parallels to St. Paul's language about boasting will be found in Ignatius, *ad Polycarp*, cap. v., also in Clem. *ad Cor.* xxxviii.

[2] The change from οὐθέν εἰμι to οὐδὲν ὠφελοῦμαι should be noticed.

of moral value.   Those who have had much to do with either the collection or distribution of "charity" know how often it is given as a salve to conscience, because the donor "feels happier for having given."   To give from a sense of duty is very different.   But to bestow charity that it may minister to our satisfaction, or, possibly, that our action in so doing may win for us the approbation of others or public recognition, is fatal to ourselves. Charity was given, asceticism was practised, even martyrdom was actually courted in the early ages as passports to heaven.   This view of charity may have passed into the Church from the later Judaism, in which almsgiving actually became a synonym for righteousness.[1]   The propitiatory value of asceticism in itself, even of self-immolation or desire for martyrdom, were ideas which the Church assimilated from heathenism.   From self-sacrifice for the sake of others, inspired by a genuine love for God and man, these practices were in spirit widely different.

Verses 4–7.   "Love suffereth long, is kind. Love is never[2] envious, never boastful, never puffed up, never behaves unbecomingly, is never self-seeking, never exasperated, never reckoneth up her wrongs, never rejoiceth at unrighteousness, but

---

[1] See Hatch's *Essays in Biblical Greek*, pp. 49–51, where both the O.T. and N.T. uses are fully discussed.

[2] By the insertion of "never" and "always," we get the full force of the present tenses.

rejoiceth with the truth.   [Love] is always bearing, always believing, always hoping, always patient."

These four verses must be taken together. In them "Love" is personified, much in the same way as "Wisdom" is personified in Proverbs viii., but with a difference. The qualities of wisdom are intellectual and moral, those of love are entirely moral,[1] and are the qualities specially characteristic of the human nature of our Lord.[2] This last fact is the keynote to St. Paul's teaching and that which makes love in this chapter synonymous with "Christianity." Our ministerial life must be modelled upon the ministerial life of Jesus, it must be wholly inspired by His spirit, His motive power, and final purpose; hence the qualities— the ethical virtues—described and suggested in these verses, are the virtues with which our life as His ministers must be suffused and which we must, in conduct, express. This makes every one of these assertions of St. Paul of quite exceptional importance. Yet though there is in the passage no direct reference to intellectual gifts, the qualities here enumerated are essential

---

[1] An interesting example of the moralising of every faculty and function of life by Christianity.

[2] "We have but to substitute 'Jesus' for 'love,' the person for the thing personified, and Paul's panegyric becomes a simple and perfect description of the historic Jesus. As a literal portrayal of the character of Jesus it cannot be surpassed." *The Fifth Gospel*, p. 153.

for a truly Christian use of such gifts, and probably, as he was writing, St. Paul had in his mind the want of these qualities in the way the members of the Corinthian Church used their intellectual endowments. St. Paul's words should always remind us of "how close a connection subsists between the right and effective use of intellectual gifts and the moral and spiritual state of the heart."[1]

When we turn to a consideration of the actual words used by St. Paul, we notice at once how difficult it is, except by paraphrase, to give in English an adequate rendering of the original. The Divine nature and origin of μακροθυμία is asserted in St. Luke xviii. 7.[2] If we might use the word, as we use its opposite, it is "long-tempered." To this somewhat passive quality is added the active χρηστότης,[3] which is also referred to as a Divine quality in Tit. iii. 4. Both these qualities must frequently be exercised by the minister of Christ when he is sorely tempted to act otherwise.[4] No one knew better than St. Paul the trial of dealing

---

[1] T. C. Edwards *in loc.*

[2] The moral character of the Father and Christ are one. St. John x. 30, xiv. 9.

[3] The words occur together in Gal. v. 22. "*Longanimis* est in malo ab aliis profecto ; *benignus*, in bono ad alios propagando." Bengel *in loc.*

[4] Chrysostom (*De Sacerdotio*, iii. 13) has some excellent advice on the necessity for the minister of Christ being one who is not easily made angry.

with ἄτοποι ἄνθρωποι.[1] The life of our Lord is one long witness to the virtues here attributed by St. Paul to love.

Those who have had long and wide experience of the ministerial life, and who are quite honest with themselves, know how peculiarly liable it is to the next four temptations to which St. Paul asserts that love does not succumb. ἡ ἀγάπη οὐ ζηλοῖ, οὐ περπερεύεται,[2] οὐ φυσιοῦται, οὐκ ἀσχημονεῖ. "Love never envies." To some men what is termed "success" seems to come early and in large measure, and sometimes, especially in the English Church (where "patronage" is in so many different and (occasionally) irresponsible hands), what is apt to be regarded as "success" cannot always be said to be deserved. Then the hard and earnest worker who toils, often for many years, with little or no "recognition" of his work, may be tempted to "envy."

Of the next two words the first seems mainly to refer to manner and the second to disposition. Both are the temptations of the successful, or of those who presume upon or are proud of their position. The first might be rendered "soundeth its own praises," or "acts with

---

[1] 2 Thess. iii. 2.

[2] Vulg., "non agit perperam." About the exact significance of the word there seems to be some doubt. In Marc. Aurel. v. 5 περπερεύεσθαι follows ἀρεσκεύεσθαι.

ostentation," and perhaps especially in the way of speech : the second seems rather to have reference to the feeling of which the speech or manner is the expression ; " conceited " is probably not a bad English representative for the original. Unfortunately, the clergy in country villages or poor parishes are constantly tempted mentally to measure themselves with those whose advantages have been very small ; they rarely have the opportunity of coming into close contact with those who in education and attainments are greatly superior to themselves. They must remember the law which seems to state that it is dangerous to a man's character for him to live almost entirely in the society of those whom he is tempted to regard as beneath him.[1] To live for long with impunity in this position requires a peculiarly careful self-discipline. Of all men he should maintain through the best literature a constant converse with intellects and powers greater than his own.

The last word of the four, ἀσχημονεῖ, is one of wide application.[2] We may yield to the

---

[1] A frequent instance of this is seen in Europeans who live among and have to deal with what are termed the inferior races.

[2] Under this head we may place a whole gradually-descending group of tendencies, from simple thoughtlessness to the most aggravated and worst forms of impurity and lust. The root-idea of ἀσχήμων is " deformed." In the N.T. there seems to be in every instance a connection, close or distant, with weaknesses or sins of the flesh. In I Cor. xii. 23 the Vulgate renders τὰ

temptation to "unseemliness" in many ways
and to very various degrees. But unseemliness of behaviour is always selfish and therefore
essentially unchristian. As selfish, it is radi-
cally opposed to love. It is wholly inconsistent
with the love of souls, for its tendency is to
destroy instead of to save. In any want of
"seemliness" in conduct there is a want of
σοφία. The true corrective is given in Eph.
v. 15, "Look therefore carefully how ye walk
(ἀκριβῶς), not as · men unskilled in the true
art and practice of conduct, but as men skilled
therein."

In verse 5 we have three more temptations
which love overcomes. First, "Love is never
'self-seeking,'"[1] but rather is always "other-
seeking"; it is infinitely altruistic, as was
Christ. The picture of what Christ did, in

ἀσχήμονα by *quæ inhonesta*; in Rom. i. 27, τὴν ἀσχημοσύνην is
translated *turpitudinem*. There is a warning of Chrysostom
(though used in a different connection) which it is well for a
pastor to bear in mind in all intercourse with women, πλείστης
οὖν κἀνταῦθα δεῖ τῆς ἀκριβείας, ὥστε μὴ τὴν τῆς ὠφελείας ὑπόθεσιν
μείζονος αὐτῷ γενέσθαι ζημίας ἀφορμήν (*De Sacerdotio*, iii. 18). For
a much wider use of ἀσχημοσύνη, see Plato, *Repub.* iii. 401 A.
(where it is opposed to both σώφρων and ἀγαθός).

See an admirable chapter in Bishop Moule's *To my Younger
Brethren*, on "The Daily Walk with Others" (ii.), where he writes :
"We clergy are *trusted* to an extraordinary degree in personal
intercourse with female parishioners. . . . Do not think a strong
word of caution in this matter out of place and out of scale.
Carelessness of even appearances here may wreck a life ; it may
certainly blight an influence."

[1] *Non studet sibi*, nec sibi ab aliis studeri postulat. Bengel.

Phil. ii. 5 ff., and which follows the exhortation "not looking each of you to his own things," is the ideal example of this activity of love. In this Epistle (x. 33) St. Paul puts before us his own practice, "not seeking mine own profit, but that of the many." To make a ministry for Christ an occasion for self-profit or self-advancement is at once to make it unchristlike. The world, from its familiarity with the object of self-profit, is quick to detect this spirit in the ministry. Where it is detected the pure love for Christ and righteousness is questioned. The influence of the ministry for good is weakened, if not lost.

Secondly, "Love is never easily provoked," *i.e.* to anger. For the wrath of a man worketh not the righteousness of God,[1] whose promotion and increase is the object of those who work for Christ. Again and again is ministerial work spoiled and ministerial influence lessened by faults of temper.[2] Herein lies one of the

---

[1] Jas. iii. 20. "The thought that it is God's righteousness brings out the absurdity of man's hoping to effect it by mere passion." Mayor *in loc.*

[2] See an admirable address by the late Dean Church on "Temper," delivered to the Junior Clergy Society, and printed in *Cathedral and University Sermons*, pp. 194 ff. We may also remember these words of Chrysostom. "θυμὸς δὲ ἄγριος εἴς τε τὸν κεκτημένον εἴς τε τοὺς πλησίον μεγάλας ἐργάζεται συμφοράς." *De Sacerd.* iii. 13. To the objection that sometimes "it is impossible to keep your temper" reply, Der Mensch kann was er soll; und wenn er sagt er kann nicht, so will er nicht. *Ars Pastoria*, p. 4.

greatest of all needs for constant self-discipline. We do not show temper towards those we regard as our superiors; why should we show it towards our equals, or towards those whom we are inclined to regard as our "inferiors"?

Thirdly, "Love never reckoneth up its wrongs" (οὐ λογίζεται τὸ κακόν). The Greek is capable of more than one rendering. "Taketh not account of evil" is that of the Revised Version, which, in substance, is not very different from the one I have adopted. "Love does not make a mental note and lay up in its memory the contempt shown by one, the indifference shown by another, the intention to wound betrayed by a third."[1] To allow ourselves to act in this way is to defeat the end of our ministry; we seek fellowship with men for their good; we must be careful not to interpose a barrier between ourselves and them, or to take away from ourselves the opportunity for effecting our purpose. To be misunderstood and to be thwarted was the daily experience of our Master; St. Paul also constantly suffered in this respect. Shall we expect to escape it?

In verse 6 we are told that " Love never rejoiceth at [or over] unrighteousness," but always "rejoiceth with the truth." The first assertion points to a most subtle form of temptation. The words could only have been written by one who had a

---

[1] Marcus Dods' *First Corinthians*, p. 302.

deep insight into both human nature and the peculiar temptation of those who are placed in a position of some relative importance. Frequently it happens that one man rises through the fall of another. In business, in politics, in professional life men "make mistakes," they are guilty of follies, it may be they commit crimes, in consequence their reputation is lost: then comes the opportunity of their competitors. Unfortunately such an experience is not wholly unknown within the ministry. But what of the conscience of a minister of Christ who could secretly rejoice at the failure of a fellow-minister?[1] We surely ought to regard every "failure" of a minister of Christ, from whatever cause it may happen, as the failure of a champion of righteousness. His defeat is consequently a victory for unrighteousness. Which of these is our object —personal advancement and success or the advancement of righteousness? It is the entering in of the fatal suggestion of possible self-advancement that can alone make St. Paul's assertion applicable to the ministry. But he who knows his own heart, or anything of the hearts of others, knows only too well how Satan with his wiles will undermine and

---

[1] Upon the "rocks" on which the ministry may be wrecked Chrysostom adduces "ἡδοναὶ ἐπὶ ταῖς τῶν συλλειτουργούντων ἀσχημοσύναις, πένθος ἐπὶ ταῖς εὐημερίαις, ἐπαίνων ἔρως, τιμῆς πόθος (τοῦτο δὴ τὸ μάλιστα πάντων τὴν ἀνθρωπείαν ἐκτραχηλίζον ψυχήν). de Sacerd. iii. 9.

attack spheres which should be strongholds for Christ.

The opposite spirit of mind is always to rejoice with the truth. These words suggest many applications. It may not be over-refinement to see a contrast in χαίρει and συνχαίρει, the first being personal and selfish, the second the feeling of true joy, social joy. Again, the opposition of ἀδικία and ἀλήθεια is suggestive.[1] Here, as so often in the New Testament, ἀλήθεια approaches in meaning "the ideal"—that which is meant to be. If St. Paul, as we may well suppose, was familiar with Christ's designation of Himself as the "Truth," the words at once suggest mutual, combined rejoicing at the onward progress of the work and cause of Christ, whatever that progress may personally cost us.[2] Another application is as follows:—The "truth" may have an intellectual reference. We may have "pinned our faith" to some theory or doctrine or interpretation. Further knowledge, gained by others, may have thrown at least a doubt, if it has not wholly discredited our own interpretation. It may require no small amount of self-sacrifice and humility on our part to own that we are wrong, to give up our views which may have become widely known, and upon which, in all good faith and earnestness, we may have laid much stress in

---

[1] ἀλήθεια and ἀδικία are contrasted in Rom. ii. 8.

[2] St. John iii. 26 ff.

public. But the Truth, and the progress of the Truth, must be first, and unselfishness — true love — bids us, not merely give up our own views, but actually rejoice, though at our own discomfiture, that Truth has been advanced. I must not give other applications, though many a curious page of history supplies evidence of the apparent inability of men called to the ministry of Christ, and having a desire to further its work, to "rejoice with the truth."

In verse 7 we have four more activities of love. It always "bears," always trusts, always hopes, is always patient. In each case the range of love's activity, whether intensively or extensively conceived, is defined by πάντα. Love has no limit, it neither knows nor makes exceptions. στέγει is doubtless capable of a double interpretation— either "hides" or "bears not resentment" (vulg. *suffert*). This latter interpretation is probably correct. If so, then the difference between it and ὑπομένει will be that between refusing to be crushed by a superimposed weight and refusing to cease holding out against some opposing force. The verse may be said to emphasise the strength of love under four aspects, thus " Love carries an infinite burden, has infinite faith, infinite hope, infinite endurance." All these four virtues are essential requisites for ministerial work. Without these, service to Christ cannot be adequately rendered. The four words which follow gather up the results of the four virtues, and express these as one, ἡ ἀγάπη οὐδέποτε πίπτει. The strength of love is infinite, therefore love never faileth. The four previous clauses may be otherwise expressed thus :—To the burden it will bear, to the faith it possesses, to the hope which inspires it, to the endurance it exercises, love refuses to put a limit. We remember how St. Peter once asked our Lord about the limit of our forgiveness, and the answer he received.[1] Here again causes of failure to live the true life of Christian service are clearly revealed. We either shun or sink under burdens far too easily ; we need an increase of faith—based upon an increased knowledge of God in Christ ; we are not sufficiently "hopeful" ;[2] the limit of our patience and endurance is far too soon reached. To understand the words "love never faileth" we must remember that the same man who wrote them wrote also, "I can do all things in Him Who strengtheneth me."[3] These words must be understood to imply the imperishable nature of the strength of Christ. Love is as imperishable as its source. Christ is love personified, and as long as the Person remains so must that which

---

[1] St. Matt. xviii. 21 ff.

[2] If I may paraphrase a well-known saying of Bishop Lightfoot's : A wider knowledge of what God has done among men, for them and through them, should be a "rare cordial" to those who are inclined to have little hope.

[3] Phil. iv. 13.

He personifies. " I and my Father are one,"
and " God is love." So the chain is complete.
The exhortation may be quite simply expressed,
We must have more of Christ, more of the
Divine in our ministry, and therefore in ourselves.

Verse 8. " But whether there be prophecies,
they shall be brought to an end ;[1] whether there
be tongues, they shall cease ; whether there be
knowledge, it (too) shall be brought to an end."

The permanence of love, the essential nature
and characteristic of Christ, is here contrasted
with the temporal nature of the charismata,
which, as various gifts and manifestations and
modes of operation of the One Spirit (of Christ),
are temporal according to the special need of
each. At the Parousia the need for all these will
have passed. Then, we may believe, the Divine
Love will find other modes and other channels
for its expression. For the sake of his argument
St. Paul is probably using the strongest examples
of which he could think. The Corinthians knew
how highly he prized prophecy, indeed more than
any other of the χαρίσματα properly so called.[2]
He knew how highly they prized the " glosso-
laliæ." Of the essential value, indeed necessity, of
γνῶσις there could be no doubt. Certainly the
Corinthians would not be inclined to admit it.

---

[1] καταργεῖν is a favourite word with St. Paul. Here it occurs four
times in four verses ; the contrast with ἡ ἀγάπη μένει is striking.

[2] I Cor. xiv. I ff.

In this verse there is a deep truth implied—one which it has been most difficult for the Church, and especially difficult for the ministry in every age to learn :—The all-important is the presence and the power of Christ in the Church, in the ministry, and in its work. The methods whereby that presence is manifested, and the particular form of the channels whereby the power is conveyed, and the ways in which the work is done, are subject to change.[1] But history gives us proof after proof of the truth of St. Paul's teaching, from the days of Stephen down to the present time. Few lessons which the minister of Christ has to learn are harder, indeed more painful, than to discriminate between essentials and non-essentials, between the substance and the means whereby the substance is imparted.

Verses 9, 10. " For our knowledge is imperfect and our prophesying is imperfect, but when the perfect (state of things) is come, that which is imperfect shall be brought to an end."

Every word breathes the experience of the earnest minister of Christ ; every word should be an inspiration for ourselves. We must recognise how terribly imperfect is our know-

---

[1] The Gospel is not "a second Levitical Code." The N.T. is "full of principles of the most instructive kind ; but the responsibility of choosing the means was left for ever . . . to each Ecclesia, guided by ancient precedent on the one hand, and adaptation to present and future needs on the other." Hort, *Christian Ecclesia*, p. 232.

ledge, and therefore our interpretation and exhortation which is based upon it. To recognise this imperfection is the first step towards enlargement and improvement. Again the field of knowledge (and all knowledge, rightly regarded, is knowledge of God) is wide, and there are many workers therein. Surely it is well that the days even of pretension to encyclopedic knowledge have passed. Neither knowledge, nor truth, nor skill are the monopoly of any one body of workers,[1] nor indeed is the expression of these. Useful exhortation and inspiration may be based upon many a fragment of the truth, if only it be clearly recognised that it is but a fragment. The word ἔλθῃ in verse 10 should be noticed. St. Paul does not say "shall have come into being," but "shall have come," *i.e.* to us. That which we approach "comes" to us. Here again is a call for effort towards progress. If, as has been suggested, ἔλθῃ has a reference to the Parousia, the summons is still more urgent —to prepare ourselves and others for that which is approaching. We must also notice that though "Love" is not mentioned in these verses it is all the time present in the background, as the true motive power for desiring increase of knowledge, and improvement in exposition and power of exhortation.

---

[1] Job's sarcasm (xii. 2) should be remembered—

אָמְנָם כִּי אַתֶּם־עָם וְעִמָּכֶם תָּמוּת חָכְמָה ׃

Verse 11. "When I was a child I used to speak as a child, I had the mind of a child, I used to think as a child : since I have become a man I have put away childish things."

St. Paul's words are still full of the contrast between immaturity and maturity, of the need of progress, growth, and development. There is no shame in having been a child,[1] of having been marked by all that "childishness" suggests. But all which marks such a stage or condition must be left behind. Many references have been found in the words, for instance, to the prae-conversion and post-conversion periods of his life, to the *glossolalia* and the *gnosis*, but such references seem to be at least far-fetched. The words rather express an earnest exhortation to growth, and one capable of wide application. Essentially they enforce our Lord's condition, "except ye become as little children," etc.[2] ("Become," but not continue to be.) Except ye show both the possibility and the process of growth ye shall in no wise enter into the kingdom of God. I have more than once referred to our proofs of

---

[1] Many editors quote as a parallel—

> Sub nutrice puella velut si luderet infans,
> Quod cupide petiit, mature plena relinquit.

Hor. Ep. ii. i. 99.

But the following line surely better expresses St. Paul's thought—

> Nec lusisse pudet, sed non incidere ludum.

Ep. i. xiv. 36.

[2] St. Matt. xviii. 3 ff.

St. Paul's own growth as witnessed in his Epistles. And here, again, though not mentioned, the presence and power of love as the impulse to growth is implied. For love impels us to grow into clearer understanding of the One we love, into closer communion with Him. Even in the details of the verse there is a lesson. We must grow in our powers of expression. The minister should make effort after this—that he may make Christ more clearly manifest. We must also grow in our way of thinking,[1] in capacity and exercise of intelligence. Lastly, we must grow in the still deeper faculty of the reason, in ability to understand and justify to ourselves and others the ways of God. St. Paul might, when he wrote this chapter, see an immense difference between what he was then and what he had once been, but he was the last man to be content with or rest upon any present condition or achievements. Years after this he wrote οὐχ ὅτι ἤδη ἔλαβον ἢ ἤδη τετελείωμαι, διώκω δὲ εἰ καὶ καταλάβω ἐφ᾽ ᾧ καὶ κατελήμφθην [2] (by the urging, impelling, constraining, attracting power of love); so he adds,

Verse 12. " For now we see through [3] a mirror

---

[1] Meyer states the difference between ἐφρόνουν and ἐλογιζόμην to be that between "device and endeavour" on the one side and the reflective intelligence (Verstandesthätigkeit) on the other.

[2] Phil. iii. 12.

[3] The image is behind the mirror, so God is behind nature, and

obscurely (in a riddle), but then face to face ; now I know imperfectly, but then I shall know[1] as I am known."

These words express a very noble creed—the faith in which every earnest seeker after truth lives and works. And let us remember that this belief in the ultimate attainment of truth is again founded on conviction of the Divine Love. Only through the power of love will the process of truth seeking be so pursued that the object desired will be attained. This faith implies two conditions — humility[2] and love, which were perfectly fulfilled in Him who is the Truth, and Who, inspired by love, humbled Himself to come among men to "bear witness to the Truth." This faith must govern the life and conduct of every minister of Christ, and in both his life and his conduct these two conditions must be satisfied. And with him love of the truth must be seen to be synonymous with love of man, for both are love for the ideal for man, realised in man.

Verse 13. "And so faith, hope, love continue ; [only] these three, and of these the greatest is love."[3]

---

human life ; we see Him through the most perfect of all mirrors— the human life of Jesus. Cp. Rom. i. 20.

[1] Especially with reference to a moral knowledge in ἐπίγνωσις, see Westcott, *Ephesians*, p. 23.

[2] "A life devoted to truth is a life of vanities abased and ambitions forsworn." Dr. Hort, *The Way, the Truth, and the Life.*

[3] "Amor proximo plus *prodest*, quam fides et spes per se. Ac Deus non dicitur *fides* aut *spes* absolute, *amor* dicitur." Bengel *in loc.*

If faith means "trust," then our faith in God will be greater hereafter than now.   And as faith grows so will hope in which it issues, for we cannot but believe that the future will be what the present must be, a state of progress; and progress implies hope, as hope is the condition of progress.   Love will abide, for love is eternal, for God is love.

For ourselves these final words of the chapter, like so many other sayings of St. Paul, must be a standard and a mirror whereby we may examine ourselves.[1]   These are the three "theological"

---

[1] "To see the beauty, fruitfulness, and sufficiency of love is easy, but to have it as the mainspring of our own life most difficult, indeed the greatest of all our attainments.   This we instinctively recognise as the true test of our condition." M. Dods, *First Corinthians*, p. 308.

In one of the most beautiful pictures in the *Purgatorio* (Canto xxx. 22 ff.), where Beatrice and Dante meet in the Earthly Paradise, and Beatrice is clothed with the colours of the three "Theological" Virtues, it is interesting to notice that the sight and presence of Beatrice (who may represent Theology) seems to awaken in Dante the consciousness and exercise of these virtues.

> E lo spirito mio . . .
>
> .   .   .   .   .
>
> Per occulta virtù che da lei mosse
> D'antico amor senti la gran potenza.
> Tosto che nella vista mi percosse
> L'alta virtù, che già m'avea trafitto
> Prima ch'io fuor di puerizia fosse,
> Volsimi alla sinistra col rispitto
> Col quale il fantolin corre alla mamma
> Quando ha paura o quando egli e'affitto.

Here L'alta virtù may well be "hope," and rispitto seems to mean "trust."

virtues, and we must see that they remain with us and are in us. Apart from them we cannot do our work for Christ. We must have faith in God and in man, in man's possibilities and in God's purpose for man. We must have hope. Where it is wanting, or where it seems to be growing faint, there we must be shutting our eyes to what justifies it. Love is the one foundation and the one reason for our ministry ; it is the one motive power for all our service.

Chapter 7

THE PRAYERS OF PAUL

ἀδιαλείπτως προσεύχεσθε.—I THESS. v. 17.

τῇ προσευχῇ προσκαρτεροῦντες—ROM. xii. 13.

ἀδιαλείπτως μνείαν ὑμῶν ποιοῦμαι πάντοτε ἐπὶ τῶν προσευχῶν μου.—ROM. i. 9.

ἰδοὺ γὰρ προσεύχεται.—ACTS ix. 11.

THE prayers of every true Christian, could we hear them, would be of the nature of a self-revelation. They would reveal his conception of God, the quality of his faith in God, also his ideas of the possibilities of those for whom he prayed, including himself. They would be a revelation of his thoughts, his convictions, his aspirations, his intentions, his hopes, and also of his efforts. The true Christian prays before he works ; he prays for guidance, direction, and control, as well as for success. He also prays, while he works, for a constant renewal of strength to persevere. To him prayer and work are inseparable, for both are of the nature of communion with the Divine Will. In both prayer and work he loses himself ; he merges his personality in the Divine purpose, but only to find himself privileged to further that purpose more effectually. The greater a man's feeling of responsibility in life, and the more real his faith in God's guidance and strength, the more earnest will be his prayers.

All this must be specially true of the Christian minister, with his greater responsibilities, and his life dedicated to the learning, making known, and the promotion of God's purpose in the world. It was certainly true in a very special degree of St. Paul.

The immense change of spirit which came over him at his conversion is thus described, "Behold he prayeth." The words are extremely suggestive. Read in connection with their context they seem to say, "His whole attitude towards both God and man is changed." Not that Saul, the Pharisee, had been unused to pray. Like every pious Jew he had, probably three times daily, been accustomed to repeat at least the substance of the *Shemoneh Esreh*.[1] Nor would it be right to say that until his conversion St. Paul's prayers had been "conventional." Saul the Pharisee was far too earnest a man for that to be true of him. Perhaps the change in his prayers may be best explained by remembering his altered views of "righteous-

---

[1] שְׁמוֹנֶה עֶשְׂרֵה. Upon this see Schürer, *History of the Jewish People*, E.T. div. ii. vol. ii. pp. 85 ff., where a translation is given. See also Westcott, *Hebrews*, pp. 206 ff., where also is a translation.

ness "[1] the word which describes a man's con
ception of the right attitude to God.   Still it would
probably be true to say that had we asked St.
Paul the meaning of the words addressed to
Ananias[2] he would have replied, "Then for
the first time I knew what real prayer meant,
what it was intended to be."   The similarity in
such fundamental traits as zeal, earnestness, and
reality of St. Paul's character after and before his
conversion, needs no proof.   Indeed many of the
objects of his prayers in these two very different
periods of his life were probably identical.   It
was his *spirit* which became changed when his
conceptions of God's nature and of His relation
to men (as these were revealed to him in Jesus
Christ) were so entirely altered.

I shall not enter upon an investigation into the
Jewish, or early Christian conceptions of prayer, or
into the customs of prayer in St. Paul's day.   But
before examining the prayers in St. Paul's Epistles,
I would try to point out briefly, first, St. Paul's
conception of " prayer," and secondly the stress
which he laid upon it,—the importance he attached
to it.

1. In Acts xxii. 17, 18, St. Paul speaks of
himself as having been praying in the temple ;[3]
immediately afterwards he states how, while he
was so engaged, the Lord Jesus spoke to him.[4]

---

[1] Phil. iii. 9.
[2] Acts ix. 11.
[3] προσευχομένου μου ἐν τῷ ἱερῷ.
[4] ἰδεῖν αὐτὸν λέγοντά μοι.

Here prayer is regarded as a colloquy with the Divine.

In 1 Thess. i. 2, 3, we seem to have a wide interpretation given to prayer, "We give thanks to God unceasingly for you all, making mention of you at the time of (ἐπὶ) our prayers . . . in the presence of our God and Father."[1] The words "making mention" in Eph. i. 16 are immediately followed by "That the God of our Lord Jesus Christ . . . may grant to you a spirit of wisdom . . ." Hence "making mention" may be held to imply intercession[2] for something for those of whom he "makes mention." Thus "prayer" as used by St. Paul may be said to include thanksgiving, intercession, and consciousness of the presence of God, and of other's needs.

It is well known that the Shemoneh Esreh, with the substance or foundation of which, as I have said, St. Paul must have been familiar, is called *the* prayer,[3] and that it includes praise (blessing), confession of faith, prayer for knowledge, wisdom, understanding, etc., also supplication, and also execrations, though these last may be later than St. Paul's time.

In Rom. viii. 26, St. Paul speaks of the co-operation of the Holy Spirit in prayer, "The

---

[1] Bengel's note is ἔμπροσθεν = *coram*. constr. cum *recordantes*.

[2] See Armitage Robinson's note on μνείαν ποιούμενος, *Commentary on Ephesians* (Kregel Publications, 1979) p. 149.

[3] הַתְּפִלָּה.

Spirit also helpeth our infirmity, for we know not how to pray as we ought, but the Spirit Himself maketh intercessions for us, etc." In verse 7 of the same chapter we have the mind which is inimical to God ; in verse 9 we are told of those in whom the Spirit may dwell ; in verse 14 ff. we read " as many as are led by the Spirit of God, these are sons of God, etc." Putting these verses together we conclude that the chief object of prayer is to do the will of God.

In 1 Cor. xiv.[1] 14 ff. we read of the connection between prayer and the understanding : verse 14 seems to give an instance of what St. Paul means by "the edifying of the Church,"[2] and both blessing and thanksgiving[3] may, in the light of the passages previously quoted, be regarded as parts of "praying." All these instances show that St. Paul attached a wide meaning to what we term prayer.

2. The stress which St. Paul laid upon prayer, how important he considered it, is clear from the following passages :—

(1) Among the activities absolutely incumbent upon the Christian, described in the picture of the practical Christian life in Rom. xii., we have, " As far as your prayer is concerned be devoted."[4]

(2) Immediately following the description of the

---

[1] προσεύξομαι δὲ καὶ τῷ νόι.

[2] ἄκαρπος to be understood actively, μηδενὸς ὠφελουμένον (Basil).

[3] vv. 16, 17. See Westcott on the " Biblical Idea of Blessing," *Hebrews*, p. 209.

[4] τῇ προσευχῇ προσκαρτεροῦντες : the datives are datives of relation.

armour of the Christian warrior in Eph. vi. 11 ff.,
we have (in verse 18 f.) a rule for the use of this
armour.[1] It must be used in a certain spirit.
The Christian soldier "must use the vital powers
and instruments of warfare, which he has received,
in increasing prayer."[2] The spirit of prayer must
rule the whole aggressive Christian conduct, and
more especially the wielding of the word of God.
The passage, as indicating the prayerful spirit
which must govern the "ministry of the word,"
is rich in suggestiveness. Bishop Westcott points
out how "the universality of the duty as to mode,
times, persons, is enforced by πάσης, παντί, πάσῃ,
πάντων; and how we have "the nature of the
prayer" defined as "constant, spiritual, resolute,
and manifold."

Other examples of St. Paul's insistence upon
the duty and necessity of the practice of prayer
will be found in Phil. iv. 6; Col. iv. 2, 12, etc.

In his wide application of the nature of prayer,
and in his earnest teaching of the necessity for it
at all times, St. Paul supplies useful admonition
to ourselves. It is so easy, amid the stress of
what is termed "work," to forget the one condition
whereby the Divine, or "spiritual" power in our
work may be retained. We think, and contrive,

---

[1] διὰ πάσης προσευχῆς καὶ δεήσεως: the first is addressed to
God only, and includes the element of devotion; the second is
general in its application, and includes some general request.

[2] Westcott *in loc.*

and study, and toil ; we meet with what the world calls failure and success ; we exercise the intellect, and pour out in large measure our physical strength ; with an increasing number of men their pastoral work is certainly the conscientious discharge of a professional calling ; but without constant prayer,—regular communing with God and reference of all to Him,—the " virtue," the essentially Divine quality of our work, must be wanting. The Divine nature and the unique responsibility of our labours are forgotten. We are then apt to represent ourselves rather than our Master, for it is much easier to profess to speak in His Name than actually to do so, which implies that He is indeed speaking through us. We may *say* " thus saith the Lord," but men easily detect whether we have striven to obtain the means whereby so to speak, whether when we come to speak to them, we come from " the presence of the Lord." [1]

I now pass to a brief consideration of some of St. Paul's prayers.

(1) Rom. i. 8–12 : " First I offer thanks to my God through Jesus Christ (Who as mediator

---

[1] Cf. Aug. *De Doctr. Christ.* iv. 15 " et haec se posse, si potuerit, et in quantum potuerit, pietate magis orationum, quam oratorum facultate non dubitet, ut orando pro se, ac pro illis, quos est adlocuturus, sit orator ante quam dictor. Ipsa hora jam ut dicat accedens, prius quam exserat proferentem linguam, ad Deum levet animam sitientem, ut eructet quod biberit, vel quod impleverit fundat."

presents all our prayers and praises) about you all, because your faith (your Christianity or allegiance to Christ) is being announced in all the world (I hear of it everywhere). For God is my witness, to Whom I render holy service in my spirit (the living inner sphere of that service which is no mere outward form) in preaching the good news of His Son (the outward sphere in which the spiritual service is rendered), how unceasingly I make mention of you at (the time of) my prayers, beseeching (Him) if somehow now at last a way shall be prospered to me in the will of God to come to you. For I am longing to see you in order to impart to you some spiritual gift of grace,[1] with a view to your (further) establishment (in the Christian faith and life); that is, that I may be mutually encouraged among you, each of us by the other's faith, yours and mine."

The thoughts helpful to the pastor from this self-revelation of the Apostle's heart and aims are many: First, and not least important, is the tone of thankfulness and encouragement, a tone we must cultivate and express whenever possible. From force of circumstances we are often tempted to forget to look upon the brighter side. Secondly, we must notice the clear definitions of the spheres of service: (1) our moral self-consciousness: our service must be a heart-

---

[1] ἵνα τι μεταδῶ χάρισμα ὑμῖν πνευματικὸν.

service, which includes a mind-service and a will-service ; (2) all that has to do with the propaga-tion of the gospel. We may recall St. Paul's definition of his office in verse 1 "as separated to the gospel," therefore his life was dedicated to (the purpose of) the gospel : we may compare 2 Cor. x. 14, "we were the first to come unto you in (the cause of) the gospel";[1] Phil. iv. 3, "they laboured with me in the (furtherance of the) gospel"; also 1 Thess. iii. 2, "our brother and God's minister in (the work of) the gospel." Thirdly, we may notice St. Paul's habit of re-membering, in his prayers, those for whom he worked. To pray for a work or a person is to connect these with the Divine ; and this cannot fail to increase the sense of our responsibility towards them ; for anything we can connect with the Divine must be sacred and therefore important. Fourthly, the object of the visit St. Paul wished to make was to impart some "spiritual gift of grace." As from the Apostle, so from every minister of Christ, there should proceed "virtue." Christ's promise of living water proceeding from the believer[2] was true of St. Paul : it must be true of us. The minister of Christ "must himself become a centre and abounding source of spiritual influence and bless-ing to others." Here the object of our efforts is

---

[1] So R.V. marg. (see Plummer's note *in loc.*)

[2] St. John vii. 38.

clearly set forth—the enlargement and strengthening of the Christianity of those among whom we work. Lastly, the final sentence is very interesting, especially if read as a corrective to what has immediately preceded it.[1] St. Paul does not wish his readers to feel that he is assuming a position of spiritual or official superiority to them. He knows of the dependence of the teacher on the taught, of the preacher on his hearers, of the worker upon those for whom he works.[2] The fulness of meaning in συμπαρακληθῆναι must on no account be lost. What was true of Christ[3] is true of His ministers. Their work, at least to some extent, is dependent on the spiritual atmosphere, and on the faith of those for whom they work. They are able to give in proportion to what they receive. St. Paul is not ashamed of making this clear. His very assertion of it may be regarded as a delicate hint to his readers that they also have a responsibility towards him. We, too, must insist on the fact that the prosperity of the great cause for which, by their Christian profession, both minister and people are pledged to strive, depends upon their co-operation, upon the encouragement they give to

---

[1] See Sanday and Headlam's note *in loc.* We may say that both pastor and people, teacher and taught, contribute to the atmosphere in which work is done. The physical analogy of an invigorating or "bracing" atmosphere is suggestive.

[2] "We can only give back in rain what we receive in dew."

[3] οὐκ ἐδύνατο ἐκεῖ ποιῆσαι οὐδεμίαν δύναμιν, St. Mark vi. 5.

each other. This truth the pastor must not fail to set clearly before those over whom he has oversight.

I would next consider the two great prayers found in the Epistle to the Ephesians—the first in chapter i. (vv. 15–19), the second in chapter iii. (vv. 14–19). These prayers must be considered together, for the second is certainly complementary to the first, if it is not an actual resumption of it.

i. (15–19). "For this cause I also having heard of the faith which is among you in the Lord Jesus, and which (is manifest) towards all the saints, cease not to give thanks for you, making mention of you when I pray, that the God of our Lord Jesus Christ, the Father of [the] Glory,[1] may grant to you a spirit of wisdom and revealing[2] in the knowledge of Him, that, having the eyes of your heart (*i.e.* mind) enlightened, ye may know what is the hope of His calling, what the wealth of the glory of His inheritance in the

---

[1] δόξης is not unconnected with σοφίας (which implies knowledge) and ἀποκαλύψεως for both imply light, which seems to be an essential quality in "glory." [In these prayers I consider only those thoughts which bear directly or indirectly upon the Pastoral office.]

[2] "It is a teaching spirit, rather than a teachable spirit which the Apostle asks that they may have" (Armitage Robinson, *Ephesians*, p. 38). (But I think he is wrong in interpreting πνεῦμα here directly instead of mediately, of the Holy Spirit. It is rather the teaching spirit through which we teach ourselves and others which the Teacher Spirit imparts to men, whom He uses as His instruments.)

saints, and what the surpassing greatness of His power toward you that believe according to the energy of the might of His power, etc."

St. Paul begins, as in Rom. i. 8, with a thanksgiving. "It was his habit to think of all that was fairest [1] in the lives of Christian people ; . . . he had a keen eye for goodness ; . . . however sternly he rebuked them for their sins, he rejoiced heartily in every manifestation, however faint, of a genuine desire to do the will of God." [2]

The words "a spirit of wisdom and revealing" (or of "revelation," if the active cause be not forgotten) are difficult because they are capable of various interpretations. First, what is the meaning of πνεῦμα ? According to Bishop Westcott [3] it is, "that through which the principle or power or feeling or characteristic, to which it is referred, becomes effective in the man" ; [3] he

---

[1] Psychology teaches us to dwell on the good rather than on the evil.

[2] Dr. Dale, *Ephesians*, pp. 128, 129.

[3] *Ephesians*, p. 22. By his use of the word "communicate" Westcott seems to admit the active sense in ἀποκαλύψεως. If we understand σοφίας of "skill" (as I think we must) the active sense of ἀποκαλύψεως seems necessary.

The following considerations may help also to make clear this difficult phrase—one of those phrases whose difficulty, and therefore whose true meaning, we may fail to notice simply from familiarity.

σοφία I believe must be active : why should ἀποκάλυψις be passive ? compare Rom. xi. 33. St. Paul surveys God's work and exclaims, Oh the depth of the wisdom and the knowledge (γνώσεως) of God ! The world-order is the product of these two *powers* in God. In Eph. i. 8 we have ἐν πάσῃ σοφίᾳ καὶ φρονήσει. Φρόνησις is

continues, "the spirit of wisdom and revelation will be that spirit, that influence and temper through which wisdom and the materials for growth in wisdom enter into" (and, I would add, are *active* in) "human life." Through this spirit the Christian is at once able to test and to receive and to communicate Divine truths."

From personal experience, and therefore from personal possession, St. Paul must have known the value of what he prays others may enjoy. If the minister of Christ seeks that his people may enjoy some privilege or blessing, surely he should from experience know the value of this. What is needful for them must be needful for him. On the other hand, what he has found useful for himself he must inspire them to seek after, and he must help them to obtain. The boon which St. Paul here prays that his readers

---

surely an active quality—a power in human nature. The same is true of σύνεσις in Col. i. 9.

Bengel, as so often, is illuminating. "Idem Spiritus, qui est promissionis, in progressu fidelium est etiam sapientiæ et revelationis. Sapientia in nobis operatur sapientiam : revelatio (operatur) cognitionem. Also the following words of Bishop Gore (*Ephesians*, p. 80) are helpful. "The spirit of 'wisdom and revelation' vouchsafed to us is to enable us to apprehend in a measure the divine 'wisdom and prudence' (i. 8) manifested in God's work of creation and redemption." Trench, *N. T. Synonyms* (p. 341), says ἀποκάλυψις includes not merely the thing shown and seen, but the interpretation or unveiling of the same.

In Christianity the process—which may mean the exercise of human faculties under the sanctification of the Divine—is often of not less value than the result.

may possess is thus an essential element in the Ministerial equipment.

If, then, we interpret σοφία as efficiency, and ἀποκάλυψις as an exercise which calls for efficiency in its use, and, if we remember that " ἐπίγνωσις has always a moral value," then the meaning of this first petition will be as follows : The Christian's object both for himself and others must be growth in the knowledge of God,[1] for this knowledge tends to fulness of life ; this growth in knowledge implies a spirit—an influence producing a temper —marked by the possession of efficiency and by the coming into life of the contents of the Divine revelation, which are to be efficiently used.   And the Christian minister, like St. Paul, must pray, not only that this spirit may be granted to him, he must strive to foster this spirit in others, and to make it effective in them.

If we combine such sayings as "they shall all be taught of God,"[2] "this is life eternal that they may know Thee,"[3] and "the lips of the priest should keep knowledge,"[4] then the application of this petition to the ministerial life becomes

---

[1] " This knowledge can never become final. All that can be learnt of the course of Nature and History becomes, under the action of the 'spirit of wisdom and revelation' a disclosure of fresh truth as to the character and purpose and working of God." " The eternal life itself consists in this. In this lies the real glory and hope of experience and labour." Westcott, *Ephesians*, p. 23.

[2] St. John vi. 45, from Isa. liv. 13. The Hebrew is suggestive לִמּוּדֵי יְהוָה ("disciples of the Lord ").

[3] St. John xvii. 3.   [4] Mal. ii. 7.

clear. The responsibility of every minister of Christ to make effort to obtain what is here asked for is equally plain. The minister must be an instrument through which this work, as every other work, of the Spirit is accomplished. This particular work is the efficient revelation of Christ through whom God is known.

St. Paul's next petition is that the eyes of the hearts of his converts may be so enlightened that they may be able to know what is the hope of God's calling, etc.

Here, again, St. Paul evidently starts from the experience of what he personally enjoys. And what the Apostle had found of surpassing value in his life, the minister of to-day will find of no less price. St. Paul refers to a personal condition, which he describes as the great perceptive faculty (τοὺς ὀφθαλμοὺς) of heart and mind,[1] of feeling and intellect being made, and being kept, vigorous by the action of "a spirit of wisdom and revealing." The dependence of this efficiency of vision upon the Spirit which produces efficiency generally and which enables the process of revealing to proceed, must be noticed. It is only through the action of God's

---

[1] καρδία "expresses the whole personality of man," Westcott. Driver's note on Deut. iv. 29, "if thou search after Him with all thy heart and with all thy soul," is "The phrase denotes (substantially) the entire spiritual being of man, the 'heart' being in the psychology of the ancient Hebrews, the organ of intellect, and the 'soul' being the organ of the desires or affections."

Holy Spirit that the perfection and sanctification of the highest faculties can take place.

Dr. Dale [1] points out that "there is something in this passage to discourage the Christian preacher." Growth in Christian truth and life demands a condition in his hearers which he cannot assume. "On most other subjects, if a speaker has a clear understanding of the truths he is trying to illustrate, and if he has any faculty of exposition, he can be tolerably sure of being able to make his meaning clear to every intelligent listener. A Christian preacher can have no such confidence." His hearers must be "taught of God." Spiritual truths can only be understood by those who possess in some measure the Spirit. We have not only to teach men, we have to impart the Spirit to them."

St. Paul deals with this subject in 1 Cor. ii. 12 ff., where he asserts that he and his fellow-Christian teachers have received the Spirit which is of God,[2] that they might know the things that are freely given to them by God. These things they speak, not in words which man's wisdom teacheth, but which the Spirit teacheth. If we add to these words our Lord's saying, "That which is born of the Spirit is spirit,"[3] we see

---

[1] *Ephesians*, pp. 144, 145.   [2] τὸ ἐκ τοῦ Θεοῦ.

[3] ἐκ τοῦ πνεύματος πνεῦμά ἐστιν : St. John iii. 6. Bp. Westcott says, "The quickening power is the Spirit. The idea of nature passes into that of person."

that the Spirit is conveyed to man by God, though often through spiritually-endowed men. Hence the paramount importance of the Christian preacher or teacher being thus endowed, and to such a high degree that from his own fulness he can impart to others. This is why the minister must keep open those channels of grace by which the supply of the Spirit is vouchsafed to him.

St. Paul now proceeds to describe the object of the enlightenment which he prays his readers may possess. He would have them know what is the hope of God's calling, what the wealth of the glory of His inheritance in His saints, and what the exceeding greatness of His power towards us who believe.

We may assume that St. Paul had in his teaching, in Ephesus and the neighbouring cities, dealt with these subjects, which certainly need attention and exposition to-day as then. With the nature of these subjects I must not deal at length, but I first notice how one object of St. Paul's prayer is that his converts may have practical experience of that Divine *power* which God wrought in the Christ,[1] raising Him from the dead.[2] I draw attention to these last words,

---

[1] Notice the definite article. The Resurrection was no isolated event, but a great deed—as part of an age-long process, the whole of which manifested the "power" of God.

[2] The key to what this power should mean for us is found in

because as the beginning of St. Paul's prayer dealt with knowledge, so the end of it deals with power. Here again is a lesson for the minister of Christ. Alike for himself and his people, he must pray for knowledge, but not for knowledge for its own sake, only that it may issue in *power*. To-day in the world we have a thousand examples of this sequence. We can see on every side how knowledge is the essential preliminary condition for both the possession and the exercise of power. This condition is equally true in the spiritual sphere, where Divine knowledge must be acquired and used if we are to possess and utilise Divine Power.

The second prayer in this same Epistle really opens with the first verse of chapter iii., but is immediately interrupted by thoughts suggested by the words, "the prisoner of Christ Jesus on behalf of you Gentiles," which describe St. Paul's present position. The intervening verses, from 2 to 13, contain a short fragment of spiritual and ministerial autobiography, which explains how St. Paul came to be where he was. These verses are unusually rich in suggestion of ministerial ideals, but I must pass on to the prayer, which runs thus, "For this cause I bow my knees to the Father, from whom every fatherhood in heaven and on earth derives its name,

---

Col. ii. 12, "ye were raised through your faith in the operation of God who raised, etc." The moral conclusion is asserted in v. 13.

that He may grant to you according to the wealth of His glory to be strengthened with power through His Spirit in the inward man, that the Christ may dwell permanently[1] in your hearts through [the] faith : that having been (and continuing to be) rooted and grounded in love ye may be sufficiently strong to comprehend with all the saints what is the breadth and length and height and depth, and to know the love of the Christ[2] which surpasseth knowledge, so that ye may be filled unto all the fulness of God."

Between this prayer and that found in the first chapter there are many similarities. In both we have a seeking after both knowledge and power. In the first, personal enlightenment leads to a living consciousness of the Divine power. In a very real sense the prayer of the true prophet[3] will always be, " Lord, open their eyes that they may see the power by which they are surrounded, and through which they may be strong." And this prayer will be accompanied by effort to ensure the personal assimilation of this power. In the second prayer the need of

---

[1] κατοικῆσαι; whereas παροικεῖν implies a *temporary* sojourn.

[2] Again notice the definite article. The love which is the characteristic of the Christ. On a connection between what "love," Messiah, and prophecy should imply, see Davidson, *Old Testament Prophecy*, pp. 1 ff. God is love, and both prophecy and the Messianic Rule imply the entrance and abiding of love in the midst of human life.

[3] 2 Kings vi. 17.

the Divine power comes first, and it comes as a condition of ability to apprehend[1] "the whole range of the sphere in which the Divine wisdom and love find exercise." Then we must know the *love* — the essential characteristic of the Christian life—which fills this sphere. The final end (here, as always) is the perfection of the individual in the society, and the measure of this perfection is human nature so filled with the Divine (as in the Christ) that there is left neither space nor opportunity for anything less or lower than this.

This prayer, I believe, expresses nothing less than St. Paul's aspirations for himself, and if for himself then also for others. It explains, too, the object and nature of his efforts. It shows us after what he is striving, and after what he would have others strive. The prayer is invaluable to the worker for Christ, and to those called to teach in Christ's name, for it describes what must be their aspirations and efforts on behalf of themselves, and for those for whom they are responsible.

There is one application of this prayer, an application suggesting a rich inspiration for ministerial work, which must by no means be overlooked. I refer to its *social* teaching.

The keynote is struck in the words πᾶσα πατριὰ. Every group of men knit together by

---

[1] For this meaning of καταλαμβάνεσθαι, compare Acts x. 34.

common relation to one origin (father)[1] is of the nature of a brotherhood. Therefore I would understand ὑμῖν (in ver. 16) as "to you as members of a community." Then we see at once how St. Paul asserts that the true community life depends upon the realisation by each individual[2] of the Divine strengthening. In these days of highly complex organisations within the Church, and of belief in Acts of Parliament to effect social regeneration, it is more than ever important for us to assert the absolute necessity of *personal* sanctification, and the need for *personal* consecration. Ultimately, by a Divine law, the welfare of the community depends upon the ethical character of every individual within it.

The next petition may be rendered, "that all which the Christ should mean may dwell in your hearts (the seat of character) through the Christian faith." The meaning of τὸν χριστὸν is far more comprehensive than had the Apostle written simply Χριστὸν. Those to whom he writes are now members of the Messianic society. The character of each individual must be ruled by the Messianic King, for the "heart"[3] is the seat of His authority. Therefore the conduct (which is the expression of the character) of each must be such as befits a citizen of the Messianic kingdom. We must remember all that ὁ χριστός

---

[1] And therefore *par excellence* every Christian community.
[2] Implied in τὸν ἔσω ἄνθρωπον.   [3] St. Luke xvii. 21.

meant to St. Paul,[1] and we must interpret the term here in agreement with its significance in the rest of the Epistle. Also we must not forget that one great object of this letter is to prove to its readers that they had been admitted into the ancient, but only now for the first time "fulfilled," Messianic commonwealth.[2] We may say that τὸν χριστὸν here refers to both a truth and a power embodied in a person, but to be realised in a *community* of persons *each* of whom individually realises that power. The term ὁ χριστός thus contains a philosophy of history, and a belief in a social order as well as in a historic person. It suggests an ideal community ; but this will only come into existence through all that " the Christ " means finding a home in and ruling the inner life of the individual.

The social aspect is again emphasised by ἐν ἀγάπῃ, which is the characteristic virtue both of the historic Person and of the ideal State. St. Paul says " rooted and founded," because love is that from which all true life springs ; it is also the essential condition of all social stability. The social ideal is also prominent in verse 18, for when St. Paul says " with all the saints " he is not praying that his hearers may enjoy some individual privilege but a common (*i.e.* a social)

---

[1] See the chapter on " The ' Christ ' of St. Paul," in my *Social Teaching of St. Paul*, pp. 77 ff.

[2] The Messianic society of the O.T. and N.T. is one.

endowment.[1] I pass on to consider the somewhat strange idea of being " fully strong enough "[2]
to know the love of Christ. If knowledge is a
source of strength, strength is equally an essential
condition for full knowledge, and especially to
know what the love of Christ really is. We have
only to reflect in order to see this. When St.
Mark left St. Paul in Pamphylia he had not
strength sufficient to learn from personal experience what the love of Christ implied to St.
Paul, what it demanded from him. The student
who would pursue truth through the toil of
acquiring knowledge must have much strength,
both in the way of physical endurance and in will
power. To know the love of Christ we must
walk with Christ, we must climb with Him to
heights inaccessible to those infected with the
weakness which any measure or form of
selfishness produces. Those who succumb to
a temptation may have little idea of its real
strength ; it is only those who resist it successfully,
those upon whom it has put forth all its force, who
know this. The strength of Christ alone enables
us to know, from close and continued communion
with Him, what is the love of Christ.

Finally, the social idea is very evident in the
last petition, which must be interpreted, "that

---

[1] σὺν πᾶσιν τοῖς ἁγίοις.

[2] ἐξισχύσητε, a ἅπαξ λεγ. in the N.T. ἰσχύς occurs in i. 19, vi.
10, and 2 Thess. i. 9.

ye may severally[1] be so fulfilled that the Divine fulfilment is realised." May not this "Divine fulfilment" be the realisation of the ideal "Christ" society in which the purpose of God, through the embodiment of the righteousness of God in a great universal society, is fulfilled?

Looking back over these two prayers together, we see that St. Paul's desire for his readers is threefold—first, knowledge; secondly, strength; thirdly, that both should issue in that love of Christ which is essential to complete all life, whether individual or social. For both minister and people there are no greater needs to-day. Without knowledge we cannot either teach or guide; without spiritual strength we cannot help to make others strong; without both of these the love of Christ, with all that it implies, and unto which it issues, cannot be realised. In regard to knowledge, our present position has striking analogies to that of St. Paul. Like him we have suddenly come into the possession of an immense accession of new knowledge—a further development in the revelation of the mystery of God has been granted to us. To St. Paul the new knowledge was the truth of the universality of the Gospel. To us—paradoxical as the statement may seem—it is the universality of the Divine Law which we now see pervades the universe and rules in every

---

[1] See Westcott's note *in loc.*

sphere. The message of this, which we have to declare and explain to the world, is that upon the knowing and doing of God's will depends all welfare. Christ, filled with the Divine love, gave His life to bring this message to men, and to give them the power to obey it. To the giving of this message, and to helping men to live according to it, must his ministers dedicate their lives to-day. For only thus can the purpose of God be fulfilled.

In the first chapter of the Epistle to the Colossians (verses 9 ff.) will be found one of the most beautiful and complete of all St. Paul's prayers. In it is set forth the ideal Christian character[1] which St. Paul desires for his readers at Colossæ; hence we may say it sets forth that character which those must cultivate who would be examples to the flock, for "like produces like." It evidently expresses St. Paul's own ideal, and it would be difficult to find a higher ideal for those who to-day are engaged in the same work as his. This is the prayer.

"For this cause we also, from the day we heard, cease not praying on your behalf and making supplication that ye may be filled with the [full] knowledge of His will by all wisdom and spiritual intelligence, that ye may walk worthily of the Lord so as to please [God] in

---

[1] Maclaren, *Colossians*, p. 38 (in the Expositors' Bible).

all ways, bearing fruit in every good work and
growing by the [full] knowledge of God, strengthened according to the might of His glory unto
every [kind of] endurance and long-suffering,
giving thanks unto the Father who hath made
us competent for the share of the lot of the saints
in the [Divine] light."

Here, again, the first condition is fulness of
knowledge of God's will.   For right conduct,
adequate knowledge must always be a primary
and essential condition.   We saw that ἐπίγνωσις
seems always in the New Testament to be used
exclusively in reference to facts of the religious
order, and specially in reference to the knowledge
which we are enabled to gain of God and of His
purposes for man's salvation.[1]   In a very true
sense all knowledge of nature and of man, of
science, history, and experience, is knowledge of
God's will, and every addition to our knowledge
is an addition to our knowledge of the Divine
will.   All knowledge[2] should be pursued with the
object of enabling us more perfectly to do that
will, and of giving us power to help others to
do it.   The Christian teacher can have no higher
or more comprehensive aim than this.   If we
bear in mind this unity of aim of all knowledge,
then the evil division between " secular " and

---

[1] Westcott, *Ephesians*, p. 23.   Cp. 218 f.
[2] The unity of all " Knowledge," as of " Truth," should be
maintained.

" sacred " knowledge vanishes. Then also the range of subjects upon which the Christian teacher may preach is enormously enlarged. All depends upon the spirit in which a subject is treated, and the end or aim with which it is taught or expounded. From this it will be seen that the range or extent of the preacher's own knowledge cannot be too wide.

St. Paul next adds ἐν πάσῃ σοφίᾳ καὶ συνέσει πνευματικῇ.[1] Bishop Lightfoot paraphrases the passage thus : " That ye may grow more and more in knowledge till ye attain to the perfect understanding of God's will, being endowed with all wisdom to apprehend His verities and all intelligence to follow His processes, living in the mind of the Spirit, to the end that knowledge may manifest itself in practice," etc. I believe that Lightfoot is entirely right in taking ἐν here as instrumental, and that σοφία and σύνεσις are not spheres of knowledge, but instruments whereby knowledge is obtained and used.

The next clause, commencing with the words " that ye walk worthily," evidently expresses the

---

[1] The following notes of von Soden are helpful—

(a) " Vielmehr zeigt die Epexegese 10–12 deutlich, dass θέλημα die göttliche Norm für das praktische Verhalten der Christen bezeichnen will."

(β) σύνεσις ist ohne σοφία nicht zu erreichen ; sie ist die Gabe, das Rechte und Verkehrte zu unterscheiden, σοφία die Fähigkeit, überhaupt die Wirkenden Kräfte, deren Gesetze und Effecte zu begreifen, um darnach das eigene Leben zu ordnen."

consequence, first, of being filled with the knowledge of the Divine will; and secondly, of using this knowledge in a way which is described as "with all wisdom and spiritual understanding." The art or practice of life, that is conduct, is one which needs both skill *generally* and sanctified intelligence. This skill assumes the knowledge of God's will; it also assumes that this knowledge is applied under the inspiration and guidance of the Holy Spirit. This "skill" is absolutely essential for a useful ministerial life, but it is often wanting even where knowledge is present. Briefly, St. Paul's desire for his readers—which also expresses his own aspiration—is knowledge of God's will applied under the Spirit's sanctifying guidance, so that our conduct shall be worthy of Christ with the aim of being well pleasing to God. Our life's walk must be in entire agreement with our profession.[1] It must be well pleasing to God, as is the conduct of children who desire to do their father's will. As Dr. Maclaren says: "This is the unique glory and power of Christian ethics, that it brings in this tender personal element to transmute the coldness

---

[1] Compare the fifth question in the ordination of priests. Prayer and Holy Scripture may be regarded as primary sources for learning God's will. The study of the World and the Flesh is study, not so much of a wrong subject, but study pursued in a wrong spirit and from a wrong attitude. "There is absolutely no trace in Paul's thought of that later tendency to divide life into sacred and secular, to limit the religious life to a part of human nature." *The Fifth Gospel*, p. 146.

of duty into the warmth of gratitude."[1]   The last
words supply two tests or standards of conduct.
First, is it worthy of Christ, our one sufficient
standard of conduct?   Secondly, is it strictly
according to God's will as that will is revealed
to us?   The special need of entire Christlikeness
in ministerial conduct, and the constant need of
asking, "Is this or that action or plan worthy of
Him?" must not be forgotten.   We cannot hold
Him up to others unless we copy Him ourselves.

After ἀρέσκειαν come three participial clauses[2]
which, from their symmetrical arrangement, may
be regarded as descriptive of conditions of the
true life-walk.   The first asserts that the Christ-
like life must be rich in effect.   But if it is to
be fruitful it must be enriched by that which will
enable it so to be.   For example, teaching
(so-called) often ceases to be fruitful or effective
because the teacher has ceased to acquire knowledge.   The conduct of each age is a product
of the knowledge of each age.   With the growth
of the knowledge of God's will new forms of
the service of God should be suggested.   Unless
we keep abreast of the knowledge of our age we
cannot "serve our generation."

The second clause, "strengthened with all
strength," etc., points to another side of human
(and ministerial) experience.   Knowing and doing

---

[1] *Colossians*, p. 44.
[2] I accept Bishop Lightfoot's punctuation.

are not the whole of life. We have also to *bear* and to be patient. Endurance and long-suffering are virtues which the minister of Christ must manifest, like his Master. Both demand strength in large measure. This strength must be sought from God, the source of all strength. Of the might of God's glory[1] we have abundant evidence, and this might is the measure of the strength available for us. We specially need this strength, for our endurance and long-suffering must not only be manifested, they must be accompanied with joy. Our endurance must not be that of despair, nor our long-suffering that of exhaustion. Both must be accompanied with cheerfulness. To manifest this under such conditions makes upon us an exceptional demand.[2]

The third clause tells us our life must be one of thankfulness, for our position (and our work) is a privilege, and as such it must be regarded. We have been made competent (or sufficient) to obtain the portion of the lot of those who are sanctified, and this in the kingdom of light. Here, as so often by St. Paul, the ideal is treated as the actual. The reason for this is given by

---

[1] "The 'glory' here, as frequently, stands for the majesty or the power, or the goodness of God, as *manifested* to men." Lightfoot *in loc*.

[2] This is specially applicable to the sometimes exhausting labour of pastoral visitation. We must, if possible, take a cheerful spirit to the sick, the suffering, and the oppressed.

ἱκανώσαντι.   Upon us, through a Divine endowment, have the possibilities been bestowed.[1] These final words (for St. Paul now, as in other cases, passes from prayer to meditation) seem specially applicable to the ministry.   Our work is often hard; it is apt to be full of difficulties, discouragements, and disappointments, and upon these we are apt to dwell.   But there is another aspect of our work.   We live and work in what is, comparatively, a region of light, and our lot, to some extent, is among consecrated men, though many of these need to be reminded what consecration must involve.   Our work is also a privilege, for we share it with Christ and with all His faithful followers.   For this work we have received a sufficient endowment, *if* we use and *improve* it.   For all this there is surely much reason for thankfulness.

In the first chapter of the Epistle to the Philippians (verses 9–11) there is a short prayer which sets forth a very beautiful ideal of the Christian life, and in which, again, St. Paul seems to reveal an aim he had placed before himself. This prayer may also well express the aspiration of those who, as ministers of Christ, would follow in the Apostle's steps.   The prayer which may

---

[1] The thought is explained by a reference to 2 Cor. iii. 5, 6. "Our 'sufficiency' (ἡ ἱκανότης ἡμῶν) is from God, who also hath made us sufficient (ἱκάνωσεν) as ministers of a new covenant."

actually be said to represent St. Paul's view of Christianity[1] runs thus : "And this is the purport of my prayer, that your love[2] may abound yet more and more in knowledge and all perception ; that ye may approve the things that are excellent ; that ye may be pure and not causing others to stumble against[3] the day of Christ ; filled with the fruit of righteousness, which is through Jesus Christ, unto the glory and praise of God."

The ministerial life must be a Christian life to a very high degree. Its characteristic virtue must be love, and, in this life of abounding love, there must be advanced moral knowledge and intense keenness of moral perception. In a very true sense love sharpens all the faculties, whereas selfishness and want of sympathy blunts them all. Few virtues are more essential to him who has the care and guidance of souls than the moral αἴσθησις. It will hardly exist without ἐπίγνωσις, which it applies to the finer details of the individual life. It also fulfils itself in the various phases of Christian tact,[4] a quality which it is easy to despise, but which more often than not means that effort is being made to understand the feelings and point

---

[1] Jordan, *The Philippian Gospel*, p. 60.

[2] ἀγάπη, used here absolutely as a synonym for " Christianity."

[3] εἰς.

[4] That gentleness of touch (from Lat. *tango*)—

> Quam manibus osseis tangit
> Crystallianam phialam frangit.

of view of others. The cultivation of moral
αἴσθησις, of which ἀγάπη, as well as ἐπίγνωσις is an
essential preliminary condition, may be regarded
as a paramount necessity in the useful ministerial
life. The emotional, the intellectual, and the
æsthetic faculties will all be cultivated in the well-
balanced life, but they will all be consecrated to
a moral end—to the increase of righteousness.
We constantly meet with men who are comparative failures simply from the lack of development of one or other of these essential factors in
the Christian life, which is the really human life
at its best. Enthusiasm is essential, but so are
also intelligence and taste, and much enthusiasm
to-day is at least misapplied, and fails to be
permanently effective because it lacks these
essential complementary conditions.

If I may digress for a moment I would draw
attention to the fact that in all these prayers
St. Paul lays especial stress upon the cultivation
of certain endowments of human nature, he seems
to pay particular attention to the cultivation of
powers. In this, of course, he emphasises the
utilitarian aspect of the Christian life as a διακονία.
Beneath this lies a deep truth. We are apt to
dwell on ends and results; St. Paul dwells on
processes, and on the powers or faculties by
means of which these processes take place.
Here we see the immense stress he lays upon
character, and upon the value of human nature in

itself.   No lesson is more important for this age.   As mechanical contrivances have taken the place of handicraft for producing certain results, the character in work and the moral effect of the work upon the worker are both being lost. There is no longer place or opportunity for either. The photograph has taken the place of the portrait ; the furniture, the carving, the decoration of our houses and public buildings are now the products of machinery : one and all lack character.

The same evil has infected our religious work. Elaborate organisation takes the place of personal dealing ; and admirably, though mechanically, performed services, the place of preaching and teaching.   Individuality, and so character, is here as elsewhere being crushed out by machinery.

In verse 10 St. Paul passes to the object of $\epsilon\pi\iota$-$\gamma\nu\omega\sigma\iota\varsigma$ and $\pi\hat{a}\sigma a$ $a\ddot{\iota}\sigma\theta\eta\sigma\iota\varsigma$.   Both are essential for all the constant and important decisions which we are called upon to make daily.   Life has been defined as a continuous series of moral choosings. We must always be testing and approving or rejecting,—approving " after examination had " of the absolutely best, and rejecting all beneath this.   Character is both made and discerned in this process.   Right choice both demands and makes character ; and conduct is the expression of the choices we have made.   St. Paul's standard of conduct is high.   It must be flawless in itself ; it must be harmless with regard to others ; it must be the conduct of those who are preparing for the day of Christ. In verse 11 St. Paul sums up the secret, and aim, and result of such a life. It is a life filled with fruitfulness which is the product of righteousness. In this word righteousness, which is here used in a somewhat unusual sense, we seem to have an implicit exhortation to the necessity of *moralising* all the faculties of life, the emotional, intellectual, æsthetic powers ; which is yet another reminder that the character of the process is not less important than that of the result. The words τὸν διὰ 'Ιησοῦ Χριστοῦ state how these faculties may be moralised—by the presence and power of Christ in the life, by vital union with Him. Then, and only then, will the true aim of all human endeavour be realised—the manifestation and exaltation of the essential nature of God and the right appreciation of this by man. There is no saying the minister of Christ needs more carefully to remember than this—*Gloria Dei Vivens homo.*

Chapter 8

PAUL ON PREACHING

ἀπεστειλέν με Χριστὸς . . . εὐαγγελίζεσθαι.—I COR. i. 17.

οὐαὶ γάρ μοί ἐστιν ἐὰν μὴ εὐαγγελίσωμαι.—I COR. ix. 16.

συνείχετο τῷ λόγῳ.—ACTS xviii. 5.

As a minister of Christ, St. Paul was above and before everything else a preacher. He tells us that Christ sent him forth from Himself with a commission to preach the gospel.[1] To fulfil this commission was his life's work. To this all other aims and activities were subservient: beside this all else was secondary. He claimed no praise for preaching. "If I preach the gospel, I have nothing to glory of, for necessity is laid upon me; for woe is unto me if I preach not the gospel.[2]

After many years of ministerial work, St. Paul described[3] how, at the time of his conversion, he received his commission as a preacher. As a preacher he is to stand upon his feet, in an attitude of readiness to listen, to serve, to speak,

---

[1] I Cor. i. 17.   [2] I Cor. ix. 16.   [3] Acts xxvi. 15 ff.

to go.[1] Christ appeared to him, to place him in His hand[2] as an instrument to do His work in the special capacity of a witness[3] of the things wherein He hath seen Christ and the things in which Christ will yet appear unto him. Every word should be carefully noticed. For at any time the Christian preacher, if true to his office, can only bear witness to the things in which he has already seen Christ, though he must always be expectant and observant, for he knows not in what things in the future Christ may yet reveal Himself to him. The Divine in Nature and the whole revelation of Science, so called ; the Divine in History, including the whole content of the Bible ; the Divine in daily experience, including the Divine in our own nature as witnessed to by Conscience : all this must be the subject of our testimony. The Vision of God ever has been, still is, and always will be, "the call"[4] of the true prophet. The full description of the "apostolic" mission of the preacher contained in the one word ἀποστέλλω must not be forgotten—I send thee forth with the full commission of the *legatus a latere* to represent Me, and to speak for Me, and, while I send thee, I go with thee.[5]

Now we come to a list, or description of the

---

[1] Compare Ezek. ii. 1.   [2] προχειρίσασθαί σε.

[3] καί in v. 16 should be translated "even."

[4] See a university sermon by Bp. Westcott printed in *Christus Consummator*.

[5] *e.g.* Acts xviii. 10.

objects towards which St. Paul's preaching was to be directed, which he was to make effort to effect. First, he must arouse attention,[1] he must get men to see what he saw, in order that they might turn themselves[2] from a life lived in an atmosphere of darkness, of ignorance and moral stupor, "toward[3] the light," which symbolises knowledge, truth, purity, fellowship, safety, and joy.[4] Christ and Christianity, the preacher must show, mean all these. It was the effect of light proceeding from Christ that caused St. Paul so far to turn himself that he who had been absolutely certain that he must persecute was now ready to ask "what shall I do, Lord?"[5] Also, men must be led to turn themselves from an (unconscious) recognition of the authority of Satan,[6] and cast themselves in faith upon God; in order that they might receive (the privilege and benefit of) remission of sins, and a portion among those who are sanctified, and who owe their position and condition to their faith in regard to Christ. All these objects of the preacher may be brought under two heads—first, to produce *repentance*, with a view to a change of conduct; second, to produce *faith*, whereby

---

[1] There is a close connection between attention and interest, and "it is the first duty of a preacher to be interesting." (Archbishop Magee.)

[2] ἐπιστρέψαι in v. 18 is middle.   [3] εἰς.

[4] Westcott, *Epistle of St. John*, p. 17.   [5] Acts xxii. 10.

[6] ἐξουσίας, in v. 18, is explained by 1 John v. 19.

men may be able to persevere in this conduct.
Repentance will, of course, imply the reception
and assimilation of new knowledge ; and faith,
which issues in obedience, will imply the accom-
panying privileges of membership in the Christian
Society. The preaching is at once doctrinal and
ethical. It contains an appeal to the individual
conscience and reason :[1] it is destined to produce
such conduct as is compatible with membership
(and its privileges) in the community of the
sanctified.

To this description of his commission and of
the objects of his preaching, St. Paul immediately
adds a summary of his life's work from the time
of his conversion until the day on which he
spoke. To an ever-wider circle of hearers[2] he
continued to announce that men should repent
and turn to (trust upon) God, practising works
worthy of repentance. Here, again, repentance
and faith are the keynotes, and it is assumed that
faith implies conduct.

St. Paul's conception of his work has its root
in his conviction of having received from Christ
a responsible commission, in the discharge of
which all the factors of a consecrated personality
must be exercised. Our knowledge of St. Paul's
life shows us under what different circumstances
and conditions he was called upon to represent

---

[1] 2 Cor. iv. 2.

[2] Damascus, Jerusalem, Judæa, the Gentiles, v. 20.

his Master.   He had to announce, proclaim, preach the gospel, teach, prophesy, and admonish as the occasion demanded, but the consciousness of his apostleship, his Divine commission, always lay beneath all.

To prevent repetition I shall not again speak of the various functions which from time to time the preacher is called upon to discharge—those of the herald, the teacher, the prophet, the ambassador, and the steward of Christ.   With these I have already dealt.   I have also pointed out St. Paul's conception of the importance, nay rather of the necessity of preaching.   Now I purpose to confine myself to considering what we can learn from him of the object, the contents, and the methods of preaching.

Briefly, St. Paul's object, as that of our Lord, is "salvation."   But this salvation is no mere personal escape from the evil consequences of sin; it is safety "within the Messianic Kingdom."[1]   This is the portion, or lot, or inheritance of Christ's loyal servants, or subjects. But how shall men be loyal to One in Whom they have not believed? And faith or belief, which is both the basis of loyalty and that by which loyalty is maintained, implies knowledge. How shall men know without a preacher?[2] Hence the first object of preaching must be to

---

[1] κλῆρον ἐν τοῖς ἡγιασμένοις, Acts xxvi. 18.   Compare Eph. i. 18.
[2] Rom. x. 14 ff.

impart knowledge. This, of course, often means much less than to teach[1] in the full sense of the word. From the Gospels we learn that our Lord first announced and then taught.[2] But to impart knowledge implies first the possession of knowledge by the preacher or teacher, and must also imply the power to create, when necessary, the conditions under which knowledge may be assimilated.[3] Hence St. Paul's first object in preaching is simply to make Christ known, to cause men to know what was essential about Him. Anything which would promote or spread this knowledge was to St. Paul a cause for satisfaction.[4] To give Christ a wide publicity, so that men could not plead ignorance about Him, or suffer from the results of that ignorance,[5] seems to be the meaning of προεγράφη, "placarded" or "evidently set forth" in Gal. iii. 1. Again in Col. i. 25, when St. Paul is speaking of the discharge of his stewardship towards the Gentiles, he describes it by such terms as "manifestation," "making known," "proclaiming."[6]

---

[1] To "teach" means "to show how to do."

[2] Compare St. Mark i. 14, with i. 21.

[3] This is why it is so important that all preachers and teachers should have at least some elementary knowledge of the principles of psychology.

[4] Phil. i. 18.

[5] "Kein Mensch, der einmal einen Strahl von Seinen Lichte in sich anfgenommen hat, je wieder so werden kann, als habe er nie etwas von Ihm gehört." Harnack, *Das Wesen*, p. 1.

[6] Note the words πληρῶσαι τὸν λόγον, ἐφανερώθη, γνωρίσαι, καταγγέλλομεν.

To-day I believe that the results of Christian preaching, and so the influence of our ministry, are less than they should be from a common neglect of this primary and elementary duty. Preachers do not neglect it wilfully, but because they assume that in a so-called Christian land and among professing Christians the necessity for it no longer exists. They assume that the knowledge of their hearers in reference to the facts of the life of Christ, as found in the Gospels, is equal to their own. But examination into the actual state of the case will often reveal, even among so-called "educated" people, a re-markable ignorance of the contents, not merely of the New Testament, but of the Gospels. An easy proof of this assertion may be obtained by putting young people of the so-called "upper" classes, who come to be prepared for confirma-tion, through a brief examination upon the details of the Gospel story.

The most important elements in this proclama-tion St. Paul briefly summarises in 1 Cor. xv. 1 ff.—the death and resurrection of Jesus Christ. But this passage shows that St. Paul did not confine his proclamation to the *facts* of Christ's life, and that he did not regard that life as an isolated event. This is proved by his twice repeated "according to the Scriptures."[1] His reference to these, at least for Gentile hearers,

---

[1] κατὰ τὰς γραφάς in both verses 3 and 4.

would have been meaningless had he not made
known to them such passages as dealt with the
preparation for the Incarnation. His method
of reference to the Scriptures is much more
clearly seen in his address at Antioch in Pisidia,[1]
in his speech to the people from the stairs of
the Temple,[2] and in that before Festus and
Agrippa.[3] The course of history, so far as it
was known to St. Paul, which led up to the
human life of Christ, and the consequences of
that life, and especially of its great events—
the Crucifixion and Resurrection—were evidently
among the contents of his preaching. Indeed
in a very true sense the identity of "the Christ
of faith" with "the Jesus of history," may be
said to be the special message of St. Paul.
Among other consequences this identification
carried with it the conviction of the continuity
of the Divine society of prae-Christian Israel
with the society of believers in Jesus.[4] This,
again, from several passages in his epistles,
where a knowledge of it is assumed, must have
been among the contents of St. Paul's preaching.[5]

---

[1] Acts xiii. 16 ff.   [2] Acts xxii. 1 ff.   [3] Acts xxvi. 2 ff.

[4] Just as the word Messiah had to the Old Testament writers a
social, as well as a personal significance, so had the *adjective* ὁ
χριστός to St. Paul. See my *Social Teaching of St. Paul*, p.
78 ff.

[5] On St. Paul's frequent use of γνωρίζειν, γνῶσις, etc., see note
on p. 17. In 2 Cor. xi. 6, St. Paul assures the Corinthians he
was not ἰδιώτης . . . τῇ γνώσει.

To-day the preacher has every reason to seek to possess, and to copy St. Paul's example in freely employing, a wide knowledge of history. We can hardly attribute to St. Paul a "philosophy" of history[1] in the exact sense in which the word is generally understood to-day: but certainly to him, so far as his knowledge went, "all past history was a pre-paration for the Incarnation," and to him the all-important matter was the world-wide "appropriation of the results" of that central event of all history.[2] From our rapidly growing knowledge of the past, and from our increasing sense of the unity and continuity of history, we can see, to a degree which was impossible to him, how the experiences of other nations besides the Jews were contributing to the preparation for the one Universal Religion. Also, we can point out, from our knowledge of history subsequent to St. Paul's own time, how the appropriation of true Christianity, or the failure to make use of it, has been one of the principal factors in the destiny of many nations as well as of countless individual lives.

Besides the chief facts of our Lord's life and the preparation in history for the Incarnation, St. Paul in his preaching frequently

---

[1] See Sanday and Headlam's *Romans*, p. 342.

[2] See Westcott, *Introduction to the Study of the Gospels*, p. 47 ff.

referred to his own personal experience of Christ. The Epistles, we must remember, are in a very true sense written sermons, and to these, as well as to his addresses in the Acts, we may refer for the *contents* of his preaching. In every Epistle we shall find there is a large element of autobiography or self-revelation, and often this is rather indirect or implicit, than direct and explicit. In his various letters he describes his actions and the motives for these,[1] his conduct before and after his conversion, he reveals his inward experiences,—what he had thought and felt in the old Jewish life and in the new Christian life, also the forces and convictions which had produced in him such a mighty change. References to his old life will be found in Acts xxii. 3–9, xxvi. 4–12; Gal. i. 13, 14; Phil. iii. 4–7; 1 Cor. xv. 9, etc. References to his new life will be found in the continuations of each of these passages. All these are explicit references to an actual change of conduct. But still more important are the many allusions, both direct and indirect, to states of mind,[2] and to changes of thought and feeling,[3] and, above all, to what may be termed *spiritual* experiences.[4] I think there is little doubt that in Romans, chapters v.

---

[1] *e.g.* 2 Cor. i. 8, 23 ff.; ii. 12 ff.; Phil. ii. 25 ff.
[2] *e.g.* Phil. i. 19 ff. [3] *e.g.* 2 Cor. vii. 8.
[4] *e.g.* 2 Cor. xii. 1 ff.

to viii., St. Paul is throughout speaking from a very deep and real personal experience ; this is especially true of chapter vii. Allusions to personal experience and personal feeling will be found especially numerous in Second Corinthians, the most autobiographical of all his letters. In this constant appeal to personal experience, St. Paul shows us that he knew how both to interest and to touch his hearers. He also reminds us that we are to be, not merely the channels, but the instruments, even embodiments and expressions of revelation. In short, we may say that the speeches and writings of St. Paul contain a revelation of Christ mediated, not only through him, but actually *in* him. The life and the preaching of the minister of Christ to-day must both be of the same nature. Every teacher who has a knowledge of psychology knows, first, the much greater interest which the hearer takes in the recital of the personal and the concrete, than in that of the imaginative, or theoretical, or abstract ; and, consequently, the greater effect of the former ; [1] and, secondly, he knows the far greater effect of the indirect or partial, where the hearer's own effort is called out to supply something, than of the entirely direct

---

[1] Compare Carlyle's dictum, " When a true man will speak of actual experiences from his heart, other men will listen to him."

or complete, where no such effort is demanded. The indirect method, which leaves much for the hearer or learner to supply for himself, was a very favourite method with our Lord— the Model for all teachers : indeed, it may be said to be the essential characteristic of His parabolic teaching. To-day, and often the more indirectly and implicitly the better, the preacher must still use personal experience and give personal testimony.[1]

From its evidence of personal experience we are naturally led to another aspect of St. Paul's preaching—that of testifying, or bearing witness. This is a duty which is often overlooked by the preacher to-day, yet it is essential, if our object is to be attained. We, like the apostle, have to put a case before the world (or before our congregation) as before a jury. We wish to obtain a verdict of "proven." St. Paul knew that he had not only to tell the gospel story, he had to asseverate, to give solemn testimony to its truth in the sight of God, and in the presence of men. " It is conviction which convinces," and we must so give our testimony that men cannot but feel that we are entirely convinced both of its truth and of its import-

---

[1] " The inner fundamental character of Christian preaching as a *personal testimony* is inalienable from the idea of preaching." Christlieb, *Homiletic Lectures on Preaching*, p. 90. (The whole of the chapter on the Meaning and Nature, the Scope and Aim of Preaching, is well worth study.)

ance.   Unfortunately there is much so-called
preaching which certainly does not impress the
hearer in this way.   Twice [1] St. Paul commences
an exhortation to Timothy with the solemn words
διαμαρτύρομαι ἐνώπιον τοῦ Θεοῦ, where he seeks to
impress upon him the vital importance and
sacredness of his work.   The second of these
exhortations refers to preaching, to the different
forms it must take, and the reasons for it.

Besides heralding, or proclaiming and testifying,
St. Paul speaks of his preaching as including
warning or admonishing and also teaching.[2]
First of admonishing;[3] the need for this is
frequently urged by St. Paul.   He speaks of it as
his own practice and also as a ministerial duty.[4]
It is to perform the office both of a father[5] and of
a brother,[6] also of one who as a citizen[7] has the
good of the community at heart.   It is a treatment that all need, and that must be mutually
performed.   By it the minister no less than the
layman from time to time is benefited.

St. Paul joins admonishing and teaching
together as elements in preaching.[8]   "The first,"
it has been said, corresponds to repentance, the

---

[1] I Tim. v. 21 ; 2 Tim. iv. 1.   For διαμαρτύρεσθαι, see Luke xvi.
28 ; Acts xx. 21, 23, 24 ; xxiii. 11 ; xxviii. 23 ; I Thess. iv. 6.

[2] Col. i. 28.   (See Lightfoot's note *in loc.*)

[3] For νουθεσία, see I Cor. x. 11 ; Eph. vi. 4 ; Titus iii. 10 ;
for νουθετεῖν, see Acts xx. 31 ; Rom. xv. 14 ; I Cor. iv. 14 ; Col. i.
28, iii. 16 ; I Thess. v. 12, 14 ; 2 Thess. iii. 15.

[4] I Thess. v. 12.   [5] I Cor. iv. 14.   [6] 2 Thess. iii. 15.
[7] Rom. xv. 14 ; I Thess. v. 14.   [8] Col. i. 28.

second points to that which corresponds to faith ; the first has to do with the "moral" side, the second with the "intellectual" side of preaching. In these divisions there is an element of truth ; but they are not entirely satisfactory, for νουθετεῖν, which means literally "to apply the mind to," assumes an intellectual as well as a moral act, and "faith" is something very different to a mere assent to an intellectual proposition. The more correct view is to regard admonition as a necessary preliminary condition for effective teaching.[1] Christian progress, or, under another simile, Christian edification, requires a foundation. Much in the old life must be given up, or "put off," ere the new life can make satisfactory growth. The law, with its negative precepts, must still precede the positive teaching of the Gospel. The work of John the Baptist is still necessary to prepare for the coming and the indwelling of the Christ. And the minister to-day learns from experience how frequently failure arises from attempting to build on an imperfect foundation, from trying to graft the new life on an insufficiently prepared stock.

St. Paul was a great *ethical* teacher, with a deep knowledge of human nature ; hence he was very conscious of the value, indeed of the necessity of discipline. This was the reason why he laid

---

[1] In psychological language it is to bring a subject into the centre or focus of the field of consciousness.

such stress upon admonition. He knew how much pleasanter and how much more easy it is to teach men new truths than to bid them look into, and reform their actual present conduct; he knew how difficult it is to induce men to make a stern personal effort to eradicate sins, bad habits, failings, narrow-mindedness, and prejudice. Yet this most necessary work must be done, and it must be done in reference to individuals as well as in general admonitions addressed to a congregation of professing Christians. St. Paul's epistles are full of warnings against various dangers, and of rebukes against different kinds of errors.[1]

In Colossians i. 28, we must be careful to connect ἐν πάσῃ σοφίᾳ with νουθετοῦντες as well as with διδάσκοντες, and to understand the words as meaning "with all (or, every kind of) skill." For of all the tasks which the working pastor has to perform, none requires more "skill" than to admonish with good effect.[2] For we have so to admonish as not to alienate, indeed so that we actually gain additional influence over those we

---

[1] The too great readiness to let the new settle among the old has been productive of much evil. Cp. *e.g.* Israel's history after the conquest: the history of the Early Church from the second century, and especially after the "conversion" of the Empire. In the thoroughness of Nehemiah's work (note the process implied in iv. 10, ὁ χοῦς πολὺς, which must be cleared away, and in his treatment of the mixed marriages) we see the proof of his statesmanship.

[2] And it is impossible, unless in our own life we supply what we demand in others, for "Nihil est enim quod minus ferendum sit quam rationem ab altero vitæ reposcere eum qui non possit suae reddere."

admonish. It is here that the chief difficulty lies. St. Paul draws attention to it in 2 Thess. iii. 14, 15.[1] We have to "remind men of their duty" and of all that duty means, and to do this always implies at least some degree of blame for duty neglected; and blame, as we know, is always easily resented. We have to produce some feeling of shame, and yet we must not forget that the one we admonish has a "brother's" position with, if not a brother's feelings, yet a brother's rights. Another instance of St. Paul's thoughtfulness and care will be found in 2 Cor. ii. 6 ff., where the Christian actions described by χαρίσασθαι καὶ παρακαλέσαι (encourage) are enjoined, while the danger suggested by καταποθῇ must be carefully avoided.

From admonishing St. Paul passes to *teaching*. "The Christian ministry in the Apostle's view is distinctly educational in its design."[2] We cannot lay too much stress on the teaching function of the ministerial or pastoral office, especially in these days when there are so many temptations to neglect it. There is so much else to be done which seems to be of more urgent and immediate importance,[3] and which certainly promises quicker,

---

[1] See Lightfoot's note *in loc*.   [2] Maclaren, *Colossians*, p. 142.

[3] If we might translate *re* by what so many ministers term "work," there is a much needed warning in the lines—

"Perdidit arma, locum virtutis deseruit, qui
Semper in augenda festinat, et obruitur re."

Hor. *Ep*. I. xvi. 67, 68.

more tangible, and more visible results. Then we must remember that many of "our hearers make the task of teaching more difficult by ill-concealed impatience with sermons which try to discharge it."[1] But so long as we remember that teaching was one of the chief functions of our Lord's ministry,[2] we shall see the importance of making it a chief factor in our own. Men are slow to take in new ideas, but it is ideas which ultimately govern conduct, and the chief end of teaching is to obtain an entrance for ideas, to impart and explain them, so that, through them, conduct may be changed. History proves that however little immediate success may wait upon a "teaching" ministry, yet from the first days the men of permanent and ever-widening influence have been the teachers in the Church.

It is interesting to notice that one of the earliest[3] pictures we have of St. Paul's ministerial activities shows him (in conjunction with St. Barnabas) "teaching much people"; and that the

---

[1] Maclaren, *Colossians*, p. 143. The preacher may learn this from "The Prologue for the Theatre" in *Faust*; *e.g.*—

> "Beseht die Gönner in der Nähe!
> Halb sind sie Kalt, halb sind sie roh.
>
> .   .   .   .   .
>
> Sie zu befriedigen ist schwer."

[2] St. Matt. iv. 23, v. 2, vii. 29, ix. 35, xiii. 54, etc. Notice how frequently the imperfect ἐδίδασκεν (as describing our Lord's *practice*) is used.

[3] Acts xi. 26.

last activity [1] in which we see him engaged, as the curtain falls upon his history, is "teaching the things concerning the Lord Jesus Christ with all boldness." In 1 Cor. iv. 17, St. Paul joins τὰς ὁδούς μου τὰς ἐν Χριστῷ with πανταχοῦ ἐν πάσῃ ἐκκλησίᾳ. [In Acts xiii. 1 we find a list of prophets and teachers where, if Meyer is right in his interpretation of the use of the conjunctions, Saul (St. Paul) is enumerated as a teacher.] We must also notice the place occupied by "teachers" in the two lists of those who exercised a particular function in the Ecclesia and on its behalf.

(1) 1 Cor. xii. 28. "And God hath set (for His own use, ἔθετο) some in the Church, first apostles, secondly prophets, thirdly teachers"; then follows a list of "practical" activities. There has been much discussion over the exact meaning of this verse. It seems best, at least here, to understand "apostles" in the narrower sense of the word; prophets, according to the estimation of their gift by St. Paul and the Early Church, naturally come second. But it is well to remember that while there would be teachers who could not claim to exercise the function of the apostle and the prophet, these two would both constantly discharge the function of teaching.[2] In verses 8–10

---

[1] Acts xxviii. 31.

[2] The help of the Holy Spirit in teaching must always be remembered. See Westcott's notes on John xiv. 26 and xv. 26. Also see St. Matt. x. 20. Henrici's note on διδασκάλους is, " Diese hatten

of this same chapter Dr. Hort sees a reference to teaching. Here "the function of teachers," he thinks, is subdivided "under three different qualifications, what are called "an utterance (λόγος) of wisdom," "an utterance of knowledge," and "faith."[1] If this be so, we have an instructive insight into St. Paul's view of the necessary qualifications for the teacher.

(2) Eph. iv. 11. "And He gave some as apostles, and some as prophets, and some as evangelists, and some as pastors and teachers." A question at once arises here whether we have four or five classes of men who perform certain functions. The original, which substitutes καί for τοὺς δὲ before διδασκάλους, seems to be in favour of St. Jerome's view that the pastors and teachers are the same—"and some, pastors who are also teachers." The men who have oversight and have the care of settled bodies of Christians must be "apt to teach." In 1 Tim. iii. 2 we are told distinctly that the one who has oversight (τὸν ἐπίσκοπον) must be διδακτικόν. In 2 Tim. ii. 2 the thoughts of "witness," "trustworthiness," and "ability to teach" are combined; and trustworthiness is certainly essential for the discharge of the pastoral office, for anyone to whom is committed care and oversight. In 2 Tim. ii. 24

die Gabe des heil. Geistes, das Evangel, in verstandesmässiger Lehrentwickelung vorzutragen."

[1] *Christian Ecclesia*, pp. 158, 159.

we read that "the Lord's servant"—evidently, from what precedes, one who performs a public function in the society—must be διδακτικόν and also παιδεύοντα (with educational ability), and that he must also have as his object the imparting of μετάνοιαν (which at least assumes additional knowledge) εἰς ἐπίγνωσιν ἀληθείας, a qualification which seems to imply a somewhat advanced stage of teaching ability.

Before we leave St. Paul's very comprehensive expression of his conception of preaching, found in Col. i. 28, 29, we must notice yet another responsibility which the words ἐν πάσῃ σοφίᾳ throw upon the preacher. The aim set before himself by St. Paul is a lofty one, being nothing less than to present every man perfect (τέλειον, fully developed) in Christ. To attain this object, which must be ours, as it was his, will require infinite skill alike in admonishing and in teaching. Both these may therefore be regarded as an art which has to be constantly practised, and therefore must be carefully acquired. St. Paul implies by the words he uses that the practice of both will involve labour (κοπιῶ) which is actually of the nature of a struggle (ἀγωνιζόμενος). St. Paul certainly does not make light of the difficulty of his task, or of the labour and skill which it demands. Do ministers of Christ to-day, as a rule, prove by their conduct that they are equally convinced of what their object requires from them?

Do we bring to our preaching, in all its various parts, all the skill available ? Can such words as "labour" and "struggle" be applied to our methods either of the acquisition or the exercise of skill ?

I pass to another thought suggested by St. Paul's language. He speaks of his struggling being "according to Christ's working which worketh in me powerfully." The little word κατά is full of suggestion. Are we always careful that our striving is strictly in accordance with Christ's method and direction of working? The Divine power, as manifested in Christ, always works according to definite rules or laws and in certain definite directions, all ordained by God Himself. Here I make two assumptions, the justification for which is being strengthened, by our growing knowledge of the sciences of man and of society, day by day. First, that the laws for successful teaching and for right dealing with men are as surely ordained by God, are Divine laws, as are the "laws of motion"; and that ignorance of them, or carelessness to obey them, is as certainly attended with evil effects—loss of welfare in the fullest sense of the word—as is ignorance of, or disobedience to, any so-called physical law. Secondly, that these laws of human nature (*e.g.* which deal with teaching and the formation of character), to the knowledge of which we are coming by the strictly scientific method of induction, were taught by Christ by revelation, and absolutely obeyed by Him through His complete union with the Divine.[1] By St. Paul, too, these laws (*re* teaching and dealing with men) were both known and obeyed. He knew them by revelation; he was able to obey them through his close union with Christ.

But we must not think only of κατά, which defines the mode, we must think of τὴν ἐνέργειαν, the force. We work according to law in order that we may utilise the Divine power. Here, again, between the " spiritual-moral " and the physical there is a close and instructive analogy. In every sphere of work it is realised to-day that man's success depends upon his careful utilisation of the forces (or force) of " nature." The Christian minister's success depends upon an equally careful and intelligent utilisation of the ἐνέργεια of Christ.[2] To apply this is his task, but this utilisation implies knowledge and skill. Here we have the strongest of all reasons for study and self-discipline.

To-day we hear many complaints of the " ineffectiveness " of ministerial work, indeed of the ministry itself. We hear also of the want

---

[1] For more upon this subject and upon its value for Christian Apologetics, see my *Social Teaching of St. Paul*, pp. 90 ff.

[2] ἐνεργεῖν, ἐνέργεια, and their cognate words in the N.T., are always used with a moral or spiritual connotation. They bring out the idea of " personal " power, and have reference to action (even if Satanic, 2 Thess. ii. 9, 11) in the human sphere.

of energy in Christ's ministers. Our word "energy" (especially in the more scientific sense) is not a bad substitute for the Greek, and effectiveness is the result of the presence and wise application of energy—mental, moral, and spiritual. Our preaching often lacks effectiveness from want of these three forms of energy. To possess energy we must be united with the source of energy. Here, as so often, the cause of failure lies in a wrong relationship. We are not near enough to our Master: our union and communion with Him is not sufficiently vital—" The measure of our power is Christ's power in us." In Eph. iii. 7 the two conditions, κατὰ τὴν δωρεὰν τῆς χάριτος and κατὰ τὴν ἐνέργειαν τῆς δυνάμεως αὐτοῦ, are strictly parallel. As Bishop Westcott says, " St. Paul's service as a minister of the gospel was determined by two conditions : the original gift of the grace of God that was given to him, and the continuous working of God's power in him." [1] Our responsibility is to see that we are always in such a close relation with Christ that a continuous supply of His Divine energy is passing into us.

Finally St. Paul, as a preacher, teaches us to keep a definite end in view. And our end must be the same as his — to "present every man perfect in Christ Jesus," [2] where perfect means

---

[1] *Ephesians*, p. 47.

[2] ἵνα παραστήσωμεν πάντα ἄνθρωπον τέλειον ἐν Χριστῷ.

" morally complete," [1] which, of course, implies first, the " removal of all defects," whether arising from character or circumstances, and secondly, the complete possession of all that belongs to human nature as God meant it to be. Everything in our preaching which is calculated to further this end is justifiable, but nothing else. The purpose supplies us with a sufficient test of what is and is not permissible in preaching. Dr. Hort's definition of the Christian as the perfect man is true ; but this perfection is attainable only " in Christ," through union, growing into identification, with Him, such identification of life and spirit as is described by St. Paul when he says, " It is no longer I that live, but Christ liveth in me."

There is yet another function of the preacher upon which St. Paul lays great stress,[2] and which St. Luke constantly describes him as discharging,[3] viz. giving a message of good tidings. It has been asserted that, except by the missionary to the heathen, this function of the preacher is much neglected to-day. To this it has been replied that the need for "evangelistic" preaching in

---

[1] Or morally "fully developed."

[2] 1 Cor. i. 17, ix. 16, xv. 1 ; Gal. i. 16, etc.

[3] Acts xiii. 32, xiv. 15, 21, xv. 35, etc.

The translation of $\epsilon\dot{\nu}\alpha\gamma\gamma\epsilon\lambda\dot{\iota}\zeta\epsilon\sigma\theta\alpha\iota$ (even in the R.V.) is much wanting in uniformity ; e.g. Acts xiii. 32, " We bring you glad tidings of " ; Acts xiv. 21, " preached the gospel " ; Acts xv. 35, (simply) " preached." See p. 148.

our own country is past. When a country is
"Christianised" the work of the missionary pure
and simple—that of bringing good tidings—is
over; what is now required is rather interpretation, application, exhortation. But such a view
shows forgetfulness of two facts: first, that
great numbers of people in our own country are
still, as I have already shown, very imperfectly
acquainted with the contents of the gospel;
secondly, that even greater numbers are apparently unconscious of the possibilities which
the gospel message asserts; and these possibilities
are surely of the nature of "good tidings."
People as yet very dimly realise how the acceptance of the gospel and obedience to its
principles would increase the happiness of the
individual and the general welfare of society.
St. Paul gives a very complete description of
his conception of his ministry in Eph. iii. 7 ff.,
where he speaks of his being called "to bring
to the Gentiles the good tidings of the inexplorable wealth of the Christ." "Through the
accomplishment of his special office of evangelising
the Gentiles, St. Paul was called to show how the
truth made known to him met the various needs
of men." (Westcott, *Ephesians*, p. 47.)

Perhaps there is no preaching more required
to-day than that which speaks of the possibilities
which the gospel offers to men. We have only
to think of the immense amount of unnecessary

evil which surrounds us, and which causes such
infinite misery and trouble, we have only then
to think how acceptance of the conditions laid
down in the gospel for human welfare and
happiness, how obedience to these would cure
by far the greater part of all this,—we have only
to see all this in order to be convinced of the
need for our constantly enforcing this aspect of
our message. The message of the possibility
of the forgiveness of sins (of the removal of the
causes of evil), of the possibility of comparative
moral safety, of the possibility of peace among
those who are at strife with each other, and of
the abolition of all forms of oppression, must be
a message of good tidings. And we must show
men that the gospel, not only explains the
conditions under which all these good things
may be realised, but offers the power whereby
they may be accomplished.

The above is, I know, a very imperfect account
of St. Paul's conception of the methods, contents,
and objects of preaching, but I trust it may at
least be sufficient to show of what immense
importance he considered both the office and
the work of the preacher to be. Perhaps there
is no single word which conveys more clearly
the tremendous nature of the task committed to
the preacher than the word πληροῦν. The
minister of Christ can have no nobler aspiration
than to be able to say, with as much truth as

possible, when he comes to look back upon any sphere of ministry, πεπληρωκέναι τὸ εὐαγγέλιον τοῦ Χριστοῦ.

The three following instances of εὐαγγελίσεσθαι show in what different ways the function may be discharged :—

Rom. xv. 20. By the work of the missionary pure and simple. " Making it my aim so to preach the gospel, not where Christ was already named (ὠναμάσθη)."

Rom. i. 15. By the further unfolding of the fuller meaning of the gospel, and of the possibilities which it offers. The readers of the Epistle to the Romans needed to have the glad tidings preached to them in this sense.

1 Cor. xv. 1. " I explain the nature and import of the 'evangel' which I evangelised to you," etc. Here, as the chapter shows, the evangel does not refer simply to the good news of the *fact* of the resurrection, but of the whole *possible consequences* of the life and death and victory of Christ to us.

Chapter 9

PAUL ON PROPHECY

ὁ δὲ προφητεύων ἀνθρώποις λαλεῖ οἰκοδομὴν καὶ παράκλησιν καὶ παραμυθίαν.—1 COR. xiv. 3.

ὁ δὲ προφητεύων ἐκκλησίαν οἰκοδομεῖ.—1 COR. xiv. 4.

ζηλοῦτε . . . μᾶλλον δὲ ἵνα προφητεύητε.—1 COR. xiv. 1.

THE whole subject of prophecy in connection with Christianity, from the opening of New Testament history to the present time, including a study of its existence and the necessity for it among ourselves, calls for much more careful examination and treatment than it seems so far to have received.

I cannot enter upon such an examination now. In virtue of my present purpose I must confine myself first to a brief study of what we can gather from St. Paul's teaching upon the subject, and then to a consideration of some of the practical lessons which the Christian minister to-day may learn from this.

Not a little confusion has arisen from our considering separately what we learn about prophecy in the Old and New Testaments, also from our regarding too often what I may term the *extravagances*[1] of prophecy as the natural phenomena of the power. Another caution much needed in regard to this subject is that we should pay more attention to the phenomenon or evidence of prophecy itself than to the particular terms which at different times are used to describe it.

We must start from the postulate that essentially the religion of the New Testament and that of the Old are the same. In both there is assumed the revelation of the will of an ethical (or righteous) God to man, who (it is also implied) has a capacity for understanding and doing that will. Then if Christianity has not perpetuated any institution of Old Testament religion, we may assume either that this institution was not of the essence of the religion, or that it was ordained to meet the needs of a particular and temporary condition. Such an institution was the Aaronic priesthood, such was also the Ceremonial Law. These may be regarded as national institutions of the Israelitish people, to whom the revelation of which we are speaking was first made, and to whom it was at one time practically confined. These were institutions which, under certain conditions, were useful, even necessary, during certain periods in the growth or development both of the people and of the religion.[2]

---

[1] *e.g.* among the Montanists.

[2] For many thoughts in this chapter I am indebted to Dr.

But religion implies not only a revelation of the will of God, and a capacity in man to receive that revelation, it also implies some means whereby God communicates His will. May we not then assume that, if the religion is meant to be universal, the means employed by God for communicating His will must also be universal? In other words, shall we not find that if the Divine will is communicated to man it will be communicated—whether directly or indirectly—through means or channels which are universally possessed by man, and therefore through certain faculties which are of the essence of human nature? We shall also find from history that as man's conception of God rises, that is becomes more ethical, man more and more certainly realises that it is through the highest faculties—the reason, the conscience, and the will—that the Divine will is communicated to him.[1]

In its essence prophecy, or the prophetic faculty or power, assumes the existence or possession of nothing but what is possible to all men. It is not necessarily conditional upon any external accessories, indeed in the case of the greatest prophets—Samuel, Elijah, Amos, John the Baptist —and especially in the case of our Lord Himself,

A. B. Davidson's *Old Testament Prophecy* ; also to his article on "Prophecy" (Old Testament) in Hastings' *Bib. Dict.* ; also to Robertson Smith's *Prophets of Israel*.

[1] "The prophet rose to be God's one appointed organ of utterance." Davidson, *Old Testament Prophecy*, p. 107.

these were conspicuously absent. Generally the appeals, or exhortations, or revelations which we term "prophecies," were made by men of the people, who were without any special advantages of birth or position ; and in every case, whether in the Old Testament or the New, we shall find that the appeal was made to the reasonable and moral faculties of the hearers. Again, we shall find, both in the Old Testament and the New, that, from the human point of view, the prophets were men of unusual observation, perception, and insight, and that generally they were men with a large knowledge of human nature, also of the conditions of their time,[1] and therefore of the probable sequence of events. From the Divine point of view they were men who were in unusually close communion with God (or with the Holy Spirit), though this communion (except in the case of our Lord) was not at all times equally close or strong.

Possibly the most complete definition of the position and function of the prophet in the Old Testament is contained in these words of Amos : "Surely the Lord GOD will do nothing, but He revealeth His secret unto His servants the prophets? . . . the Lord GOD hath spoken, who can but prophesy?"[2] Another illuminating passage is the wish of Moses, which seems to point

---

[1] *e.g.* the review of the nations in Amos i. and ii.
[2] Amos iii. 7, 8.

forwards to an ideal, "Would God that all the LORD's people were prophets, that the Lord would put His spirit upon them!"[1] In both these passages a very close communion with the Divine, and a very strong influence from the Divine upon the prophet, is clearly implied.

Throughout the New Testament we have evidence of the existence of prophecy during the whole of the period with which it deals. Zacharias "is filled with the Holy Ghost," and prophesies;[2] John the Baptist is termed a prophet;[3] our Lord is not only regarded as such by the people,[4] but claims the office for Himself;[5] in St. Peter's speech on the Day of Pentecost[6] he asserts that "that which hath been spoken by the prophet (Joel), I will pour forth of (ἀπό) my Spirit upon all flesh, and your sons and your daughters shall prophesy," was the explanation of the phenomenon whereby men had heard "the members of the infant Ecclesia" so speaking that they could understand the mighty works of God; there are

---

[1] Num. xi. 29. "The whole episode is an important illustration of the belief that Jahweh did not confine His gifts to particular persons or classes, . . . the belief in the free range of the Spirit, in the possibility of all men, irrespective of class or place, coming under its influence, and so into close relation with God, is one of abiding value, and what it was capable of becoming may be seen in Jeremiah's great prophecy (xxxi. 33 f. : cf. Ezek. xi. 16 f.). G. B. Gray *in loc.*

[2] St. Luke i. 67. [3] St. Matt. xi. 9; St. Luke vii. 26.

[4] St. Matt. xxi. 11; St. Luke vii. 16.

[5] St. Matt. xiii. 57; St. Mark vi. 4.

[6] Acts ii. 16 ff.

"prophets and teachers" in the Church in Antioch;[1] in First Thessalonians, First Corinthians, Romans, Ephesians, in the Revelation of St. John, and in Second Peter[2] the existence of prophets and prophesyings is asserted. And in none of these writings is their existence so mentioned as to lead us to think that it was regarded as something extraordinary, but rather as belonging to the normal life of the Church, indeed almost as an element in its life essential for its *bene esse*.

I believe that if we take every mention of prophecy in the New Testament we shall not be going beyond what can be proved if we assert that the simple definition of "a revelation or expression of the will of God" is applicable to each and all. Further, if we consider the subject in St. Paul's writings and in connection with his work, we may safely state that the influence or action of the Holy Spirit is always assumed. It was the Holy Spirit who called upon the members of the Church of Antioch to separate[3] Paul and Barnabas from among the prophets and teachers in the Church for a special work; when Agabus prophesies St. Paul's imprisonment[4] he commences his warning by "Thus saith the Holy Spirit." In First Thessalonians the charge not to despise

---

[1] Acts xiii. 1 ff.

[2] 1 Thess. v. 20; 1 Cor. xiv.; Rom. xii. 6; Eph. ii. 20, iii. 5, iv. 11; Rev. xi. 18, etc.; 2 Pet. iii. 2.

[3] Acts xiii. 2.   [4] Acts xxi. 11.

prophesyings follows immediately upon the words "quench not the Spirit." In 1 Corinthians xii. the gift of prophecy must be thought of in connection with the preceding words about "diversities of gifts, but the same Spirit," and also in close connection with the assertion that "the manifestation of the Spirit (whatever form this may take) is given to every man to profit"[2]—for his own benefit and that of the community. In 1 Corinthians xiv., where St. Paul deals most fully with the nature and purpose of prophecy, he does so in connection with other gifts of the Spirit. In Ephesians prophets are mentioned three times ; in each case we may say that, besides their ministry towards the Church being regarded as specially important, the action or influence of the Holy Spirit, if not definitely stated, is at least implied :—(1) In ii. 20 those who are being built into the building of which apostles and prophets are a foundation are being built-together into a Divine habitation ἐν πνεύματι ; (2) in iii. 5 that which is now revealed is revealed to Christ's holy apostles and prophets ἐν πνεύματι ; (3) in iv. 11, where "prophets" are mentioned among Christ's special gifts to the Church, it is impossible in the face of verse 4[3] (as it is also in Rom. xii. 6)[4] to doubt, even if the action of the Holy Spirit is

---

[1] 1 Thess. v. 19, 20. [2] 1 Cor. xii. 4, 7, 10.

[3] ἐν σῶμα καὶ ἐν πνεῦμα.

[4] ἔχοντες δὲ χαρίσματα . . . εἴτε προφετείαν . . .

not expressly mentioned, that "His work is recognised in the formation of the Church."[1]

We must not fail to notice that in four
instances, where St. Paul mentions those who
exercise ministerial functions in the Church, or
on its behalf, he places "prophets" immediately
after "apostles." As the directness of the Divine
commission is the peculiar endowment of the
apostle, so the Divine inspiration is the special
mark of the prophet. In this connection we
may notice the expressions,[2] "This charge I
commit to thee, my child Timothy, according to
the prophecies which went before on thee, that
by them thou mayest war the good warfare"; and
"Neglect not the gift that is in thee which was
given thee by prophecy with the laying-on of
the hands of the ministry." In both these cases
I believe that "prophecies" and "by prophecy"
refer to utterances revealing the will of God's
Holy Spirit,—probably fervid exhortations given
by those present,—which might be regarded as
the channel of the χάρισμα which was given from
a Divine source to Timothy for his work.

From all these passages we may conclude that
the "prophets" of the Apostolic Church were men
who were in exceptionally close communion with
the Holy Spirit,[3] and also that by "prophecy"

---

[1] Westcott, *Ephesians*, p. 58.   [2] 1 Tim. i. 18, iv. 14.

[3] Though the closeness of this communion probably varied
from time to time.

is meant an utterance of the will of God (a revelation), or a speech conveying a spiritual influence from God,[1] ministered or uttered to the Church or to individuals[2] by men who were prophets. All this proves the truth of Dr. Davidson's contention that "there is no ground for supposing that New Testament prophecy should differ from that of the Old Testament; indeed, the truth of his assertion of "the manifest identity of Old and New Testament prophecy."[3]

I will now consider what St. Paul teaches us of the *use* of prophecy, and at the same time I shall try to show how a certain kind of preaching to-day may be calculated to supply for us what in the Churches of the Apostolic age was supplied by prophecy. This short study may, I hope, direct some towards supplying the need of more "spiritual" preaching, and to the urgent necessity on the part of the preacher for seeking a closer and stronger communion with God's Holy Spirit, and for deeper inspiration by Him. This communion and inspiration are absolutely essential for the preacher, if the most important objects of his mission are to be attained.

St. Paul asserts in 1 Cor. xiv. 3 that he that prophesieth—one prophesying—speaks, *i.e.* conveys through his words, οἰκοδομὴν καὶ παράκλησιν καὶ

---

[1] Words are the vehicles of ideas, which may be regarded as motive powers.

[2] *e.g.* Timothy.　　　　[3] *O.T. Prophecy*, p. 118.

παραμυθίαν, which the R.V. translates " edification and comfort and consolation." This rendering is unfortunate ; for to-day "comfort"[1] and "consolation" have become practically synonymous. If we translate παράκλησιν by "encouragement" in the sense of "heartening" or strengthening, we may retain "consolation" for παραμυθίαν,[2] and understand by it the help of sympathy which is the special need of those who are weak or broken in spirit. Each of those three helps may be regarded as spiritual. That which is spiritual is "born of the Spirit," and παράκλησις, as the word implies, is the special function of the Paraclete. Then "building up" in 1 Pet. ii. 5 is directly connected with the thought of a "spiritual" house and "spiritual" sacrifices ; while the action of the Holy Spirit in producing παραμυθία is closely connected with that described in Rom. viii. 26 as "helping our infirmity." The point upon which I would lay special stress is that the preacher to-day, like the prophet of old,[3] must

---

[1] It was different when Ps. cxlvii. 13 was rendered, He "comforteth" the locks of Thy gates.

[2] παραμυθία only occurs here in the N.T. ; παραμύθιον only in Phil. ii. 1, where it is gentle, persuasive power, such as the consoler uses to assuage sorrow. παραμυθεῖσθαι occurs in John xi. 19, 31, where it is used of the consolation offered by the Jews to Martha and Mary. In 1 Thess. ii. 11 it is the fatherly sympathy offered to the immature ; in 1 Thess. v. 14 it is the sympathy to be extended to the faint-hearted (at Thessalonica probably mourners).

[3] "The prophet's function most nearly corresponded to that of the preacher among ourselves." Davidson, *O.T. Prophecy*, p. 106.

make these three objects his, and to do this he must be a "Spirit-filled" man, who can, by imparting the influence of the Spirit, actually do the Holy Spirit's work.

St. Paul next tells us (in verse 4) that he that prophesieth edifieth the Church, that is, a Christian assembly or congregation, so that the prophet has a *social* mission.[1]

In verse 6 St. Paul asks, "What shall I profit you unless my utterance take the form of revelation, knowledge, prophecy, or teaching? In considering this verse we must remember that St. Paul has in his mind both a likeness and a contrast. The one who speaks with tongues and the one who prophesies are alike under the influence of the Spirit, and therefore in a more or less ecstatic state;[2] but the one who prophesies is employing the gift or possession of the Spirit much more usefully. We must lay stress upon the words "What shall it profit you?" which contain a caution very necessary for the preacher. He may have in his mind a sermon which may have upon both himself and his congregation an effect similar to the one which the *glossolaliae* seem to have had upon the Corinthians—both speakers and hearers. The preacher may be very proud

---

[1] This may be said to be the main work of the Old Testament prophets.

[2] This does not imply a mechanical use of the prophet by the Spirit. *O.T. Prophecy*, p. 126.

of this sermon, in its composition he may have "soared to the heights," it may actually have edified himself, it may be destined to produce admiration, even a measure of wonder and excitement in his hearers;[1] but when he remembers that to each one the Spirit is given for profit (πρὸς τὸ συμφέρον) quite generally, he will see the necessity of ruthlessly putting aside this sermon in favour of one which will more nearly satisfy the conditions which St. Paul lays down.

In this 6th verse St. Paul may be said to be speaking of the means or channels of profit. He names four of these, which may be divided into two pairs—revelation being evidently the source of prophecy, as knowledge is of teaching; indeed we may say that just as teaching assumes knowledge, so does prophecy assume revelation.

From this an important question arises, for some have asserted that with the close of Revelation the very possibility of prophecy naturally ceased. They would say with Davidson:[2] "Prophecy did not confine itself merely to interpreting, it *added*," and they would ask, what can we add to the contents of revelation contained in

---

[1] Chrysostom's advice to the preacher is useful, "μὴ τοίνυν μήτε ὁ τῆς διδασκαλίας ἀναδεξάμενος τὸν ἀγῶνα ταῖς τῶν ἔξωθεν εὐφημίαις προσεχέτω, μηδὲ ἀπὸ τούτων τὴν ἑαυτοῦ καταβαλλέτω ψυχήν· ἀλλ᾽ ἐργαζόμενος τοὺς λόγους, ὡς ἂν ἀρέσειε τῷ Θεῷ (οὗτος γὰρ αὐτῷ κανὼν καὶ ὅρος ἔστω μόνος τῆς ἀρίστης δημιουργίας ἐκείνων, μὴ κρότοι, μηδὲ εὐφημίαι). *De Sacerd.* V. vii.

[2] *O.T. Prophecy*, p. 99.

the New Testament? Can we add to the faith which was once for all delivered to the saints.[1] But to ask this seems to me to contradict the teaching of our Lord concerning the work of the Holy Spirit, Who "shall guide us into all the Truth,[2] and Who shall show us τά ἐρχόμενα the things which are coming." With these words we may compare, "He shall teach you all things."[3] If we believe in the continuous and progressive revelation of God, through the Holy Spirit, we shall also believe that the function of the prophet, as the revealer, to be continuous in the Church, because while ἀποκάλυψις continues, προφητεία must also continue. The possibility of reconciliation between those who affirm and those who would deny this lies here. The fundamental principles of the faith have been given once for all and are incapable of addition, but the amplification of these principles, their logical and necessary developments, are still being revealed. As Dr. Davidson says, "the prophets never represent themselves as the heralds of truths, or an order of things wholly new. They stand on certain old and acknowledged foundations. The novelty of their teaching goes no further than to indicate how the

---

[1] Jude 3.

[2] St. John xvi. 13 (Westcott's notes on this passage contain some valuable thoughts for the Christian minister and teacher). The truth is assumed to *exist* in all its fulness.

[3] St. John xiv. 26.

old truths are to be adapted to new circumstances, and how amidst necessary modification their essence is to be preserved." [1]   An interesting parallel has been drawn between the Old Testament prophets and the scientific discoverers and teachers of the present day. If the laws of Nature—using the words in their widest sense as the laws which everywhere pervade the universe—are laws of God, then what is termed the *discovery* of these laws by man may, from the opposite point of view, be regarded as a further revelation of the will of God, in answer to man's effort to discover that will.   For upon obedience to these laws—including those of Sociology, Psychology, and Ethics—the welfare of the individual and of society depends.   The man who points to the meaning of these laws, shows their Divine origin, and earnestly appeals to people to obey them, is discharging an office not entirely unlike that of the biblical prophet.

In verses 24 and 25 St. Paul points to another function of the prophet.   If there come within hearing of prophecy (where men are prophesying) one antagonistic in spirit to the faith, or uninstructed in it, the result upon him may be conviction of sin, and also his being brought to judgment ; the man is brought to himself, his true nature and his sins and needs are revealed to him, and the result of conviction is confession

---

[1] *O.T. Prophecy*, p. 103.

and acceptance of the faith. Here, again, the effect attributed to prophecy, to the action of men inspired by the Spirit, is similar to the effect elsewhere attributed to the Spirit Himself, *e.g.*, " He shall convict the world in respect of sin . . . and of judgment,"[1] with which we may compare St. Paul's words, " the Spirit Himself beareth witness with our spirit."[2] Between such " spiritual " preaching as is designed to effect that change in the man "far from God" which will bring him to the feet of his Heavenly Father, and the effects of prophesying here described by St. Paul, there is surely a very close similarity.

In verse 32, in the words "the spirits of the prophets are subject to the prophets," lies a useful lesson. Reasonableness, self-possession, and self-control are marks of the true prophet. The impulse which comes upon him to prophesy is different from that which comes upon the heathen pythoness or sibyl, who acted "as a lyre played by an invisible hand." The "spirits of the prophets" are doubtless the spirits or minds of the prophets under the influence of revelation. As Davidson says : " The prophets can command themselves. . . . There is no suspension of consciousness or of reflection here— only elevation."[3] Upon this subject Davidson has some most helpful teaching for the man

---

[1] St. John xvi. 8 ff.   [2] Rom. viii. 16.
[3] *O.T. Prophecy*, p. 121.

who aims—surely a worthy aim!—to be a "spiritual influence" as a preacher. If we study carefully the phenomena of prophecy we shall find mental elevation and strong mental concentration. We shall also find in the greatest prophets a striking calmness, "as Moses received the Divine word without perturbation, so he uttered it in all composure and serene calmness."[1] The same was true of our Lord in a still higher degree, for "He always spoke calmly and with no excitement, enunciating His great principles with an unruffled dignity." Hence "the very ideal of prophecy is to receive the Divine communication unperturbed by the nearness of the Divine, and to deliver it with a calm confidence in its truthfulness and its certainty to prevail."

I now return to the three instances in which prophets are mentioned in the Epistle to the Ephesians. It is interesting to find this threefold reference to prophets in that Epistle which, above all others, deals with the fundamental nature and permanent constitution of the Church. In all three instances, as I have already noticed, the mention of "prophets" is preceded by that of "apostles"; in the third instance is added a mention of, first, "evangelists," second, of "pastors and teachers." A short study of these three passages will suggest many thoughts in reference to the meaning, the responsibility, and

---

[1] *O.T. Prophecy*, p. 124.

the exercise of the prophetic function in the Church to-day.

(*a*) Chap. ii. 20. There is no passage which more certainly assumes the essential unity of the Church of the New Testament with that of the Old than this. From the preceding verses we see that to St. Paul the Christian was the one in direct descent in the Messianic society; the Jew who had not embraced Christianity was no true spiritual son of Abraham, Moses, and Isaiah. In both Old Testament times and in St. Paul's day it was, first, men who live close to God and who have received from him a Divine commission; and, secondly, men to whom the Lord revealeth His secrets, who were the true foundation stones in the Divine society; and so, surely, it must be now. As, before the Incarnation, Jehovah the invisible Divine King, so, since the Incarnation, He who sits enthroned in the Heavens, is the one fundamental Basis, and the one Crown of the whole spiritual edifice. As the Head is [1] in heaven and the body still upon earth, performing the will of the Head, that body must have on earth organs through which the will of the Head may be executed, also organs through which may be declared revelations from the spirit of the Head. The necessity for such organs and for the discharge of their functions surely exists as much to-day as it did in the apostolic age.

---

[1] See Armitage Robinson's *Ephesians*, pp. 43 f.

The Divine commission and the Divine inspiration—each mediated through suitable instruments—are still the true foundations of a society whose claims must be Divine and spiritual. To-day these claims are being frequently challenged ; it lies with us not merely to assert, but to substantiate them ; and they must be proved not merely by a statement that we belong to some historic institution of which they were true in the past, or that from such an institution we have, by descent or transmission, received some supernatural power or authority. I say nothing against such assertions, except that by the world to-day they are regarded as insufficient justifications for our position. The world asks for other proofs. It says, show us that you are doing the work of apostles, prove to us that you are revealing the will of God for man. Then the world will still listen, as it has listened in every age. It listened to Chrysostom and Ambrose and St. Francis of Assisi ; it listened to Luther and to John Wesley. And it will listen to us if, like each of these, we can prove that we have a Divine commission and a Divine message.

(*b*) Chapter iii. 5 ff. The chief subject of this passage is the grandeur of the revelation made in St. Paul's own age to Christ's holy apostles and prophets[1] by the Spirit. Westcott's para-

---

[1] ἐν πνεύματι. Meyer's note is "The Holy Spirit is the Divine Principle *through which* the ἀπεκαλύφθη took place." He compares I Cor. ii. 10, διὰ τοῦ πνεύματος.

phrase is illuminating : " to those whom God charged with an authoritative office and endowed with spiritual insight.[1] But we must not overlook verse 4. " Whereby ye may be able, as ye read, to perceive my understanding in the mystery of the Christ, which was not made known in other generations to the sons of men as now it has been revealed," etc. The particular mystery of the Christ to which St. Paul here refers was the incorporation of the Gentiles — the essential mystery of the Christ [or Messianic] society, or purpose[2] or dispensation in that age. But *this* mystery does not exhaust the mysterious (in the true sense of the word) in connection with that society. There are mysteries connected with the ideal society (which is at once human and divine) still waiting to be revealed through some divinely chosen and equipped instrument whereby God's Holy Spirit may speak to men. We must also notice the stress here laid upon the office of the understanding both in νοῆσαι and in τὴν σύνεσίν μου. St. Paul was a prophet in regard to this particular revelation ; as such he uses his understanding and demands that his hearers shall use theirs.

By those who believe that God is to-day, in a very special sense and in many various ways

---

[1] Bishop Westcott could not mean to suggest (as the sentence seems to do) that he regarded the apostles and prophets as identical !   [2] τοῦ χριστοῦ is adjectival.

(πολυτρόπως), speaking to us, the ability to discharge the function of the prophet is of all abilities the one most to be desired, and therefore most sedulously to be cultivated. At the same time, we must remember that the attempt to discharge it involves a tremendous responsibility. The qualifications for its exercise can be learnt from St. Paul. Are they wholly out of our reach? Among them is the cultivation of the spiritual understanding, "the most valuable, perhaps, of all the gifts of the Spirit, the one most greatly to be sought, in order that by it each one of us may gain the watchful eye, the understanding heart, the soul open to God, ready always to learn from the manifold experiences of life how we can apply to each case that comes before us the unsearchable riches of the Christ."[1]

(c) Chapter iv. 11. From another point of view I have elsewhere dealt with this important passage. The passage deals with the Christian life in the Christian society, and with the "harmonious growth" of the society. It contains no indication to show that St. Paul regarded either the circumstances in which it was written or the lessons he was trying to teach as of an exceptional or a temporary character. It would be much more true to say that the conditions described are those of "all the days" of the Church on earth, and that the lessons are just

[1] Bishop Creighton, *The Mind of St. Peter*, p. 159.

those most needed in every period of the Church's history. To enable the members of the society to become useful men and women, and to build up the society, two[1] objects which have to be attained through the equipment of all the members, Christ gave to the society certain men to perform certain necessary functions in the society.

Has Christ ceased to give men endowed by Himself, by His Spirit, to the Church for this work, which is His work? Only when men in response to His call have ceased to give themselves to Him. Of the men He gives some are Divinely commissioned for some definite purpose, others are endowed with prophetic power, others have ability to carry and to tell the message of the good tidings, others are gifted with the qualities necessary for the exercise of pastoral care and instruction. Have we not here what is practically an exhaustive list of the spiritual functions of the ministry?

In his commentary on this passage Dr. Armitage Robinson writes :[2] " The official ministry rises in importance as the first generation of apostolic and prophetic teachers passes away, as

---

[1] Which are yet one. St. Paul knows that only out of perfect members can a perfect society be constituted, and that the perfection of the society tends to maintain the perfection of the members.

[2] *Ephesians*, p. 98. Yet in an article on *Christian Prophets* under " Prophetic Literature " in the *Encyc. Bib.* Dr. Robinson writes : " In its most spiritual element the gift of prophecy may be said never to have become extinct in the Christian Church." (See this and the following paragraphs, vol. iii. col. 3887.)

the very designations of 'apostle' and 'prophet' gradually disappear, and as all that is permanently essential to the Church of the apostolic and prophetic functions is gathered up and secured in the official ministry itself." But have these apostolic and prophetic functions been so "secured"? That they were meant to be *discharged* and therefore in some measure possessed by the ministry of the Church in every age, I feel certain.[1] We have evidence, and we thank God for it, that here and there they are very fully discharged by men living close to Christ, ready to execute His commission, and faithfully to represent Him, by men also full of the Holy Spirit, who, by the most careful observation of the signs of the times and the needs of men, are able to reveal God's will as that revelation is increased from year to year. But we are still far from the realisation of Moses' ideal, even with regard to the ministers of the Church. The greatest need to-day, for the extension of Christ's kingdom, is that of more men in whose lives the adequate discharge of the apostolic and prophetic functions shall be found.

To-day far too many of the "official" ministers of the Church are engaged, I will not say in useless works, but in discharging the lower and less important functions of the ministry to the

---

[1] To see that this is so is possibly the greatest responsibility laid upon the Church, and especially upon the leaders in the Church.

frequent neglect of these higher functions, and consequently to the grievous spiritual loss and spiritual impoverishment of the Church. One of my chief objects in calling attention to St. Paul's "ideals of ministry" is to induce men called to the ministerial office to covet more earnestly and to strive with more devotion after the "greater" gifts and, perhaps, in view of the present need, most of all, the gift of "prophecy."

Chapter 10

PAUL ON WISDOM

ἡμεῖς δὲ κηρύσσομεν Χριστὸν . . . Θεοῦ σοφίαν.—1 COR. i. 23, 24.

ἐν σοφίᾳ περιπατεῖτε . . .—COL. iv. 5.

THIS is a quality, or possession, or endowment connected by St. Paul with the *discharge* of the pastoral office which demands very careful consideration. Speaking of himself and his fellow-ministers, St. Paul says,[1] "A wisdom indeed we utter (as well as the rhetoricians) among the mature believers,[2] a wisdom not of this world, nor even of the rulers of this world, who are coming to nought ; but we utter God's wisdom (that which consists) in a mystery, that which hath been (and still in a measure continues) hidden, which God fore-ordained before the ages to our glory." Again, in 1 Cor. iii. 10, St. Paul speaks of himself as "a wise master builder" ; and in Col. i. 28 of his "admonishing every man and teaching every man with all wisdom."[3]

In his first prayer for his converts in the

---

[1] 1 Cor. ii. 6, 7.   [2] ἐν τοῖς τελείοις (τέλειος = fully developed).

[3] See p. 325.

Ephesian Epistle St. Paul prays[1] that God may
give unto them "a spirit of wisdom and revelation[2] in the knowledge" of Him (*i.e.* God). In
the similar prayer in the Colossian Epistle he
writes,[3] "We do not cease to pray and make
request for you that ye may be filled with the
knowledge of His will in all spiritual wisdom
and understanding." Thus wisdom is evidently
a quality or possession which he is most anxious
they should have and exercise. "Is it so," he
asks indignantly,[4] "that there cannot be found
among you the one wise man who shall be able
to decide between his brethren?" He would
have the word of Christ dwell in his readers
"richly with all wisdom."[5] Also they must
"walk with wisdom towards those that are outside"[6] the Church.

If St. Paul felt wisdom to be so very necessary
for his converts, we may feel sure he judged it
to be specially necessary for those who ministered
in a position of responsibility.

But St. Paul is even more insistent upon the
necessity of the possession and exercise of wisdom
than his actual words at first sight seem to

---

[1] Eph. i. 17.

[2] Note that in Rom. xi. 33 we have σοφίας καὶ γνώσεως;
Eph. i. 8, σοφίᾳ καὶ φρονήσει; Col. i. 9, σοφίᾳ καὶ συνέσει; ii. 3,
τῆς σοφίας καὶ τῆς γνώσεως; Jas. iii. 13, τίς σοφὸς καὶ ἐπιστήμων.
In each ease σοφία is the first member (as also generally in the
O.T.). Does not this suggest that σοφία is the prime condition
which enables us to acquire or use other powers or faculties?

[3] Col. i. 9.   [4] 1 Cor. vi. 5.   [5] Col. iii. 16.   [6] Col. iv. 5.

suggest. Many of the sentences in which he uses the words "wise" and "wisdom" are parts of arguments, in which a strong contrast between two kinds of wisdom, or of wisdom proceeding from two different sources, is implied. In 1 Cor i. 20 we have "the wisdom of the world," implying the existence of another wisdom: in i. 26 we have "wise after the flesh" (κατὰ σάρκα) in contrast to a wisdom of a higher standard: in ii. 13 we have "man's wisdom" (ἀνθροπίνης σοφίας): in iii. 19, "the wisdom of this world" (ἡ σοφία τοῦ κόσμου τούτου). Every one of these passages may be said to imply not only the existence, but the need of the exercise of another kind of wisdom—that termed in i. 30, σοφία ἀπὸ Θεοῦ, in ii. 7 Θεοῦ σοφίαν, or the real wisdom implied in ἵνα γένηται σοφός in iii. 18.

What then is this true and highest kind of wisdom, the Divine wisdom, which minister and people alike should possess and exercise? The answer to this question demands a brief examination of the New Testament use of certain terms, and it may, I venture to think, lead to at least a slight modification of the meaning which these are very commonly supposed to bear.

Many of the interpreters of the New Testament seem to have approached their study of wisdom, as found in its various books, through what they have learnt of its meaning from Aristotle. The *locus classicus* is found in Arist. *Eth. Nic.* vi.

cap. 7 : " We give the term wisdom in the arts
to the most consummate masters of the several
arts ; we call Phidias wise as a sculptor and
Polyclitus as a statuary." Here Aristotle seems
to be in entire agreement with the New Testament
use. A little further Aristotle says, δεῖ ἄρα τὸν
σοφὸν μὴ μόνον τὰ ἐκ τῶν ἀρχῶν εἰδέναι, ἀλλὰ καὶ περὶ
τὰς ἀρχὰς ἀληθεύειν. ὥστ' εἴη ἂν ἡ σοφία νοῦς καὶ ἐπιστήμη, ὥσπερ κεφαλὴν ἔχουσα ἐπιστήμη τῶν τιμιωτάτων.
Here I think Aristotle is to some extent parting
company with the New Testament conception.
But when we come to the words, " Wherefore
Anaxagoras and Thales and such men are said to
be wise but not prudent (τοὺς τοιούτους σοφοὺς μὲν
φρονίμους δ' οὔ φασιν εἶναι) when they are
seen to be ignorant of their own interests, and are
reputed to know things extraordinary, surprising,
difficult, and superhuman, but useless (ἄχρηστα),
because they have no human good in view "—
when we come to this conception of σοφία and
σοφός, we have, I think, travelled far from the
New Testament idea of wisdom.

In using the words " wise, wisdom," etc., in
connection with the teaching of the New Testament, or in connection with Christian teaching
generally, we need to be specially careful, because
it is so easy either for the writer or speaker to use
these words in a sense foreign to their biblical
meaning, or for a reader or hearer so to understand
them. The two following extracts will show this :—

" Wisdom is the power of regarding things as they are in themselves, and understanding the power of discerning their true relations as they come before us.   Wisdom deals properly with that which is spiritual and moral—with principles : understanding with that which is earthly and intellectual, with embodiments. . . . Wisdom . . . deals with that which *is* : understanding deals with that which is presented to us.   Wisdom is the support of faith, and understanding is the preparation for action." [1]

" So Wisdom and the Spirit of Wisdom is the great Light of God which explains to each man his life and his work, as far as he can understand it, and enables him to see his part and his duty towards that Body to which the Holy Spirit makes Himself mind and heart." [2]

I am quite ready to admit that these statements are capable of being so interpreted as not to be in opposition to the usual New Testament sense of wisdom.   Though I think the statement that " wisdom deals with principles,[3] understanding with that which is earthly," is at least liable to be seriously misunderstood, as is also the statement that " wisdom is the great Light of God," without some complementary assertion that wisdom is the

---

[1] Westcott, *Gifts for Ministry*, pp. 19, 20.

[2] Benson, *The Seven Gifts*, pp. 15, 16.

[3] How far is this due to Augustine's definition of σοφία as " intellectualis cognitio (?) æternarum rerum " ?   This seems to have influenced Armitage Robinson's definition on p. 30 of his *Ephesians*, " Wisdom is the knowledge which sees into the heart of things."

ability to *work* in that Light. Briefly, there appears to me in both extracts a tendency to regard wisdom rather as the essential nature of some thing,[1] than as defining the " how " of some action, even if that action be mental (intellectual), or moral, or spiritual. It is quite right to speak of wisdom as a possession in the same sense as sight and hearing are possessions. But it would be better to liken wisdom, as a possession, to the ability to run well, or to swim well, for these are possessions in the sense of qualities, they are " powers " rather than merely entities.[2]

What I would urge is that throughout the Bible, in the Old and New Testaments alike (except perhaps in a few cases in the Apocrypha, where we have at least traces of the influence of Aristotelian or post-Aristotelian philosophy), " wisdom " never loses its original meaning of ability, or skill, or cleverness, and that in every case where the words σοφός and σοφία occur we shall do well at least to keep clearly in mind the

---

[1] Compare Lightfoot on Eph. i. 8. " While σοφία is the insight into the true nature of things, φρόνησις is the ability to discern modes of action : while σοφία is theoretical, φρόνησις is practical." If "insight" means general mental ability skilfully used this is right, but not otherwise. I should in place of the final words read, While σοφία is general (ability or skill), φρόνησις is an application of this.

[2] A " power," or a skilful plan, I presume, may be an " objective thing." Only if it can be so regarded am I able to agree with Prof. Davidson's statement, " This, which is wisdom, the objective thing, is the theme of Wisdom, the Preacher." *Biblical and Literary Essays*, p. 79.

interpretation of the first as " capable," " skilled,"
" skilful," or " clever," and of the second as
"ability," "skill," or "cleverness "; though we must
remember that there is a moral and an intellectual
skilfulness as well as a physical or mechanical one.
The " wise " man of the Bible is not the mere *possessor* of some higher kind of knowledge, or of some
complete philosophy of the universe ; [1] though the
possession of knowledge is a condition of wisdom
and is essential for its exercise. The chief or
ultimate object of the Bible writers is not to
produce correctness of thought, or to give explanations of the deep problems—either of human
life or of the universe. The purpose of the Bible
is not primarily to enunciate or explain a philosophy, but to produce righteous conduct, that
is, true skill in the art of right living. This is the
key to the Bible's conception of wisdom for man.

The source of the New Testament meaning and
use of σοφός and σοφία lies in the Old Testament,
not in the Greek philosophers. The New Testament writers were Jews who still, to a great
extent, *thought* in Hebrew, even if they wrote
in Greek. I do not assert that there are no
passages in the Bible in which σοφία does not

---

[1] *e.g.* like Thales and Anaxagoras in Aristotle. It is interesting
to notice in connection with the thought of philosophy that
σοφία and its cognates never occur in the Gospel or Epistles of
St. John which (if any books do) deal with the philosophy, the
deep, underlying and comprehensive principles and explanation
of Christianity.

at least *imply* a certain philosophy, for the art of conduct implies a science of conduct, which, again, may be said to imply a philosophy of life. But, taking its use as a whole, σοφία has in the Bible a far closer reference to skill than to reason,[1] except, of course, when reason means mental skill. It implies action rather than abstract thought, and certainly rather than the *contents* of abstract thought. Even where the Bible speaks of the " wisdom " of God, the idea of ability, or skill, or cleverness (in its best sense—a sense analogous to what we mean by "genius")—the ability to imagine and create, to choose the best and highest ends, and the ability to adapt the most suitable means to these ends—is not wholly absent.

Even in its biblical sense " wisdom " does not in itself imply an ethical quality.[2] It gains an ethical significance from the source whence it proceeds, from the end or purpose towards which it is employed, and also from the method or spirit in which it is used.

The subject is one of immense importance, because, if the above interpretation of wisdom is correct, we may say that both the Church as a

---

[1] In the articles upon חָכָם and חָכְמָה in the new Oxford Hebrew Dictionary ample proofs of this will be found. See also Toy's *Proverbs*, p. xxiii.

[2] Cp. 2 Cor. i. 12. One of the best definitions of " wisdom " I know is the following from Wildeboer's *Sprüche* (p. 2) : " חָכְמָה ist die Wiesheit welche die besten Mittel zur Erreichung eines bestimmten Zieles und deren richtige Anwendung kennt."

body and the ministers of the Church as individuals are in urgent need of wisdom,[1] and that of all the qualities which they should seek to acquire none is more important. Again and again, in both corporate and individual action, we see a want of skilful conduct, due first, to an inadequate knowledge of the Divine will (so far as that will has been revealed and therefore may be known), and secondly, to a want of that discipline of life, upon which Christ laid such great stress, and which, like practice in any art, is essential if we are to perform what we know to be right.

The difference between the wisdom of God and the true wisdom of man, as these are set forth in the Bible, may be seen thus :—God's "wisdom" becomes known to us in His revelation, or in our discovery, of His skill—in His choice of purposes or ends, in His adaptation of means to these ends, as seen in the work of both Creation and Redemption, in the nature and the strength of the forces (of all kinds) which He has created, in the laws He has ordained for the governance of the universe, and upon obedience to which the life and welfare of man and society depend. And each and all of these, means and purpose or purposes alike, are infinitely righteous. Man's wisdom consists in the skill

---

[1] " Pastorum imperitia voce Veritatis increpatur."   Gregory, *Reg. Pastoral*, i. 1.

or ability with which he uses all that God has put within his power.[1] This wisdom is dependent upon far more than knowledge : it is often the means whereby we gain more knowledge. Wisdom is also dependent upon far more than effort. It is dependent upon both faith and humility.[2] Man must not only strive to gain a knowledge of the universe and of the processes in it, including the methods ordained by God for insuring his moral welfare ; man must accept and obey, he must work according to God's laws, including God's plan of redemption, whose end is his salvation. If righteousness is conformity with God's will, then righteousness is man's true wisdom. Alike in the spheres of nature and of grace man's wisdom is seen in his skilful use of Divinely provided materials and forces according to Divinely ordained laws. But this skill in both spheres has a *moral* foundation, and depends upon a *moral* character, because humility before God and obedience to God are moral qualities. The Psalmist was right when he taught that the carefulness with which a man lives from fear of breaking a law of God, and of the consequences of that breach, is the beginning of skilful or wise conduct.[3]

---

[1] This implies zeal and earnestness in making full use of his ability, and even, as such, wisdom has a moral quality.

[2] The absolutely essential qualities for all pursuit of truth and for all "scientific" inquiry.

[3] Ps. cxi. 10.

The following passages from St. Paul's writings illustrate this conception of wisdom :—Eph. v. 15. "Look therefore carefully (ἀκριβῶς) how (πῶς) ye walk : not as unskilled (or inefficient) in the art of conduct (μὴ ὡς ἄσοφοι), but as skilled (ἀλλ᾽ ὡς σοφοί)."[1] Conduct is difficult, "it is for action we were made," and our actions have effects on others. Col. iv. 5. "Walk in (or with) wisdom (ἐν σοφίᾳ) towards those outside the Church." Christian conduct, as watched by the world, and in its contact with the world, requires skill in the art of living : skill comes from careful practice, from discipline based on adequate knowledge. 1 Cor. i. 17. "Not in wisdom of words, lest the Cross of the Christ should be made void"; that is, not with display of rhetorical skill or cleverness of dialectic, which may claim the chief attention of the hearers and actually exhaust it ; and so the lesson of self-renunciation, the principle of the Christ (society), should be lost sight of. 1 Cor. i. 21. "For since, owing to the method chosen by God to carry out the purpose He had determined, the world, through its self-chosen skill (*its* method of cleverness), recognised not God, it was God's good pleasure through the (in the opinion of the world) foolishness of the contents of the proclamation[2] to save (to put into the right path) those who accepted and obeyed the Divine plan." This

---

[1] The contrast of *peritus* and *imperitus*.   [2] τοῦ κηρύγματος.

plan, the central point of which, according to St. Paul's explanation of it, was the Crucifixion, appeared to the (in his own estimation) clever Greek to be clumsily contrived. 1 Cor. i. 26. "Wise after the flesh," that is those who boast themselves to be, and by their admirers are regarded as, capable, clever, or skilful. They may be this when judged by a lower standard than the one which the Christian can accept. 1 Cor. ii. 4. "For neither my teaching nor the contents of my preaching [1] were marked by persuasive skilful language." These passages will suffice to show how strongly the idea of "skill" enters into the meaning of σοφία in St. Paul's use of the word.[2]

The following passages from the Acts evidently demand the same interpretation :—

vi. 3. "Look out therefore from among you seven men of good report, full of the Spirit and of wisdom," that is men full of the Holy Ghost, and also capable men, skilful in the conduct of practical matters.

vi. 10. "They were not able to withstand the wisdom and the Spirit with which he used to

---

[1] " κήρυγμα signifies the facts of the gospel : *e.g.* the Incarnation, Crucifixion, Resurrection, etc. λόγος is the teaching built on this." Lightfoot *in loc.*

[2] I might add, 1 Cor. xii. 8. One endowment of the Spirit is skilful speech. Note the order is (1) wisdom, (2) knowledge, (3) faith. Wisdom is a means of acquiring knowledge, upon which faith rests, and by which faith is produced.

speak,"—the combination of dialectical skill and spiritual power with which his addresses were marked.

vii. 10. Of the practical skill in conduct which Joseph manifested in the management of his own life and in the affairs of others.[1]

vii. 22. "And Moses was instructed ($\epsilon\pi\alpha\iota\delta\epsilon\acute{\upsilon}\theta\eta$) in all the skill of the Egyptians,"—not in their philosophy or abstract science or theology, but in all that he could learn from them which would make him efficient.[2]

In each of these cases wide knowledge is of course presupposed, but the idea of $\sigma o\phi\acute{\iota}\alpha$ is that of the *art* of life (founded upon a science or philosophy of life).

The following passages also gain in clearness if this thought of "skill" is remembered :—

St. Matt. xi. 19. "Wisdom is justified by her works," *i.e.* the test of skill is seen in its results, in what it accomplishes. This saying seems to be akin to our "Nothing succeeds like success."

St. Matt. xiii. 54. "Whence hath this man this skill, which is evidenced by these mighty works?"

St. Luke xxi. 15. "I will give you speech and skill to use it."

I may also add Rev. xiii. 18, "Here is the opportunity for the exercise of skill"; and

---

[1] Cp. Gen. xli. 39.

[2] Egypt was famous for its astrologers, magicians, and the like, who doubtless employed much "skill" in practising their arts.

Rev. xvii. 9, "Here is the opportunity for the intelligence which possesses skill," *i.e.* which is trained, and so capable and efficient.

There are, of course, some passages in St. Paul's Epistles in which σοφία seems to have a much deeper meaning than that of skill and efficiency ; but even upon these passages the introduction of this idea throws valuable light.

I Cor. i. 22 ff. "Seeing that Jews demand signs and Greeks seek for (what they term) wisdom : but we proclaim a Messiah crucified, unto Jews an obstacle and to Greeks mere folly : but unto those who have accepted the call (He is) Messiah the power of God (they have felt Him to be such in their lives), and the wisdom of God" (the power they have felt, and what they have now learnt of God's dealing with men in the past has convinced them how skilfully adapted is God's chosen instrument and God's chosen method to effect His determined purpose).[1]

I Cor. i. 30 ff. "Ye are God's offspring[2] (ye share the Divine nature, the Divine is the source of your life) through your incorporation in Christ Jesus, Who became unto us by His incarnation and all that followed it, not merely the impersonation or incarnation of the Divine σοφιά, but the means for our realisation and appropriation

---

[1] We must remember that Christ is not only the manifestation, but actually the incarnation of the Divine Wisdom.

[2] ἐξ αὐτοῦ δὲ ὑμεῖς ἐστε ἐν Χριστῷ Ἰησοῦ.

of the skilfully adapted purpose issuing from God for us, even righteousness, and sanctification, and also redemption."

It is most important that we should try to realise St. Paul's meaning when in these two passages he speaks of Christ, first, as the Wisdom of God, and, secondly, of our incorporation in Him as wisdom from God to us, with the explanation, " even righteousness, and sanctification, and also redemption." For I believe that it is only upon a correct interpretation of the teaching contained and implied in these sayings that we can hope to build an adequate system of Christian ethics, and also understand what St. Paul means when he says " σοφίαν δὲ λαλοῦμεν ἐν τοῖς τελείοις." [1]

St. Paul was both a strong realist [2] and a great ethical teacher. [3] He knows there is, there must be, an absolute righteousness which is the creation of the wisdom of God. Man's wisdom is seen in his effort to realise in life that perfect righteousness. Christ realised, embodied, and expressed it in His incarnate life ; indeed, God's "wisdom" may be said to have been manifested to man through this method of the expression of the Divine righteousness. But man then thought,

---

[1] 1 Cor. ii. 6.

[2] See my *Social Teaching of St. Paul*, "St. Paul's Realism," pp. 142 ff.

[3] " The first truth with St. Paul is that righteousness is salvation : and the second is that Jesus Christ is righteousness." Du Bose, *The Gospel according to St. Paul*, p. 7.

and man still too often acts, as if he thought God's wisdom in Christ to be folly. In spite of this, Christ, sent forth from (ἀπό) God, has become to man, by actual experience, "wisdom" in human life. Here, as ever, the perfect righteousness in the fullest sense of the word is the proof of perfect wisdom.

To-day the old battle between "nominalism" and "realism," if under other names, is still being fought. To-day treatises upon ethics are being written from the so-called scientific point of view, whose result is to deny the existence of an absolute righteousness, which, instead, is treated as something entirely relative.[1]

Now we believe that God's purpose for man includes not only an absolute law of the universe, but also an absolute righteousness and a perfect social state. To the Christian realist this righteousness and this social state "exist" just as surely as does any physical law.[2] In His incarnate life Christ has manifested this righteousness; in His teaching He has laid down the principles upon which alone this state may be realised.

---

[1] See an essay on "The Ethical Significance of Christian Doctrines," by J. F. Bethune-Baker in *Cambridge Theological Essays* (1905), pp. 560, 561. "On the assumption of the Incarnation we are in possession of an authoritative test of human life. The human life which the Son of God lived is the criterion by which all human lives must be judged," etc.

[2] Phil. iii. 20 ; Heb. xi. 10.

It may be some help in understanding this if we remember that one great step in the progress of revelation and in the preparation for the gospel consisted in showing[1] that righteousness and "wisdom"—true skill in living—are identical.

To make our ministerial life and teaching more really useful, our greatest need at the present time is a clearer conception of what the Divine righteousness implies and demands, accompanied by a more courageous expression of that conception. In other words, we must present to men a more adequate ethical standard; we must furnish them with deeper and more comprehensive ethical instruction;[2] also we must prove that a profession of Christianity implies the effort to realise the life of righteousness in spheres and relationships from which to-day it seems to be almost banished. Briefly, religion must be more adequately *moralised*.

Another suggestive passage on this subject is Col. ii. 1 ff., where St. Paul states how he strives that the hearts[3] of his readers "may be strengthened (or encouraged),[4] they being com-

---

[1] As in the "Wisdom" literature, *e.g.* in the LXX's extension of Prov. i. 7, where note the contrast in σοφίαν δὲ . . . ἀσεβεῖς ἐξουθενήσουσιν.

[2] On this subject see an admirable essay by the late Sir John Seeley on "The Church as a Teacher of Morality" reprinted in *Lectures and Essays*. The whole essay should be most carefully studied.

[3] In the Hebrew sense of the word.

[4] παρακληθῶσιν : under the action of the παράκλητος — the

pacted together (*geeinigt*) in love and unto all
the wealth which comes from the firm assurance
of an understanding mind, unto the knowledge
of the mystery of God, even Christ, in whom
are hidden all the treasures of wisdom and knowledge." Christ is the Divine Mystery, therefore
He is the Divine Truth—once hidden but now
revealed. And this Divine Truth must be the
Divine Ideal. Hence Christ, as the Divine Ideal
(which men are slow to understand and appreciate),
contains in Himself all the treasures of the ideal
life and of fulness of knowledge. As our Example
—the Divinely ordained Pattern, itself the creation
of the Divine Wisdom—Christ contains in Himself all the treasures of conduct, all that we ought
to do ; and as our Teacher, all the treasures of
knowledge, all that we ought to know. We may
with this compare Eph. iii. 8 ff., " To me who am
less than the least of all saints was this grace
given—to bring to the Gentiles the good news
of the inexplorable wealth of the Christ, and to
bring to light what is the dispensation of the
mystery which hath been hid from the ages in
God, Who created all things, that now to the
principalities and powers in the heavenly (spheres
or orders) might be made known through the

Spirit of Wisdom. See G. A. Smith on Isa. xi. 2, 3 (vol. i. pp. 185 ff.).
I have elsewhere pointed out how the intellectual nature of most
of the six Spirits, or the intellectual nature of the qualities suggested
by these, should be noticed. See p. 153.

Church the manifold wisdom of God." Here I would notice the parallel between "the inexplorable wealth of the Christ" and "the manifold wisdom of God." As Bishop Westcott points out, St. Paul's views upon "the scope and power of the gospel" seem to have widened with his growing experience in the course of his ministry. From this growing experience he saw how "the truth made known to him met the various needs of men." This sufficiency of usefulness was in itself a proof of the Divine wisdom. To him (and so to us) has been committed the dispensation (the οἰκονομία, the work of the οἰκονόμος) of the mystery, which Bishop Westcott explains as "the apostolic application of the gospel to the facts of experience." We must not confine this great work to the apostolic age ; it is a work which must proceed in every age of the present dispensation, indeed we may say that what was true of St. Paul must be in a still greater degree true of ourselves. Looking back over the past we can see how the gospel, when the stewardship of the Christian ministry towards it has been adequately discharged, has met human needs under a far greater variety of circumstances than even the wide experience of St. Paul could furnish. Bishop Westcott seems to regard ἡ πολυποίκιλος σοφία (verse 10) as referring to the past, for he says, "In various ways the results of the age-long discipline of 'the

people' and of 'the nations' were made con-
tributory to the universal society, and then the
Divine purpose was seen to be justified by its
fruits."[1] The scope and power of the gospel
was the proof of the inexplorable wealth of the
Christ, and this wealth was the result of *God's*
wisdom, as was also the breadth of its applicability. But the application of this wealth demands
wisdom on the part of man (man's wisdom in the
best sense) in the utilising and applying of God's
wisdom. And as in St. Paul's day so in our
own, this is the responsibility which rests upon
the Church ($\gamma\nu\omega\rho\iota\sigma\theta\hat{\eta}$ . . . $\delta\iota\grave{\alpha}$ $\tau\hat{\eta}s$ $\dot{\epsilon}\kappa\kappa\lambda\eta\sigma\iota\alpha s$,
verse 10), and especially upon the ministers of
the Church—those organs of the Body through
whom it chiefly speaks, and to whom it looks
for leadership and guidance.

The following parallel may be suggestive :—
The wisdom of God—His skill in the choice, the
creation, and the application of means to effect
certain ends (which have also been determined
with infinite wisdom)—is constantly being further
revealed by new discoveries in the physical world,
i.e. through the investigations of science. Man's
wisdom is constantly being exercised in the utilisation or application of these newly discovered
forces or substances (with their various qualities

---

[1] The past, and so our knowledge of God's working in the past,
is far more extensive to us than it was to St. Paul, hence we can
appeal to a larger and an ever-widening experience.

or properties) to human needs and to the advance of civilisation. As "nature" is a mystery of God in process of revelation, so is the Christ.[1] Now the wealth of the Christ, intrinsically and in the width of its application, may be compared to the wealth of nature : and both, in virtue of their properties, powers and sufficiency for all the needs of man, are evidence of the "wisdom" of God. As yet we are far from having exhausted the hidden treasures, the mystery of nature ; we are equally far from having exhausted the moral and spiritual and intellectual truths and powers inherent in the Christ. The work of the Church, and especially the work of the ministry to-day, as in every age, must be the further discovery, the utilisation and the application of these truths and powers to the needs of man and to the building up of the Ideal Society. This is an exercise requiring wisdom to which the ministers of Christ must devote themselves to-day.

There are spheres in which discovery is at present making rapid progress, or in which, in response to man's effort after knowledge, God is specially revealing His will and His methods of work. These are spheres which seem to lie on the borderland between the physical and the moral. I refer more especially to such fields of

---

[1] The word is here to be interpreted in the widest possible sense—as including everything to which the adjective ὁ χριστός can be legitimately applied.

investigation as psychology and sociology, the sciences of mind and of society. In the chapter on " Preaching " I have already pointed out how we are learning that in both these spheres certain fixed and definite laws rule as surely as they do in the spheres of chemistry or astronomy ; and, also, that in both there are forces at work which can only be utilised for man's welfare when these laws are carefully obeyed. What I would now emphasise is that in both the spheres of psychology and sociology these forces are largely ethical in nature, that is they issue from and are effective upon conduct. In the sphere of mind the powers of clear thinking and of sustained attention depend upon accuracy (or truthfulness), and upon self-discipline ; in the sphere of society there is the law of imitation, according to which we see the force of example, and the powers of custom and fashion, working ; again, in the sphere of society we see welfare depending on such ethical qualities as industry and perseverance, while in both spheres such powers as purity of life and temperance are mighty. Now both these spheres, as specially ethical, claim the earnest attention of those whose object in life is the promotion and increase of righteousness, the improvement of character and of social relationships—in short, the highest welfare of man.

Around us, alike in the spheres of the intellectual and of the physical and material, we

see at work an earnest search after truth, an effort
to understand, so as to be able to utilise all the
various forces and materials which lie within these
particular spheres ; we see increasing efforts being
made to employ the secrets wrung from nature
for the service of man, that is to the improvement
of man's material and intellectual condition, which
is regarded as the chief task of advancing civilisation.   Here, we are told, is evidence of man's
"wisdom" : certainly it is evidence of ability and
of skill in action.

But do we find similar evidence of a like
earnestness among ministers of religion in qualifying themselves (by arduous study) to become
efficient guides in the moral sphere, in that of
ethics or conduct?   Do we see an equal devotion
in the pursuit of the discovery and application of
"truth as it is in Jesus"?   Do we, in short, see
the same zeal applied to the investigation and
application of moral forces as we see applied to
the investigation and application of physical
forces ?   And the utilisation of these moral forces
is even more essential to the development of life
than that of physical forces.

The success of the scientific man is largely due
to careful education and technical training, to his
earnest prolongation of the process of study and
experiment all through life, to careful observation,
to assiduous collection of evidence, and to constant
exact reasoning upon that evidence.   Where is the

evidence of an equally thorough education, of an equally careful and prolonged training, of those whose life's work should be to apply the truths and powers of Christianity, the highest and purest of all ethical forces?

From this short study I draw the two following inferences: first, that St. Paul teaches us there is a Divinely ordained, a Christian ability and skilfulness which is wholly ethical[1] in nature; secondly, that this ability and skilfulness, both of thought and conduct, is absolutely essential for the adequate discharge of the pastoral or ministerial office.

The ultimate aim of the Christian pastor and teacher is to produce right conduct based upon right principles and inspired by right motives. He must recognise that there is a true art of living, founded upon a true conception and a true science of life. This conviction must lie at the basis of any satisfactory system of Christian ethics, a subject which, if the Church is to do her Divinely appointed work, must receive from her ministers far more attention in the future than it has received in the past. Those members of the Church who are called to instruct or direct

---

[1] In the "ethical" I include, of course, what is usually called the "spiritual." God is Spirit, and God is the Source of all righteousness, and God's righteousness is conveyed to man, and assimilated by man, through spiritual means. Only it should be remembered that in itself the word "spiritual" does not connote an ethical quality, though it is generally used as if it did.

others must be far more adequately equipped to discharge these responsibilities than they generally are at present. When Christianity came into the world it immensely raised the ethical standard. Much of our Lord's teaching was directly aimed at showing how miserably inadequate were the ethical standards and the ethical instruction of the accredited religious teachers among the Jews at that time. What else is the meaning of the saying, "Except your righteousness shall exceed the righteousness of the Scribes and Pharisees," etc. ?[1] When St. Paul accepted Christianity he, too, felt the utter insufficiency of the idea of righteousness, the ethical standards and conceptions with which he had been content in the past.[2] And when in the light of Christianity he looked round upon the heathen world, he was appalled by its lack of righteousness.[3] Verily there was no distinction, all had sinned, all had fallen short of the glory of God.[4] St. Paul also saw the utter inability of either Judaism or the purest and best of heathen religions or philosophies to produce an adequate righteousness.

ADDITIONAL NOTE.

It is very easy to miss the depth and the wealth of suggestiveness for both teaching and

---

[1] St. Matt. v. 20.   [2] Phil. iii. 6, 9.   [3] Rom. i. 18 ff.
[4] See Sanday and Headlam's note on Rom. iii. 23, *Romans*, p. 84.

exhortation underlying such a passage as the final doxology in the Epistle to the Romans which culminates in the words μόνῳ σοφῷ Θεῷ.

St. Paul closes this great Epistle by an ascription to God, who is able to make its readers firm — that is, steadfast, persevering, and consistent. To stablish the Christians in Rome has been the purpose of the letter. Now this stablishing must be in[1] the principles and in the conduct revealed in the gospel which St. Paul preaches, which is also the announcement[2] about Jesus Christ, which is also the revelation of the mystery kept secret through eternal times, but now made manifest, and also, through prophetic writings, made known according to the decree of the Eternal God with a view to obedience (wisdom in conduct) resulting from faith (wisdom in thought and conviction). All this must be attributed, and therefore praise for it be rendered, to the only wise God through Jesus Christ (the embodiment, or incarnation, as well as the manifestation of the wisdom of God in the ethical sphere).

The thought of God's "wisdom" as shown in

---

[1] κατὰ τὸ εὐαγγελιόν.

[2] τὸ κήρυγμα Ἰησοῦ Χριστοῦ. Meyer says : " The preaching which Christ Himself caused to go forth through St. Paul as His organ." Sanday and Headlam (*Romans*, p. 435) point out that " in this passage, still carrying on the explanation of κήρυγμα, four main ideas of the apostolic preaching are touched upon—the continuity of the gospel, the apostolic commission, salvation through faith, the preaching to the Gentiles."

the means, methods, and times chosen and used by Him runs through the passage. Man's "wisdom" lies in his ὑπακοὴ πίστεως, which involves an intelligent and skilful participation in the purpose of God, and therefore a submission to God's will.

The same thought of God's "wisdom" is present in the great exclamation in Rom. xi. 33, where, after a historical retrospect over God's method in the past, St. Paul expresses his admiration for the wisdom (the skill) and the perception of God—the skill which issues in the perception.

Thus as σοφία is a quality of God, and as God is described as σοφός, so must a true σοφία—a σοφία proceeding from a Divine Source, directed and controlled by Divine Governance—be a quality of His servants (His συνεργοί), who therefore in this sense must be σοφοί.

My readers will know what the revival of sacred learning in England owes to Dean Colet. In connection with this final verse of the Epistle to the Romans, the last words of St. Paul upon which I have ventured to comment, may I remind them of the closing words of Colet's exposition of this Epistle, and may I apply his words to myself?—"Conati sumus quoad potuimus divina gratia adjuti veros illius sensus exprimere. Quod quam fecimus haud scimus sane, voluntatem tamen habuimus maximam faciendi."

EPILOGUE

ὥστε, ἀδελφοί μου ἀγαπητοί, ἑδραῖοι γίνεσθε, ἀμετακίνητοι, περισσεύοντες ἐν τῷ ἔργῳ τοῦ Κυρίου πάντοτε, εἰδότες ὅτι ὁ κόπος ὑμῶν οὐκ ἔστιν κενὸς ἐν Κυρίῳ.—I COR. xv. 58.

αἰτοῦ σύνεσιν πλείονα ἧς ἔχεις· γρηγόρει ἀκοίμητον πνεῦμα κεκτημένος· τοῖς κατ' ἄνδρα κατὰ ὁμοήθειαν Θεοῦ λάλει· πάντων τὰς νόσους βάσταζε, ὡς τέλειος ἀθλητής· ὅπου πλείων κόπος, πολὺ κέρδος.—Ignat. ad Polycarp, i.

As I come to the end of this study of St. Paul's pastoral teaching and of his principles of ministry I am only too conscious of its incompleteness, of its many serious *lacunae*. May I ask my readers to remember that it has been written in the midst of the exacting work of a town parish, and that while writing it I have been constantly subject to the interruptions to which one in such a position is, rightly, liable. But most positions in life have their compensations. And with regard to this book I can at least claim that, as it has been written in the intervals of the daily round of ministerial duties, and in the face of their many difficulties, it has not been composed from the point of view of the theorist, who may all too easily be tempted to write of much which actually does not exist.

The details of work in every sphere of ministry are different, for these must be arranged to meet the particular local needs, and must be governed by the special local circumstances. No book, however minute its directions, can teach a man how to meet these needs, for the writer cannot know the circumstances. The personal responsibility of deciding how to deal with them for the best cannot be removed. Here the only satisfactory help will come from careful study of the circumstances themselves—such a study as St. Paul seems to have made of each of his many spheres of labour.

The application of general principles to special circumstances is the great responsibility of every sphere of life, and not least of that of the minister of Christ. This responsibility is ours in virtue of both our manhood and our Christianity, and we can neither shirk it nor delegate it. As I have shown, we are responsible men, with an apostolic and an ambassadorial commission, and with a stewardship entrusted to us. We were not meant to be machines, though, unfortunately, the tendency for even pastoral work to become more and more mechanical does seems to have grown in recent years.

To our Lord, and to St. Paul (as inspired by Him), we go for the *principles* which must inspire and control all our working. But to either we shall look in vain for such applications of these as will remove our personal responsibility.

Of the value of any Christian principle, and so of a principle of Christian ministry, we have a twofold test. First, its identity with the teaching of Christ; secondly, the evidence of its usefulness as proved by history and experience. The principles laid down by St. Paul satisfy both these tests. Those who know the Gospels know that St. Paul was speaking the truth when he said, "Be ye imitators of me *as I am of Christ.*" Those who have read the history of the Christian Church know that the usefulness of St. Paul's principles is attested upon page after page of that history. To remind my brethren, and especially my younger brethren in the ministry, what these principles are, and to encourage them to apply them in their several and widely different spheres of work, this book has been written.

I know only too well how imperfect a picture of St. Paul as a Christian pastor I have drawn. Therefore I would close with these words of St. Chrysostom: "I know not how I have been impelled to wrong him, for his excellences surpass all power of description, at least mine, as much as they who know how to speak (eloquently) surpass me. . . . The saint will judge me not by the result, but by the intention."[1]

---

[1] Ἀλλὰ γὰρ οὐκ οἶδα πῶς προήχθην ὑβρίζειν τὸν ἄνδρα. τὰ γὰρ κατορθώματα αὐτοῦ πάντα μὲν ὑπερβαίνει λόγον· τὸν δὲ ἡμέτερον, τοσοῦτον ὅσον καὶ ἡμᾶς οἱ λέγειν εἰδότες . . . οὐδὲ γὰρ ἀπὸ τῆς ἐκβά-σεως, ἀλλ᾽ ἀπὸ τῆς προαιρέσεως ἡμᾶς ὁ μακάριος κρινεῖ. *De Sacerd.* iv. 6.

SCRIPTURE INDEX

Where the reference is to consecutive verses the number of the first only is given.

(*Commented upon, or explained.*)

OLD TESTAMENT.

	PAGE
Genesis xii. 1	76
xli. 29	368
xli. 39	162*
xlv. 16	162
Exodus iii. 10 . . .	76
Numbers xi. 29 . . .	337*
Deuteron. iv. 26 . . .	204
iv. 29	285
viii. 19	204
xxxiii. 3	87
2 Kings vi. 17 . . .	289
Ezra ix. 11	127
Nehem. viii. 10 . . .	175
Esther i. 10 . . .	117
ii. 2	117
vi. 1	117
vi. 3	117
vi. 5	117
vi. 35	117
Job xii. 2 . . .	265
Psalms x. 4 . . .	99*
lxxi. 16	29

	PAGE
Psalms lxxiii. 2 . .	212, 213
cxi. 10 . . .	365
cxlvii. 13 . . .	342
Prov. i. 7 . . .	372*
x. 4 . . .	117
xi. 12 . . .	47
xviii. 14 . . .	44
Song Sol. i. 6 . . .	212
Isaiah i. 12 . . .	27
iii. 3 . . .	187*
vi. 8 . . .	76
xi. 2 . . .	153, 373
xxix. 13 . . .	80
xlii. 6 . . .	122
liv. 13 . . .	284*
lxiv. 6 . . .	29
Jerem. i. 4 . . .	76
vii. 25 . . .	127
xxxi. 33 . . .	142, 337
Ezekiel ii. 1 . . .	307
xi. 10 . . .	337
xxxiv. 23 . . .	210

	PAGE		PAGE
Hosea vi. 6	27	Micah v. 2	210
		vi. 6	27
Amos i. 1	336		
ii. 1	336	Zech. xiii. 7	211
iii. 7	127, 336		
v. 21	27	Malachi ii. 7	284

APOCRYPHA.

1 Macc. xi. 58	117	4 Macc. ix. 17	117
2 Macc. ii. 29	187	Sirach xxxviii. 27	187

NEW TESTAMENT.

St. Matt. ii. 6	210	St. Matt. xxi. 46	337
iv. 23	322	xxii. 2	124
v. 2	322	xxiii. 13	20, 224
v. 20	380	xxiii. 15	20, 224
v. 22	103	xxiii. 23	20
vi. 43	44	xxiii. 24	224
vi. 48	59	xxiii. 25	225
vii. 21	249	xxiii. 27	20, 225
vii. 29	322	xxiii. 28	224
ix. 35	322	xxiii. 29	20
ix. 36	224	xxiii. 34	224
ix. 37	25	xxiv. 14	207
ix. 38	25	xxiv. 42	216
x. 10	25	xxiv. 45	161
x. 20	323	xxv. 13	216
x. 40	223	xxv. 45	124
xi. 7	337	xxvi. 31	211
xi. 19	368*	xxvi. 38	216
xiii. 4	142	xxvi. 41	216
xiii. 25	186		
xiii. 27	124	St. Mark i. 14	146, 207, 311
xiii. 38	184	i. 15	178
xiii. 54	322, 368	i. 21	311
xiii. 57	337	i. 41	224
xiv. 14	224	iii. 13	115
xv. 9	80	vi. 34	224
xv. 32	224	vii. 7	80
xvi. 21	205	viii. 2	224
xviii. 6	224	ix. 22	224
xviii. 15	236	ix. 37	223
xviii. 21	262	ix. 42	224
xviii. 23	124	x. 45	125, 132*
xviii. 27	224	xiv. 27	211
xx. 1	25		
xx. 26	126	St. Luke i. 67	337
xx. 54	224	iv. 18	226
xxi. 34	124	vi. 8	20

	PAGE
St. Luke vi. 41 . . .	103
vii. 13	224
vii. 26	337
ix. 48	223
ix. 51	205
ix. 53	10
x. 2	25
x. 7	25
x. 16	223
x. 33	224
xii. 32	211
xii. 42 . . 162*, 163, 168*
xiii. 27	25
xiv. 32	158
xvi. 1	163*
xvi. 8 . . . 162*, 163*
xvi. 12	163
xvi. 28	318
xvii. 2	224
xvii. 21	291
xviii. 7	253
xviii. 9	47
xix. 14	158
xx. 41	197
xxi. 15	368
xxiii. 11	47
St. John i. 14 . . 155, 172
i. 48 . . . 20, 42
ii. 24 . . . 20, 42
ii. 25	42
iii. 6	286
iii. 16 . . . 104, 227
iii. 26	260
v. 36	223*
vi. 14	20
vi. 45	254*
vi. 64	20
vii. 38	279
x. 11	211
x. 14	211
x. 16	211
x. 30	253
xi. 19	342
xi. 31	342
xi. 42	223
xiv. 1	253
xiv. 26 . . 151, 323, 345
xv. 1	185
xv. 26	323
xvi. 8	347
xvi. 13 . . . 202, 345
xvi. 25	202

	PAGE
St. John xvii. 3 . . .	284
xvii. 8	223
xvii. 21	223
xvii. 23	223
xvii. 25	223
xviii. 37	32
xx. 21	223
xxi. 16	210
Acts i. 15 . . .	100
i. 25	116*
ii. 16	337
vi. 1	112
vi. 3	367*
vi. 4	134
vi. 10	367*
vii. 10	368
vii. 22	368
ix. 11	273
ix. 24	200
x. 34	290
xi. 26	322
xiii. 1 . . 149, 323*, 338
xiii. 2 . . . 78, 139*
xiii. 16	313
xiii. 25	206
xiii. 32	329
xiv. 12	75
xiv. 14	114
xiv. 15	329
xiv. 21	329
xiv. 22	177
xv. 35 . . . 17, 149
xv. 38	77
xvi. 6	78
xviii. 5	7
xviii. 10	307
xviii. 11 . . . 17, 149
xix. 8	177
xix. 21	78
xix. 23	215
xix. 25	25
xx. 3	200
xx. 17	195*
xx. 18	199*
xx. 19	177
xx. 20 . 17, 149, 196, 201*
xx. 21	318
xx. 22	204*
xx. 23 . . . 78, 318
xx. 24 . . . 206*, 318
xx. 25 . . 177, 196, 207*
xx. 26 . . . 168*, 208*

	PAGE
Acts xx. 27 . . .	202*, 209*
xx. 28	210*
xx. 29	214*
xx. 30	202
xx. 31 .	44, 196, 216*, 318
xx. 32	217*
xx. 33	219*
xxi. 10	338
xxi. 13	78
xxi. 21	149
xxi. 28 . . .	17, 149
xxii. 1	313
xxii. 10	308
xxii. 17	273*
xxii. 18	117
xxii. 25	69
xxiii. 11 .	.78, 80, 117, 318
xxiii. 30	200
xxvi. 2	313
xxvi. 4	315
xxvi. 15	306*
xxvi. 16	117
xxvi. 17	122
xxvi. 18	225*
xxvi. 22	80
xxviii. 23	318
xxviii. 30 . . .	77, 177
xxviii. 31 .	17, 149, 323
Rom. i. 1 .	75, 99, 127*, 199
i. 5	115*
i. 7 . .	98*, 104, 242*
i. 9	117
i. 11 . . .	66, 170
i. 14	226*
i. 15 . .	32, 148, 329*
i. 18	380
i. 27	256
ii. 8	260
ii. 21	153*
iv. 11	52*
v. 5	22
v. 8	227
vi. 17	96
vi. 22	96
vii. 1	48
viii. 7	275
viii. 9 . .	25, 58, 275
viii. 12	103
viii. 14 . . .	22, 275
viii. 16 . . .	22, 347
viii. 18	121
viii. 22	121

	PAGE
Rom. viii. 26	22, 44, 274, 342
viii. 28	174
ix. 1 . . .	47, 235
x. 14	146
xi. 13	123*
xi. 33 . . .	282, 357
xii. 1 .	67, 70*, 125*, 163
xii. 2	96
xii. 6 . . .	338, 339
xii. 12	275
xiii. 4	121
xiii. 6	117
xiii. 8	226*
xiv. 1 . . .	45*, 239
xiv. 17	177
xiv. 22	190
xv. 1	239
xv. 14 . . .	18, 318
xv. 16	117
xv. 19	148
xv. 20	332*
xvi. 3	174
xvi. 7	114
xvi. 9	174
xvi. 27	380*
1 Corinth. i. 1 . .	31, 75
i. 2	92, 98*
i. 4	31
i. 5	18
i. 12	31
i. 17	148, 306, 329, 366*
i. 20	358
i. 21 . . .	366*, 367
i. 22	369*
i. 23	202
i. 26	358
i. 30 . . .	358, 369*
ii. 4 . .	145*, 202, 367
ii. 6 . .	152*, 356, 370
ii. 7	358
ii. 10	22
ii. 12	286*
ii. 13 . . .	22, 358
ii. 16	58
iii. 5	121
iii. 6	183*
iii. 9 . .	174, 175, 187
iii. 10	356
iii. 16	22
iii. 18	358
iv. 1 . .	117, 164*, 167*
iv. 14 . . .	232*, 318

PAGE

I Corinth. iv. 16	.	.	30, 198
iv. 17	.	.	17, 149, 323
iv. 20	.	.	. 177
v. 1	.	.	. 236
vi. 1	.	.	. 236
vi. 5	.	.	30, 357
vi. 9	.	.	. 177
vi. 11	.	.	. 98
vi. 13	.	.	. 58
vi. 15	.	.	. 58*
vii. 10	.	.	. 79
vii. 12	.	.	. 79
vii. 35	.	.	. 118
ix. 1	.	.	. 116*
ix. 7	.	.	. 179
ix. 14	.	.	148, 229
ix. 16	.	.	306, 329
ix. 17	.	.	. 168*
ix. 20	.	.	. 72
ix. 22	.	.	. 128
ix. 26	.	.	. 58
x. 11	.	.	. 318
x. 13	.	.	. 201
x. 33	.	.	. 257
xi. 1	.	.	30, 198
xi. 28	.	.	. 190
xii. 1	.	.	. 339
xii. 4	.	.	133, 152, 339
xii. 7	.	.	126*, 339
xii. 8	.	.	22, 323*, 367*
xii. 9	.	.	. 249
xii. 10	.	.	. 339
xii. 13	.	.	. 22
xii. 18	.	.	. 145
xii. 21	.	.	. 110
xii. 23	.	.	. 255
xii. 28	.	.	. 323*
xiii. 1	.	.	. 248*
xiii. 2	.	.	. 248*
xiii. 3	.	.	. 250*
xiii. 4	.	.	. 251*
xiii. 5	.	.	. 256*
xiii. 6	.	.	. 258*
xiii. 7	.	.	. 261*
xiii. 8	.	.	. 263*
xiii. 9	.	.	. 264*
xiii. 11	.	.	. 266*
xiii. 12	.	.	. 267*
xiii. 13	.	.	. 268*
xiv. 1	.	147, 263, 338, 339
xiv. 3	.	.	218, 341*
xiv. 6	.	.	147, 343*
xiv. 8	.	.	. 179*

PAGE

I Corinth. xiv. 14	.	.	275
xiv. 24	.	.	. 346*
xiv. 32	.	.	. 346*
xv. 1	.	312*, 329, 332*
xv. 24	.	.	. 177
xv. 50	.	.	. 177
xvi. 13	.	.	. 216
xvi. 16	.	.	. 174
2 Corinth. i. 1	.	.	92
i. 3	.	.	. 66*
i. 4	.	.	. 80*
i. 6	.	.	. 235
i. 8	.	.	. 315
i. 12	.	.	. 363
i. 23	.	.	. 315
i. 24	.	.	174, 175*
ii. 2	.	.	. 235
ii. 5	.	.	. 239*
ii. 6	.	.	237, 321*
ii. 12	.	.	. 315
ii. 17	.	.	. 8, 40
iii. 1	.	.	. 141*
iii. 3	.	.	. 22
iii. 5	.	.	. 301
iii. 7	.	.	. 142*
iii. 8	.	.	. 134
iii. 17	.	.	22, 205
iii. 18	.	.	. 57
iv. 1	.	.	. 134
iv. 2	.	.	32, 309
iv. 5	.	.	. 128*
iv. 6	.	.	. 66
iv. 11	.	.	. 66
v. 11	.	.	. 32*
v. 18	.	.	. 134
v. 20	.	.	158, 159
vi. 1	.	.	. 174
vi. 3	.	.	32, 134
vi. 4	.	.	. 33*
vi. 6	.	.	18, 22
vi. 7	.	.	32, 179
vi. 11	.	.	. 235
vii. 2	.	.	. 235
vii. 8	.	.	. 115
vii. 12	.	.	. 40
viii. 1	.	.	. 139*
viii. 5	.	.	. 140
viii. 7	.	.	. 18
viii. 9	.	.	40, 227
viii. 16	.	.	. 140
viii. 19	.	.	. 141
viii. 22	.	.	. 190

	PAGE
2 Corinth. viii. 23	114*, 174
viii. 24	140
ix. 1	139*
ix. 6	140
ix. 7	140
x. 3	179
x. 14	279
xi. 2	233*
xi. 3	34
xi. 6	313
xi. 13	25
xii. 1	315
xii. 9	80, 117
xii. 15	235
Galat. i. 10	129*, 199
i. 11	148
i. 13	9, 315
i. 15	76
i. 16	66, 329
ii. 8	116
ii. 20	66, 227
iii. 1	202, 311
iii. 2	22
iii. 5	144
iii. 6	52*
iii. 8	148
iii. 15	52*
iii. 23	53*
iv. 2	167
iv. 6	22
iv. 12	234
iv. 14	66, 75
iv. 16	202
iv. 19	58*, 231*, 233
v. 1	225, 234
v. 7	234
v. 15	93, 234
v. 17	22
v. 19	53*, 58*, 176
v. 21	177
v. 22	22
v. 25	22
vi. 1	93, 120, 234
vi. 17	121
Ephes. i. 8	282*, 357, 361*
i. 10	169*
i. 13	32
i. 15	281*
i. 16	274
i. 17	17, 18, 219, 357
i. 18	310

	PAGE
Ephes. i. 19	293
ii. 4	227
ii. 20	338, 339, 349*
iii. 1	288*
iii. 2	170*
iii. 4	350*
iii. 5	338, 339, 350*
iii. 6	32
iii. 7	117, 328*
iii. 8	163, 373*
iii. 9	170*
iii. 14	288*
iii. 17	58, 227
iii. 18	17
iv. 3	339
iv. 11	66, 109*, 134*, 149*, 324*, 338, 339, 352*
iv. 12	66, 212
iv. 13	59*, 94*, 233*
iv. 15	59
iv. 20	159*
iv. 21	32, 36
v. 1	227
v. 5	176, 177
v. 15	256, 366
vi. 4	217, 318
vi. 6	129*
vi. 10	241, 293
vi. 11	179
vi. 17	32
vi. 18	275*
vi. 20	78, 158
Philipp. i. 1	31, 199
i. 3	31
i. 7	31, 234
i. 8	31, 58, 234
i. 9	17, 29, 31, 301*
i. 13	69
i. 18	311
i. 19	315
i. 24	66, 234
i. 27	69
ii. 1	84, 342*
ii. 2	234
ii. 5	10
ii. 6	130*
ii. 12	194
ii. 22	130*
ii. 25	117, 174, 178, 315
iii. 2	9, 25
iii. 4	315
iii. 6	380

	PAGE
Philipp. iii. 9 .	29, 273, 380
iii. 12 . . .	192, 267
iii. 17 . . .	30
iii. 20 . .	.30, 69, 177, 371
iv. 1 . . .	84, 234
iv. 3 . . .	174, 279
iv. 6	176
iv. 8	70
iv. 9	66
iv. 13 . .	80, 117, 262
iv. 19	234
Coloss. i. 1	31
i. 9 . .	17, 79, 295*, 357
i. 13 . . .	177
i. 24 .	.31, 33*, 35, 205, 214
i. 25 . .	31, 171*, 311
i. 27	33
i. 28	17, 32, 58*, 149, 202, 318, 320*, 325*, 356
i. 29	31
ii. 1	372*
ii. 3	357
ii. 6	156*
ii. 12	288
ii. 19	110
ii. 23	225
iii. 12	105
iii. 16 . .	17, 318, 357
iv. 2 . . .	216, 276
iv. 4	78
iv. 5 . . .	357, 366
iv. 11 . .	172, 174, 177
iv. 12	276
iv. 17	178
1 Thess. i. 1 . . .	31
i. 2	31, 274
i. 3	40
i. 5	31, 198
i. 6	31
i. 8	31
ii. 3	31
ii. 7	235
ii. 11	342
ii. 12	177
ii. 13	31
ii. 16	243
ii. 17	31
ii. 19 . . .	31, 235
iii. 2 . . .	174, 279
iii. 11	92
iv. 4	92

	PAGE
1 Thess. iv. 6 . .	204, 318
iv. 18	92
v. 1	42*
v. 6	216
v. 10	216
v. 12	318
v. 14 . .	239, 318, 342
v. 20 . . .	338, 339
2 Thess. i. 1 . . .	95
i. 3	31
i. 5	177
i. 9	293
i. 11	31
ii. 1	31
ii. 9	327
ii. 11	327
ii. 13 . . .	31, 157*
iii. 1	31
iii. 2 . . .	229, 254
iii. 6 . . .	31, 93
iii. 10	93
iii. 14 . .	237*, 321*
iii. 15	318
1 Tim. i. 4	172*
i. 18 . . .	180, 340
ii. 1	119
ii. 3	40
ii. 7 . . .	145, 149
iii. 2	324
iv. 11 . . , .	17
iv. 12	30
iv. 13	14
iv. 14	340
iv. 16	211
v. 18	25
v. 20	236*
v. 21	318
vi. 2	17
vi. 13	40
2 Tim. i. 11 . .	145, 149
ii. 2	324
ii. 3	180
ii. 6	182
ii. 21	30
ii. 24	324
iv. 1 . . .	177, 318
iv. 2	237*
iv. 7 . . .	117, 206
iv. 10	77

	PAGE
2 Tim. iv. 17	77, 80, 117
iv. 18	177
Titus i. 1	199
i. 7	167*
iii. 4	253
iii. 10	318
Philemon 2	178
9	158
19	66
24	7, 77, 174
Hebr. i. 1	87
ix. 26	240
xi. 10	36, 76, 371
xiii. 10	214
xiii. 20	211
James i. 20	257
iii. 13	357
v. 4	25
v. 7	186

	PAGE
1 Pet. i. 3	201
ii. 5	342
ii. 9	213
ii. 25	211
iv. 10	161
v. 2	210, 211
v. 5	200
2 Pet. i. 10	171*
ii. 3	145
iii. 2	338
1 John v. 19	177, 308
3 John 8	174
Jude 3	345
12	210
Rev. ii. 27	210, 211
vi. 17	210
xi. 18	338
xii. 5	210
xiii. 18	368
xvii. 9	369